SIMON ROBERTS JOINED THE ROYAL HONG KONG POLICE in 1979 and continued to serve in the renamed Hong Kong Police after the handover in 1997.

During his twenty-two years of service he worked in different departments all over the Territory. These included district crime and anti-triad squads, vice squads, Operational Command, Crime HQ, Crime Prevention, Marine, and even as a court prosecutor. During his time in Hong Kong he kept a diary and was a prodigious letter writer. He still has many of the early letters which, together with accumulated official documents, form the backbone of this book.

Simon was promoted to detective superintendent ten days before the handover. He resigned in 2002 to take up a role in the private sector, and was presented with a valedictory letter for meritorious service from the police commissioner. He is a lifetime member of the Royal Hong Kong Police Association.

Simon continues to work in the security industry and is married with two children. He now lives in England.

HONG KONG BEAT

True stories from one of the last British

police officers in colonial Hong Kong

Simon Roberts

BLACKSMITH BOOKS

HONG KONG BEAT

ISBN 978-988-77928-1-9 (paperback)
Text and photographs © 2021 Simon Roberts
Cover design and graphics by Daniel Tiller
www.mynameisdan.co.uk

Published by Blacksmith Books
Unit 26, 19/F, Block B, Wah Lok Industrial Centre,
31–35 Shan Mei St, Fo Tan, Hong Kong
www.blacksmithbooks.com

Typeset in Adobe Garamond by Alan Sargent
Printed in Hong Kong

First printing 2021

Contents

Acknowledgements

I would like to thank my brother Richard for help with photographs, and my wife Elizabeth for having such patience whilst I locked myself away writing this.

This is dedicated to my children Isabella and Henry, and my great-grandfather Joseph Roberts, the first of my family to visit Asia.

All the author's royalties from the sale of this book will be donated to the Hong Kong Police Welfare Fund.

TRIADBUSTER

Mong Kok is a seething grimy hotbed of vice, teeming with prostitutes, gambling dens, drug dealers and illegal immigrants.

Simon Roberts could be just another yuppie as he hovers outside the betting club in a seedy Hong Kong back street. Beneath the garish neon signs his business suit is immaculate, his hair neatly groomed, and his air of contented affluence contrasts strongly with the worn faces of the Chinese workers scurrying around him. Suddenly the steamy night explodes in a shower of glass and crashing debris and Simon springs into action. Gripping his Colt .38 Detective Special revolver he dashes into the betting club to help the latest victims in Hong Kong's battle of the gangland triads. The bomb is a warning for refusing to pay protection money and a second blast is threatened, but Simon is used to life on the edge.

This was how the *Sunday People* newspaper reported my life in CID in Kowloon in 1990, in a double-page full-colour spread supposedly on the real life of the Hong Kong Police.

Sadly it was all complete bollocks.

But the truth was just as interesting.

FOREWORD

I NEVER EXPECTED TO STAY in the Royal Hong Kong Police Force for twenty-two years. Like many of my compatriots I went out looking for a short-term adventure and ended up having a long term career. I am often asked now: 'What was it like?' And many people assume that I had already been in the police beforehand, or that I had family living in Hong Kong. But the truth is I was single, I was aged twenty-one and I had nothing to lose. I have met many men around my age who say that they were thinking of joining the Hong Kong Police but didn't. Many then added that they now wish they had. In the 1950s there were still plenty of foreign colonial posts for young men from Britain. By the 1970s Hong Kong was one of the last opportunities to become a member of Her Majesty's Overseas Civil Service.

From a young age I wanted to see the world and I wanted to do something interesting. Without a skill or a university education, I had to be realistic with my ambition. My opportunities were limited. But leaving 1970s Britain was my goal. Having managed to escape to Hong Kong I almost blew it by messing up my initial police exams. When I survived that early scare I decided to make the most of my opportunity in every way.

Why the Royal Hong Kong Police? Well, my great-grandfather Joseph had left home in Ireland as a teenager and joined the army. He served in Afghanistan in 1879 and later became a policeman in Liverpool. My grandfather Cecil ran away from home aged fourteen to join the army; he was only five feet tall at the time according to army records. He fought in the First World War from the Expeditionary Force in 1914 to the Battle of the Somme in 1916. My father Alec fought in the Second World War and landed in Normandy during the final offensive against the Nazis. So I guess there was always an adventurous spirit in my blood.

I did not have any objective in Hong Kong other than to enjoy life and make the most of it. I met guys who said they had five-year plans. I never even had a one-week plan, yet somehow I thrived. I've never met anyone who ended up doing what they had planned when they left school. I never manufactured opportunities and I went where I was posted. This resulted in me working for the police on land and at sea, in Kowloon and the New Territories, in uniform and CID, and in different staff postings in police headquarters.

Shortly after leaving the force in early 2002 I started to make notes about my experiences. From time to time I would recall a humorous incident and write it down. These notes grew over about ten years. Then one day, when visiting my cousin Alan, he handed me a folder with more than twenty letters I had written in the first few months when I was still at the police training school. I enjoyed reading these letters from thirty years ago. More memories came flooding back. I then remembered I had still kept letters that family and friends had sent to me in the 1980s and I re-read those too. More stories came to mind and I continuously added to my notes. These still sat idly in a folder until I finally decided to get my laptop out and try to make some sense of the assorted anecdotes. I started thinking that I had enough material to put together a story for my children and grandchildren. By the time I was finishing I thought it might make an interesting memoir. I hope I was right.

CHAPTER I

West Country Boy

SUMMERTIME IN ENGLAND lasts forever when you are eleven years old. I lay on my back in a farmer's field full of golden barley under a blazing August sun. It was the school holidays and it was my idea of paradise. I lay down hidden from view, listening to the skylarks up above me, and watching a small single-propeller RAF training plane. The pilot was flying with a display of aerobatics among the small puffy clouds in a bright blue sky. I watched it as I squinted through the sunlight, the plane high overhead doing loop-the-loop in my own private air show. Summer happiness, a very bearable lightness of being. The stress of school exams and of adulthood seemed a long way off.

This idyllic view of the world though did not last long. A year later my father lost his job as an electrical shop manager at the age of forty-nine. He spent several months unemployed and then struggled to re-establish himself when he started up a new insurance business. He had been a soldier in the Signals Regiment in World War II and had few skills other than a great work ethic. There were three children and a wife to support. It was the 1970s and we lived in the West Midlands. This was the time of Prime Minister Callaghan, strikes, picket lines, scabs, the three-day week, and large-scale unemployment. As a teenager I looked out of my bedroom window at the row of grey semi-detached houses opposite and dreamed of exotic faraway places. The wet and windy caravan holidays in bleak Welsh fields that we took every year did not inspire any glee or optimism in me. My family were struggling financially, and a university education was never even discussed. We had enough food on the table, but foreign travel was a dream.

I often resorted to fantasising about a life far away from the dull beige English suburbia.

When the sun is shining and you have money in your pocket, most places look good. In the countryside, in summer, Britain is one of the most beautiful places on earth. I had a racing bicycle with five gears that I earned for passing my '11 Plus' exams and getting into a grammar school. I loved riding for miles down country lanes, peering over hedgerows, watching rabbits and foxes in the fields, and seeing lapwings flying overhead. I fished without a licence in canals and ponds; I often stayed out all day from a young age. My mother never expressed concern about where I'd been. When I was fourteen years old I took on a paper round. I got up at 6am every morning in all weather and rode to the newsagents and filled my huge orange nylon bag with newspapers. I would try to finish before 8am to grab a bowl of cornflakes before changing into my school uniform and walking to school. When I started I earned less than £1 per week. At weekends I would often run out to see who wanted to play a game of football. There were not many reasons to stay at home. Children's TV consisted of *Blue Peter* with a dog called Shep, *Muffin the Mule* was still on TV, and was not yet considered a sexual offence. We did not have PlayStations, smartphones or laptops. Kids my age played outside. We put jumpers down for goalposts and off we went. If we did not have enough friends for a makeshift game, we would play three-and-in.

Mum had once been a fashion model and she never liked to cook. She told us this frequently. This meant she successfully avoided it. Before the invention of the microwave oven and ready meals, a boil-in-the-bag Vesta instant meal was considered a modern sophisticated delicacy. I was never convinced by the so-called meat in them which always tasted synthetic to me. We never ate out. We were too poor to have Corona soda pop delivered; I drank tap water and sometimes orange squash.

No one took drugs, except in London apparently, where LSD was fashionable. Going on a trip to us still meant getting on a bus. The most exciting thing in my early life was probably punk rock. I saw the Sex Pistols live in concert in a tiny disco in my small home town in 1977. I was up on the balcony jumping up and down with the

other punks, I thought it was going to collapse. I saw Sid Vicious
smash his guitar over a fan's head because he was spitting. I watched
as the ambulance men carried the fan out on a stretcher, his head
pouring blood as the concert continued.

After failing almost everything at grammar school I had to retake
a number of my secondary school exams and try again. I scraped
some 'O'-levels together and with no support, and no ideas what I
wanted to do, I entered the job market. There was still a depression.
Trade unions seemed to rule the country. British Leyland could not
make a car that people actually wanted to buy. The TV was full of
stories of scabs, unrest and factory closures. The country was in
transition. Heavy industry was under attack from abroad. The coal
mines were closing. Shipbuilding was failing. Our steel was too
expensive. Unemployment was at record levels. Against this cheery
atmosphere, yours truly trudged to the job centre. I was not
optimistic.

    After a few weeks of this I met Adam. He was a pipe-smoking,
balding chap in his late thirties. He was from a local water-supply
company; he must have felt sorry for me because he offered me a
job as a management trainee. I studied on day-release and obtained
a few basic qualifications. I was sent on some training courses
including one in a completely new field called 'Health and Safety'.
We also had a department called 'Work Study' which was supposed
to examine ways to make people work better and more efficiently.
It was remarkable that in a company of only 400 people we had a
team of six 'work-study officers'. It seemed many of them were
counting the days until they were sixty-five and could retire. Most
of my co-workers seemed to have a three-bed semi-detached house;
a wife called Brenda, two kids, and drove an Austin Maxi. They
had miserable caravan holidays in Wales and on weekends went
fishing.

    I looked at them and saw my future. I watched them opening
up their Tupperware boxes lovingly packed by Brenda with the
triangular pieces of Wonder loaf, processed ham, plastic cheese, and
a digestive biscuit. All washed down with instant coffee from a

thermos flask. I watched them, and I made a vow. I would never follow the same path.

If I went out with Graham from Health and Safety, we would plan our day using a large folding route map to organise our schedule. We would pack a lunch, and if it was summer, perhaps a bottle of his home-made elderberry wine. We would make our way out to various pumping stations and conduct our audits. We would have to include sewerage stations too with the smells, toilet paper, and condoms. The occasional foetus too, although fortunately not witnessed by me. The idea was to finish as early in the day as possible. Then retire to a local beauty spot. Preferably somewhere near a lake or river. There we would open the doors of his beige Austin Maxi, stretch out with our impromptu picnic and listen to a cricket match on the radio. It always seemed to be England against the West Indies in the 1970s. The best part of the working life then was that there were no mobile phones. Once I was out of the office there was no way anyone could reach me until I went back the following day.

I earned a salary, so I was paid monthly. The money went into my bank account rather than cash in hand. This was posh. I earned £180 per month after tax. I took my driving test. My father had taught me. I took my test in his Ford Cortina estate. It was quite a large car to take a driving test in. It was like a smaller version of a 1970s American design, and had an odd dashboard with a deep-set speedometer which could not be seen by the passenger. I did forty mph in a thirty limit during the test and the examiner had no idea. I passed. I bought myself my first car, a nine-year-old blue Austin Mini, for £175. I loved it. Every time I drove it, it was flat-out. I never knew a standard Austin Mini could go so fast. I could fill the tank with £4 of petrol. Ah! freedom. Freedom to go to concerts, freedom to go to football games, and freedom to chase girls.

Off to town on a Friday night. The local disco. Abba's *Dancing Queen,* how I hated that song. I would join the lads leaning against the wall watching the girls dancing round their handbags. Seeing if one of us would 'pull'. Lager was new and fashionable. A pint of Carling Black Label, or Harp, was cool. Everyone was smoking. I tried menthol cigarettes, and tried not to cough. It didn't work so

I ended up blowing more smoke out than ever went in my mouth. I ended up standing in my own private little smoke screen. If I tried to chat a girl up, they couldn't see who was talking to them. The plan was always to have a few pints of lager to build up some Dutch courage and perhaps buy a few shandies for a girl I fancied. But even better was when they bought their own. Hopefully my best friend Carl and I could offer a couple of them a lift home. Nothing ever seemed to happen though. Even when we did manage to entice a girl into the car they only wanted a free taxi service.

One night I was out with my cousin Alan. We were in Mr Pews, a small nightclub that we thought was the height of sophistication. I met a girl called Kate. She was from Wales, blonde, with cute dimples. Welsh girls are sexy. Kate had had a boyfriend before, she knew what to do. Perfect. The back of a Mini requires extreme dexterity which even my lithe eighteen-year-old frame struggled with. I needed a different car. I went to check out some alternative models. My father came to help me. Whilst he peered in the engine, I checked out the seats. I found that a Fiat 124 although being one of the ugliest cars in the world, had seats that, unlike the Mini, reclined completely flat. Clever Italians. A small lever flicked up and 'blam', the seat was instantly a flat bed. Perfect. I used to scout around for quiet country lanes and lay-bys. Once after an evening at Mr Pews and a few drinks, Kate and I ended up in the early hours of the morning at the edge of a farmer's field. It had been raining. I had driven in, and switched the engine off, carefully applying the hand brake. Confidently flicking the lever, Kate was flat on her back, and I threw myself on top of her. It's amazing how much stamina you have when you're eighteen.

Sometime later we thought it might be time to make our way home. But we had a serious problem. With our vigorous exercise, and the chassis' vibrations, the wheels had sunk into the soft earth. The car was front-wheel drive. The more I tried to reverse out the deeper the wheels sunk into the mud. We considered our options. We realised we just had to sit it out. After about an hour, we saw a car's headlamps over the hedgerows. I went out into the country lane to wave it down. The car was full of local young farmers on their way back from an institute piss-up. They saw Kate in a little white lacy mini-dress and were all too eager to help. They quickly pushed us out of the field but unfortunately I revved too hard, and much of the damp earth sprayed up over their best going-out clothes. I felt bad seeing them standing there splattered with mud. But I gave them a cheery wave as I shouted 'thanks chaps' and we were on our way at last. It was then that Kate realised her panties had been lying on the back seat all along.

My semi-retired colleague Gerald Brookes had a caravan in West Wales. Gerald was an ex-police superintendent from the West Mercia Constabulary. He was a great guy, and he taught me a lot about life. After leaving the police he took a part-time job with the water authority taking samples from rivers and reservoirs. He told me he wanted some help with his caravan maintenance. In return he offered it to me free for a weekend.

Kate and I packed our bags, stocked up on groceries and off we went to the Welsh coast. I can't remember the weather. We did not emerge from the van for forty-eight hours. It was a tiny two-berth caravan. I was nineteen years old now and getting more experienced. I eventually opened the door two days later, pale and skinny and blinking in the sudden blaze of sunlight. I noticed that a young family had moved into the caravan next to us. The husband and wife were standing outside, they simply stared at me silently. I blinked again, smiled, went back inside and closed the door.

Around this time, the BBC started broadcasting a new TV show about the Hong Kong Police. It had a mesmerising theme tune written by Richard Denton and Martin Cook. The scenes were from another world. Young British men were sweating in green uniforms and Sam Browne belts carrying revolvers and trying to enforce law and order in crazy rat-infested concrete high-rises and shanty towns. I made sure I was home every week to watch it. What a life! Guns, girls, and travel. I cannot remember ever thinking it was something I could really do. But one year later I saw an advertisement in the colour supplement of the *Sunday Observer*. A full-page advertisement. It featured a photo of a British police inspector in uniform in a street full of neon signs with Chinese characters. Underneath it said 'Be a leader. Be an Inspector in the

Royal Hong Kong Police'. I looked at the picture and re-read the advertisement. I thought to myself, why not?

I never told my parents. In fact I never told anyone, not even Kate. I went for two interviews. The first one was in Manchester and was rather comical. I'm sure they only wanted to see if I had two arms and two legs and could string a couple of sentences together. I remember them asking me: 'Do you have a problem carrying a gun?' I said I didn't. They then added: 'And what about shooting someone?' I replied: 'If it was necessary then I would be able to do so.' The answers must have been okay as I was invited down to Hong Kong House in Grafton Street, central London for a second interview. Before attending I was told to have a medical in Harley Street. It was the first and probably last time I would ever be able to attend a medical appointment in Harley Street. A very posh doctor wearing a striped shirt and bow tie told me to strip, and then with his hand over my crown jewels he told me to cough.

I then made my way to Hong Kong House in London for my interview. There were about twenty of us, and everyone looked pretty nervous. A Scottish lad asked a couple of questions. We all seemed to be white, male, young, and mostly from similar backgrounds. Generally we were the standard grammar-school boy. We were shown black and white news-reel footage of Hong Kong. We were told it was hot, humid, and rained all the time. We were fed sandwiches, there was even free beer but I didn't see anyone touch any. We were then called individually for interviews, with a board of three interrogators. I don't recall it being too taxing though. There were no aptitude tests. As I walked out of the room one of the interviewers followed me out and asked: 'Could you be ready to fly out in two months?'

They must have been desperate.

CHAPTER II

Escape to Hong Kong

I LOOKED OUT OF THE WINDOW and saw guards in green fatigues waving AK-47 machine guns. The air stewardesses walked up the aisle spraying us with insecticide to kill the mosquitoes. I knew then that I was already far away from home. The previous day I had boarded a British Airways Boeing 747 at London Heathrow Airport with a small group of prospective police inspectors. We had already stopped over in Frankfurt, and Bahrain, and were now in Calcutta. We had been in the plane for seventeen hours. England felt a long distance away.

The previous day, a damp cold morning in 1979, my father had driven me in his beige Ford Cortina to the nearest train station ten miles away from our house to see me off. My younger brother Richard had come along too. He was looking forward to moving into my bedroom. My mother and sister stayed at home. My mother seemed to be upset I was leaving, she actually cried. I suspected though that as they now had the perfect nuclear family of one son and one daughter they would be secretly pleased at the new-found space in their three-bedroom house. I carried a battered soft brown plastic suitcase which had belonged to Edith Roberts, my grandmother. She had always been kind to me. Looking back now at my original passport, which registered currency movements in the 1970s, I had £200 in my possession. This was basically my entire worldly wealth after emptying my Lloyds Bank account. I had no other assets. I had written off the little Fiat 124 a few months earlier by skidding off a country lane on black ice in the early hours of the morning. I had been going round a bend too quickly and had gone off the corner, through a hedge and hit a telegraph pole.

The pole had split the car like it was peeling a banana skin. Somehow I got out unscathed. When I climbed back through the hedge and stepped onto the road I fell flat on my back. The road was an ice rink.

So with my grandmother's old brown suitcase, my worldly belongings, and my £200, I made my way south on the train to London Euston and then over to Heathrow. The ticket cost the equivalent of about four months of an average UK wage. The flight stopped three times and took twenty-four hours to arrive at Hong Kong. There was one inflight movie shown on a small drop-down screen on the ceiling, and we were given pink plastic earphones that looked like a stethoscope. Not familiar with airline seating arrangements I was squashed into a middle seat between two other future inspectors. I tried to make myself comfortable but did not sleep much on the flight.

Having escaped from Calcutta unscathed, we eventually approached Hong Kong to great excitement. Although the skyscrapers then were no match for those today, it was still a spectacular skyline. So with Hong Kong Island and the Peak to our right and the New Territories and China on our left, we approached the chequerboard and Kai Tak. We were coming in over Kowloon City, and then after almost removing the laundry on Mrs Wong's washing line we banked sharply down onto one of the most interesting landings in civil aviation. Kai Tak Airport: mention it to one of the older commercial pilots and they become misty eyed. Pilots loved it because it was a real test of their flying skills and required extreme concentration to execute correctly. Our flight captain must have been an old China hand as our landing was smooth and stress free, unlike many of the ones you can view on YouTube. Then it hit us. Phew!, the stench of the infamous 'Kai Tak nullah'. These are the storm drains which washed excess water and raw sewage out to sea. We all looked at each other and wondered who had broken wind. Welcome to Hong Kong!

CHAPTER III

Police Training School

MY HEIRLOOM SUITCASE was safely retrieved from the luggage carousel and I made my way through immigration to be met by Chief Inspector Roy, who we later rather unimaginatively nicknamed 'Uncle Roy'. Roy was perhaps in his early forties but to us he was ancient. He was of rather slight build and had a quiff of dark grey hair. He was pleasant enough and herded all of us onto a dark blue police bus. The weather was dull, it had been raining, the buildings looked drab and grey, my first impressions were not exactly positive. To make things worse the bus was not air conditioned and I quickly realised the air quality was not equivalent to the English countryside. We were heading for Wong Chuk Hang near Aberdeen on the south side of Hong Kong Island. When I had received my appointment letter it had mentioned nine months training in 'Aberdeen'. That's not bad, I thought. I could still get the train home from Scotland at weekends before I fly out to Hong Kong!

From Kowloon, we made our way to the Cross-Harbour Tunnel which was still fairly new and charged a HK$5 toll. As we swept down into the tunnel I started to gasp – the windows were open and the bus quickly filled with diesel fumes. I tried holding my breath. With my lungs almost bursting, we emerged at last on Hong Kong Island. The scenery seemed better, the air felt cleaner, and the sun came out. As we made our way past Happy Valley I started to feel better.

At last we entered the gates of the Police Training School which was to be our home for the next nine months. The PTS looked very inviting with its pristine white buildings, green lawns and trees. We de-bussed and collected our meagre belongings. We were fourteen young men all fairly fit, but all with pasty white skin and looking rather nervous. At the time I joined, recruitment of expat probationary police was male only. A few years earlier female expat inspectors had been recruited, but due to very high pregnancy rates in the first year of appointment it was decided that the welfare cost to the force was too high.

We were led to 'J-Block', a white concrete single-storey building near the middle of the school. Inside it was a large dormitory with tiled floors and whitewashed walls. There was a row of beds on facing sides with grey metal lockers, and a pedestal fan next to each bed. Fortunately I had no notions of what to expect so was not disappointed. I opened my steel locker, and pulled out some wire hangers and switched on the pedestal fan. It was late October but still over 20°C and a lot warmer than in the UK. I put my battered suitcase on the bed and laid it over the grey blanket. I started pulling my worldly goods out and placing a few shirts on the wire hangers. Suddenly Uncle Roy came into the room and shouted: 'Everyone in the officers' mess in five minutes!' I briefly mumbled that we might be allowed a shower and a change of clothes after the twenty-four-hour flight, but was rebuffed and told, 'No – immediately. Commandant's orders!'

A few months before there had been a front-page story in the English national papers about a new inspector having his arm broken in an initiation ceremony that went wrong. Apparently the initiations involved taking the guys straight off the bus and putting them through obstacle courses or waking them in the middle of the night for drill practice. They were very imaginative, and one of the senior squad had once dressed up as a priest and led the new joiners in prayers whilst walking around the mess in a kind of midnight mass. However since the incident of the chap having his arm broken, things had become rather more muted.

When we walked into the mess the commandant was nowhere to be seen. Instead we were greeted by the squad above us at the bar, and handed glasses of cold San Miguel beer. Being tired and thirsty and still only twenty-one years old I did not mind being given a glass of beer, so I gratefully accepted and we introduced ourselves. The mess was clean and spacious with ceiling fans and lots of police plaques and of course a large framed portrait of the Queen on the wall. Outside there was a pleasant terrace with flowering trees of bougainvillea offering shade and familiar Union flags. Someone put a cassette tape of Steely Dan's *Haitian Divorce* in the stereo, the music played and the beers flowed, and somehow we all ended up in the red-light district of Wan Chai. The objective of the senior squad was to get the newcomers so drunk they would end the evening getting a tattoo. These were usually in Ricky's tattoo parlour near Lockhart Road. We lurched from bar to bar through the red velvet curtains of the girly bars in an alcoholic haze. It seemed a long way from the Welsh border counties.

On the Monday morning we were issued our kit and training uniforms which initially consisted of green shirts, white webbing belts, and short trousers with long socks and black leather shoes. The police uniform then was green in summer and dark blue in winter. We were introduced to our 'room boy' – a small plump jolly chap called Ah Wong. He would do our laundry and shine our shoes for a fixed sum each month. We were also required to swear allegiance to the Queen. This was done individually as we were called in alphabetical order into the commandant's office. He was a handsome fellow called Peter Webb who drove a beautiful old open-top MGA sports car. He also kept two little white Yorkshire terriers. Whenever I was in his office they would run around yapping and trying to nip my ankle. I suspected he had trained them to do this. We were given a Bible to hold and had to stand to attention and read off a card that we would solemnly and faithfully serve the Queen, country, and colony. In doing so I officially joined the other 660 or so expat police officers in the force at the time.

In the mess all food and drinks were signed for with chits and we settled the bill at the end of the month. Although my starting salary was only slightly more than I had earned in the UK, the top rate of tax in HK was 15 per cent so it seemed okay as long as I did not overdo the San Miguel or the jaunts to Wan Chai.

There was a small branch of the Hongkong and Shanghai Bank (HSBC) in PTS. We were all led there to open bank accounts so that our salary could be paid directly into them. My starting salary was HK$3,300 per month. Another requirement for the new trainees was to get the dreaded PTS haircut. I had anticipated a short-back-and-sides and had my hair cut short before leaving the UK. However the sight of the Chinese PTS 'barbers' sent a chill through all of us when we lined up for the electric razor shearing we would be receiving. The barbers looked as if they were heroin addicts in rehab. I watched to see if any of them displayed a modicum of ability. But sadly the uniform result was the brutal removal of any style we once had.

We had to train for longer than local recruits as the first eight weeks was devoted to learning Cantonese full time. This was in a language lab where we listened to cassette tapes whilst wearing headphones and repeating phrases ad nauseam. I found it mind numbing. One of our teachers was a middle-aged man surnamed Lee. He told us with absolute authority that there were no Chinese homosexuals. He said it was a Western disease. He also insisted that pornography was non-existent in Chinese society and again this was an unwelcome Western import. We soon found out neither of these statements were correct, but we were all too exhausted after nine hours of daily language lessons to argue. Cantonese is a very difficult language, and I had had problems even learning French. I discovered that as a white Caucasian male I would be forever known as a *'gwailo'*. This translates literally as 'ghost man'. It was not meant to be complimentary but all the expats simply adopted it, and used it themselves so it lost any derogatory connotation. We did not study Chinese characters so we wrote the Chinese words phonetically; for example, *'gai'*, meaning 'street'. However, said with a different tone it could also mean 'chicken' or 'prostitute', with obvious humorous results.

I somehow passed the oral Cantonese exam in front of an exam board in Mid-Levels. Our week in PTS was Monday to Saturday with a parade in our PE kit of T-shirt, shorts and plimsolls at 8am. We had Sunday off, if we did not transgress any disciplinary issues and have gate-guard duty.

Once we had survived the language lessons we were introduced to our local colleagues and placed into squads. We had three squads each with twelve inspectors, both local and expat probationary inspectors. We had two female inspectors in my squad. My course instructor was Roy, the chief inspector who had met us at the airport. Roy was actually a pleasant chap who did later help me a lot with my exams for which I am still very grateful. He drove a Triumph Spitfire which was pretty cool, and talked about his 'girlfriend' who turned out to be a stern woman of a certain age who reminded me of a school matron. It became clear to me during classes that our local counterparts were extremely hard working and very ambitious and not very impressed with their lazy, cheeky, hard-drinking British colleagues. They also did not like the attention we were paying to the pretty young local female inspectors.

I started to find the course very tough. I could handle the drill, and my fitness was good. In the UK I had played rugby, and each evening ran three miles after work. I could handle the weapons, and my leadership was okay. The written exams though were brutal. We had 'fortnightlys'; these were essay-style three-hour exams every two weeks. These were split into the junior, intermediate, and senior stage, and finally level one in our training. We had exams in criminal law, traffic law, gambling and vice, and Police General Orders. Considering there was an enormous amount of studying in only fourteen days from a very large syllabus it's not surprising that people failed. When I say 'people' failed, what I mean is that mostly the British guys failed. Our local colleagues would lock themselves in their rooms and study until 2am whilst we would be drinking in the mess and cramming the night before. Eventually the pressure started to tell. One by one the British lads started failing, getting homesick, getting fed up with the long hours and the discipline. Resignations started. Before we were at the halfway stage of the training three of our original intake had left. It was pretty sad to see them go. I think we all reflected on our own choices when we watched them board the bus to the airport. I failed an exam and received a warning. It was time for me to take stock. Did I really want to return to the UK? I decided I did not. It was time for me to buckle down and start taking things more seriously.

The Royal Hong Kong Police (RHKP) in the 1970s was already a paramilitary force. Early in our training we were introduced to a range of weapons. At the time, only the male officers carried firearms. The secure armoury still had the old World War II Sten gun, similar to the one carried by my father in Normandy in 1944. I tried it, it was a pig to fire, the rounds went everywhere except at the target. The Federal Riot Gun was a useful weapon for firing gas canisters or rubber bullets during riots; in training we fired traditional shotgun pellet rounds. I loved the American AR 15. This is the semi-automatic variant of the M16. Pop, pop, pop, hardly any recoil, 150 metres all rounds in a tiny group in the middle of the target, it wasn't hard with such a firearm. We spent most time with hand guns: .38 calibre Smith & Wesson and Colt revolvers. They were easy, straightforward, and simple; they were tough and hardly ever jammed. They were in use for decades before the force started moving to automatics. The revolvers were effective at close range but did not have much stopping power with the original round. We practised on the range standing up, prone, kneeling, and firing behind various objects. The main problem with a .38 revolver is that it only holds six rounds, so in later years, officers were issued with speed-loaders which held an additional six rounds. The other improvement was the introduction of more powerful hollow-point rounds. This was after several cases of violent criminals being hit by the original rounds and still managing to run away, which was rather embarrassing.

There was an 'outward bound' area at PTS on which we had to crawl through trenches, swing on ropes, and climb over walls. There was also a gas chamber. The force was well equipped for dealing with disturbances. The colony had been rocked by a serious disturbance in 1967 sparked by the Cultural Revolution in China. There had been exchanges of automatic weapons fire over the border and bombings as well as daily riots and protests against the British rule. The police had handled the situation well and had been widely praised. This was recognised by the Queen when in 1969 the Hong Kong Police was granted the 'Royal' prefix.

We also had a fully trained and well equipped Police Tactical Unit (PTU) stationed up near Fanling in the New Territories which was on standby around the clock. One of the items kept in all police armouries was CS gas. This was usually fired in canisters from a Remington shotgun during public order disturbances. Some of the more sadistic staff felt that it was important that as new recruits we should know what CS gas felt like. So we were ordered into a pitch-dark smoke chamber wearing ancient and rather useless old rubber gas masks. When in the middle of the smoke chamber we were ordered to remove the gas masks for a few seconds. The gas attacked our nasal passage, our eyes and even our skin. The burning sensation and sense of asphyxiation was unbearable. I stumbled and crawled out the other end of the chamber on all fours coughing and sweating, blinded by the gas. One of our local colleagues collapsed unconscious and had to be rushed to hospital. It took me about two hours of washing and rinsing my face and arms with cold water to partially recover from the ordeal. We were also required to fire guns but we weren't required to be shot to know what it felt like.

I usually enjoyed the firearms training. Over the nine months I fired over 300 rounds of .38 ammunition and became a fairly good shot. Even when it gradually became more difficult, firing from a longer distance, and having to fire from the side of different objects, I was able to pass the training and tests. The range course training all passed uneventfully except on two occasions. Once, one of our older British inspectors called Rupert, a former army officer and then thirty years old, decided that it would be funny to drop a live round of ammunition down the shirt of one of our trainee female officers. Many hours later at around midnight, we were still on the range, now in pitch darkness, on our hands and knees trying to find the missing bullet. We all reflected then that somehow it didn't seem quite so funny.

On another occasion, our young Scottish inspector who had struggled with his Cantonese was ordered to run down a small incline on the range, address the target with: 'Stop, don't move or I will shoot' in Chinese, and then fire off two rounds. Everyone else managed to do this without incident. But Jock became increasingly flustered with speaking the warning, and he forgot everything else. When it was his turn, he immediately drew his revolver with six live rounds, and ran down the small incline as if he was being chased by a lion while waving his revolver wildly, causing all of us to dive for cover. He slid to a halt, emptied his revolver in a burst of gunfire and then shouted: 'I shoot, stop, caution.' We all rather mercilessly fell about laughing, whilst the poor chap stood embarrassed hoping the ground would swallow him up.

As the new intake we had to be 'dined in' to the officers' mess. We had to purchase mess kits made-to-measure by a force's tailor. These consisted of a short white jacket, black piped trousers, white shirt, black bow tie, and smartly polished black dress shoes. I still have a group photo of my first mess night in which I look very serious with a pale face, and very short jet-black hair swept back. Mess nights were very formal structured affairs. The shortest and youngest members of the new intakes were allocated with special duties such as the 'duck major' who was required to 'parade the duck'. At the back of the mess some live ducks were kept in a pen. I was amazed at how tame the duck seemed to be when it was held under the arm of the young duck major and carried on top of the long tables whilst everyone cheered, shouted and thumped the table. The senior officers were piped in by one of the police pipers. The police band was always excellent, and I felt the quality of the pipers matched anything in Scotland. The band played traditional anthems and songs throughout the evening, wine and whisky flowed and speeches followed speeches. Just like the duck major, speeches were made standing on top of the long dining table. The speeches were made to welcome us as the new intake, and to say farewell to the lucky intake that were 'dining out'.

It was quite normal on these occasions for people to drink too much and for someone to run to the toilet to throw up, but there were only short amounts of time allotted for toilet breaks and it was not allowed to go for a toilet break during a speech. Cigars and pipes were smoked as if the world was about to end. Once the speeches and toasts had finished, the games began. It was squad against squad, and intake against intake, and trainees against staff. British Bulldog was very popular and very violent. This consists of one person carrying another on his shoulders, facing a similar pair with the objective to knock your carried opponent off onto the floor. There were no rules. I recall playing British Bulldog against the commandant. After a close skirmish I lost the battle. Well, I thought it the best for the sake of my career. No one wanted to be the one to fall, and various aggressive tactics and blows to the head resulted in some frightening scenes, especially when all the participants were inebriated. Mess nights were genuinely messy affairs, and usually finished in the early hours. It was a trial when we had to be inspected at the morning parade a few hours later. Our bedraggled squad was a sight to behold. I really looked forward to Sunday mornings when I could enjoy a well-earned lie-in.

Outside the gates of PTS and next to Ocean Park, the popular theme park, was Brick Hill. One of our fitness tests was the Brick Hill run. We all mustered on the parade ground in our PE kit, and on being given the order, we would run out of the gates and make our way up a path and up several hundred steps next to the cable car. The steps led all the way to the top of Brick Hill and then down the other side towards Aberdeen, where we would turn right, through Wong Chuk Hang and back through the gates next to the public housing estate. Even for a fit young person the first time is a killer. But it was one of the events that the young British inspectors excelled at. As my fitness improved I could complete the run in about twenty minutes which was amongst the three fastest in my intake. Each year there was a force-wide Brick Hill race and I recall some super fit guys doing it in about sixteen minutes. Back in the gym we had rope climbs, star jumps, push ups, sit-ups and military-style fitness training. I did forty press-ups, forty sit-ups, thirty-four squat thrusts, a twenty-inch standing jump all within a set time period and even then I only got a score of 63.2 per cent.

We also did self-defence combat training with an instructor called Button. He used to tell us to try to punch him. We never did, most of us would throw some weak half-hearted slow punch which of course he intercepted and then threw us over his shoulder. We already knew what was going to happen. One day though, Rupert, again in rebellious mood, decided to punch Button hard in the face. It connected, Button recoiled holding his face, we all winced. Rupert's satisfaction lasted about two seconds before he was put in an arm lock and his wrist bent back and almost broken.

He fell to the ground screaming with pain. Normal service was resumed. For the rest of the course we all bowed to 'Mr Button, sir'.

Leadership training mostly consisted of us put in trucks and taken up to the New Territories where we were given maps and compasses and set various objectives. Sometimes though a Wessex helicopter would come to pick us up. It landed on the cricket pitch, and we would pile on, dressed in our jungle kit of camouflage fatigues, green floppy hats, rubber-soled canvas ankle boots, with water bottles, and a small knapsack with a sandwich lunch. We would be flown over Hong Kong Island, Kowloon, and dropped off on the top of some remote hill. One of us would be told that he or she was the exercise leader and that they had to get the whole squad to a particular grid reference within forty minutes. Of course the first objective was to find out where the bloody hell we were, which was not easy surrounded by scrub on a featureless hillside. We would be out for the whole day, and the heat and mosquitoes made the task more unpleasant especially for the least fit amongst us. I did not mind these exercises though, as it was a break from the discipline of PTS.

On one occasion we were taken to the border and shown Sha Tau Kok which had been the scene of fighting and bloodshed during the insurgency in 1967. There was a fence built along the Hong Kong–China border, although in Sha Tau Kok the town straddled the border itself so one side of the street was British Hong Kong territory and the other was the PRC. It was confusing and on a few occasions British soldiers or police officers had accidentally strayed across the street and been arrested by the Chinese. I was fascinated by the place. This was only a few years after Chairman Mao had died and China was still a closed and mysterious place. I came to stand a few feet away from a member of the People's Liberation Army, a border guard dressed in the Mao uniform, green cap with red star, carrying a long, old-fashioned rifle, with a bayonet. When I looked down I noticed he had a cheap pair of white canvas plimsolls on his feet. He stared at me for a few moments in a very unfriendly way and then ambled off. It was a memorable trip and when I got back, I was still excited and wrote a letter to my parents describing the adventure.

After a couple of months in J-Block a few private rooms in the main accommodation block became available. There was an impromptu lottery and I won my own room. It was room twenty on the first floor, near the mess and facing a hillside and trees at the back. It was only about ninety square feet. It had a single bed with a brown and white patterned blanket, a small desk, a wooden upright chair, a dark leatherette armchair with wooden arms, a small dark wood wardrobe, and a fan. My own room! Although ablutions were still communal, I was over the moon. It took me five minutes to move my old suitcase in from J-Block. I still did not have an air conditioner so relied on an electric fan. In the summer the room became very hot and the mosquitoes feasted. To keep the little buggers off us we burnt mosquito coils. These hard grey coils burnt slowly and did keep the mosquitoes away but I wondered about the chemical fumes that I was breathing through the night.

We had room inspections. This was similar to army movies, where we had to stand to attention whilst one of the instructors carrying a swagger stick came in and checked everything was in order. I decided to brighten up my room by purchasing a calendar which had photos of pretty girls wearing very little. During the next inspection, the instructor went over to the calendar, thumbed through the months of the year, tried to hide a smile and left. A great result for me, as he hardly even glanced at my kit neatly folded on the bed. I also bought a small Hitachi MI stereo cassette player; it cost HK$2,200 which was a huge sum then – I think I was ripped off. A similar one would cost much less now. I still could not find cassette tapes of my punk rock favourites, The Stranglers, The Clash and Ian Dury and other legends and had to rely on friends in the UK to post them out to me.

CHAPTER IV

Exploring Hong Kong

SATURDAYS WERE OFTEN spent doing fitness training and sport and we often finished earlier as I think even our instructors needed a break. We all enjoyed getting changed into jeans and T-shirts and getting out of the school and out exploring Hong Kong itself. Even though Ocean Park was next door, I don't recall us every visiting it. Later, back in the UK, I realised that if some attraction is nearby, you hardly ever visit it. On the other side of the school was Wong Chuk Hang. This was one of the newer public housing estates and it made for an interesting excursion. Considering that many of the new Chinese immigrants still lived in wooden shanty towns on hillsides, these new estates were highly sought-after residences although they looked incredibly crowded to me. They were mainly one- or two-room flats with a small toilet and shower. Washing was placed outside the windows on long bamboo poles to dry. These small flats, often not much more than 100 square feet, had no separate bedrooms. Sleeping areas were subdivided by curtains. When you looked up to the ceiling it looked like a model railway set. The metal tracks carrying the curtains to various points to provide a limited privacy for changing clothes and sleeping. I always wondered how more intimate affairs were conducted without waking the children.

Downstairs in the public areas between the blocks there were shops and markets. People didn't really care too much about appearances and it was quite common to see local people walking around in their pyjamas. Large cockroaches ran riot, and these would be stamped on with the ubiquitous rubber flip-flops with a loud crunch, the residue leaving a slippery surface especially when it had been raining.

I saw one woman crouched down over a red plastic bucket of live frogs. A frog was taken from the bucket, its stomach split, entrails removed and carcass placed in another bucket. She was very skilled and quick in doing this. Chickens were sold alive to be killed at home unless the stall holder was requested to butcher the bird. There were shops selling cheap plastic toys, and dried herbs. Chinese medicine shops had amazing smells. With incense burning, everyone shouting Cantonese, and the cockroaches, frogs, the alien sights and sounds were enthralling.

Next to Wong Chuk Hang is Hong Kong's Aberdeen, famous for its harbour and fishing fleet. The water was full of junks and *sampans* and *walla-wallas*. Many families lived on the fishing boats permanently. Western media seems to find Aberdeen fascinating. It was obligatory for movies or music videos shot in Hong Kong in the 1970s or '80s to head to Aberdeen and film the fishing fleet. Aberdeen was also known for its floating restaurants, the most famous of which was the 'Jumbo'. Like everyone else we made our way over to its colourful decks to take a *dim sum* lunch. From that time on every expat has to take their own visitors to the floating restaurants, and it is a permanent fixture on the Hong Kong must-do list.

The long loved Gaylord Indian restaurant in Tsim Sha Tsui had opened. For a posh night out a popular place was the La Ronda rotating restaurant on the rooftop in the Furama Hotel, which was between Central and Admiralty. The views over the harbour were fantastic but the first time I went there I became dizzy.

In 1979 there were two English-language newspapers and two English TV channels. I read the *South China Morning Post* and especially the police reports by Tommy Lewis and Kevin Sinclair, both of whom seemed to have very good police sources.

Anyone investing in shares or property would have done well if they had stayed in the market. The Hang Seng Index was standing at 879 points and apartments were selling for an average price of HK$300 per square foot.

The Vietnamese refugees were becoming a problem. The merchant ship the *Skyluck* had disgorged its human cargo, and there were 38,000 refugees in camps in the colony.

At weekends I went further afield into Hong Kong Island or over to Kowloon. Going over to Kowloon meant taking the Star Ferry which on Hong Kong side was still then near Statue Square in Central. The fare was about twenty cents. It was, and still remains another essential attraction.

The new underground Mass Transit Railway (MTR) had almost completed its first line, from Central to Kwun Tong. People were saying this would have no effect on the commuter queues for the Star Ferry each morning.

The ferry very conveniently took us into Tsim Sha Tsui, 'Chimsy' for short. I walked up Nathan Road and found Sam's Tailor shop. This was an institution and in the seventies was actually run by Sam himself. Sam was a very clever business man whose family was originally from the Indian sub-continent. He befriended the bell-boys in the smart hotels and cruise ships and was often tipped off when movie stars or royalty were in town. He would then ring their room and offer a made-to-measure suit at a discount price. He always managed to have photos taken with his famous customers and proudly displayed them in his shop.

There was a story at the time that the Duke of Kent had had a suit made at Sam's and then he got into trouble with the British Union of Tailors for buying his suits in Hong Kong. I know that quite a number of new police inspectors visited to have suits and shirts made. On entering, I was immediately offered a San Miguel beer and a seat near the air conditioner. Of course by then you had no choice but to buy a suit. How could anyone refuse after such hospitality? Once he found I was in the police he would always refer to me as 'superintendent' as in: 'Welcome superintendent, please take a seat and enjoy a nice cold beer'. I suspect the young army lads who went in were all promoted to major. I did order a couple of suits and some shirts but I found the experience quite daunting. A suit cost $500. It was the first time I'd ever had anything made to measure and really had no idea what I wanted. I don't recall ever getting much use out of the suits either. I think it was more the novelty value of having a suit made at Sam's.

I visited the night markets in Yau Ma Tei and Mong Kok. The fortune-tellers, lanterns, Chinese-opera singers, joss sticks, fish ball stalls, colours, smells and sounds were otherworldly. Sometimes the multiple attacks on my senses through sight, sound and smell were so intense I pretended I was actually experiencing it all on a kind of wrap-around video screen. There were some British-style pubs that I could escape to in Kowloon. I used to enjoy Rick's Café, or I would make my way back to Hong Kong-side and catch a tram to Lockhart Road. The Vietnam War had ended a few years before and Wan Chai had been one of the popular R&R stops for the American and allied servicemen. The area surrounding Lockhart Road still had many 'Suzie Wong' type girly bars. They always put a couple of the prettiest girls out front to entice guys inside. The only time I went inside was in the early months when it was still a novelty. In the seventies the girls were all still Hong Kong Chinese girls. Many had tattoos and it was presumed they were managed by triads.

Once through the velvet curtain there was a single long bar, or one in a 'U' shape with steel dancing poles behind the bar. I knew the places were rip-off joints, and you had to keep a close eye on your bar chits to make sure extra bills were not mysteriously deposited into the glass in front of you. Unless I was in a group out on the town I kept away, they could be a bit depressing. The mama-sans were quite fearsome and you certainly did not mess with them. 'Ladies' drinks' consisted of some strange pink liquid in a champagne-type glass. One of them cost the same as about five beers and would enable the girl of your choice to sit next to you. The next step was to buy the girl out of the bar for a few hours which cost a fortune. I never did that, but I did arrange to meet a girl called Mimi on her days off on a couple of occasions. Mimi was the same age as me. She had shiny black hair with a long straight fringe. I knew guys who married bargirls but I'm not aware of one union that was successful.

Sometimes I took the tram to the Peak or a bus to Repulse Bay to see where the rich people lived. I looked at the luxury apartments and grand mansions and knew I would never be able to afford to live there. Repulse Bay was a beautiful beach with some nice little bars and was best visited in mid-week or the off season as it would be difficult to find any space on the beach on a Saturday in July.

My first Christmas in Hong Kong was quite eventful. Six of us from my intake including Dave, Craig and Jock, decided that we would make our way to Causeway Bay and spend the day in the Dickens Bar in the Excelsior Hotel. We all piled into a couple of taxis and made our way over the island. But then later sitting at the bar nursing our beers, we were all completely home-sick and miserable. In Hong Kong at that time there were hardly any Christmas decorations. No Christmas trees and no atmosphere. After enjoying a sort of festive lunch in the hotel with a couple of bottles of very sophisticated Mateus Rose, we went back to the bar for port and brandy. But there was no festive spirit so we needed a plan 'B'. In Hong Kong it was just another day. Someone came up with an excellent plan B. We went to the hotel cake shop and purchased two large fresh cream cakes for HK$20 each. Then we all then climbed in a couple of taxis and made our way across the harbour to Tsim Sha Tsui.

We were headed for 'Red Lips', an infamous girly bar which was more of a retirement home for tired prostitutes. We ordered beers, and then carefully sliced the luxury fresh cream cakes. The 'girls' devoured them like vultures, and in seconds just crumbs remained. We then staggered out into the warm evening air and somehow wandered into a massage parlour in Hankow Road. The cost of a one-hour massage was HK$45. After a lovely sauna and steam room and now dressed only in a small pair of cotton shorts I was led to a room and a lovely young woman who called herself 'Rainbow' came in to massage my tired muscles. It was an excellent massage; as she walked up and down my back her little feet and toes kneaded my shoulder muscles. Feeling thoroughly refreshed I stumbled out into the night and joined my mates. We decided to get a taxi back to Wan Chai where I ended up with Mimi at 3.30am in Disco Rock. I still have some photos of us from that Christmas Day, they bring back fond memories. It was not an English Christmas spent arguing with relatives and getting crap presents like socks and a second-hand Meccano set, but it was certainly an interesting one.

CHAPTER V

Passing out from PTS

AFTER CHRISTMAS, in the senior stage of training I would be put in charge of the squad on rotation which meant I had to march the squad to and from lessons and training. One afternoon I had to march the squad back from the parade ground to the administration block. When we were off the square I saw the room boy approaching. He was wearing his usual blue nylon shorts, grubby old vest, and rubber slippers and had a canvas bag of dirty laundry over his shoulder. I started to have naughty ideas. When we were near him I commanded loudly: 'Squad, by the right–eyes right'; an honour reserved for senior officers. The expats in the squad got the joke and gave the smartest 'eyes right' ever, but some of the locals' hands went up in a salute half-way and then they realised what was going on. Unfortunately, the drill and musketry inspector had been following quietly behind and saw me do it. I heard a shout: 'Mr Roberts, don't make a fool of me.' I was placed on guard duty on Sunday. I must have been a bit of a trouble maker, because I was 'gated' or put on guard duty quite often.

One Sunday during the summer, when suffering yet another guard duty, a young English inspector came running into the guard house, 'Quickly-call an ambulance, we've had an accident on the cricket pitch' he shouted, I dialled 999 for an ambulance which arrived within a few minutes. I ran down to the pitch to see what had happened. A young trainee inspector called Richard had been fielding on the boundary when a huge six had been hit way up in the sky. Richard had been running backwards trying to catch the ball when it flew down out of the sun and struck him in the face between his eyes knocking him unconscious. He was lying prostrate in the outfield in his white flannels. It was agreed that I should escort him to the Queen Mary Hospital. He was placed on a stretcher and I sat next to him in the back of the ambulance. About fifteen minutes later we arrived and he was admitted to an open public ward. The nurse put a bandage on his head and took his pulse. I sat down next to his bed. Within ten minutes Richard suddenly came to, and jumped out of the bed in a befuddled state. He strode up and down the ward wishing the patients a '*Kung hay fat choy*' (Happy Chinese New Year). It was late May and the New Year had occurred about four months earlier. The nurses chased him and managed to get him back to bed. He lay there with a bandage on his head. He had one eye closed and one eye open looking for an opportunity. A few minutes later he jumped up again and this time began to impersonate Frankie Howerd from an old BBC TV comedy show called *Up Pompeii*. He walked up and down the ward shouting 'Nay-nay and thrice nay' and 'Now the prologue' and other catchphrases from the show, which of course meant nothing to the locals looking on wide eyed with disbelief. Richard was discharged later in the day to the obvious relief of the nurses. I went back to PTS with him in an ambulance. I'm not sure he was ever the same again.

Once my exam results improved and I felt a bit more confident about the future I decided to buy a car. It was a British racing green MG Midget. I paid HK$6,000 for it. It was a two-seat convertible with chrome bumpers and wire-spoked wheels. I loved it. It had a manual gearbox, no power steering, and no air conditioning. I soon realised that it was probably the most unsuitable car for a place like Hong Kong. It rained a lot, which meant I couldn't put the hood down. It was often hot and humid which meant I sweated like crazy after five minutes of driving. In the winter in the New Territories, and up on the Peak it was great, but it wasn't a city car. But it was mine and it meant a certain amount of freedom.

The last set of exams before passing out of PTS is called 'Standard Ones'. All four papers have to be passed in a single sitting. In addition there were exams in leadership, Cantonese, fitness, drill, and weapons. But it was the written exams that most people were nervous about. Somehow I managed to pass them, the pass mark was 50 per cent and I remember that all my marks were between 51 and 59 per cent. But there were more failures in my intake and 'back-squadings'. Understandably the three British and one local who were back-squadded were very miserable as they had to join the intake behind us and re-do two months of training. Out of thirty-six expat and local inspectors who had started the training in our intake only twenty-three now remained.

Finally it was the day of our passing-out parade. I was very excited but also very nervous. I remember that I felt very proud, but also sad that my parents were not there to see me. I don't remember any British parents or family members coming out for any of the expat guys that year, unlike our local colleagues who had families proudly applauding. Passing-out parades in the Hong Kong Police are a big deal. There would be several hundred on the parade ground and several hundred spectators in the grandstand. The standard of drill was excellent. The police band and the pipers would be playing, the commandant would be on the dais, and usually the commissioner or one of his deputies would be present. There were march pasts, inspections, and eyes-right. A 'baton of honour' was awarded to the best inspector in the intake. I don't remember who won it, but I do remember it wasn't me. I remember our parade being pretty faultless and as we marched off our drill instructor seemed pleased. We were able to wear one silver pip on our epaulette as a probationary inspector. Exhausted, I made my way back to the officers' mess for an ice-cold beer.

CHAPTER VI

A Kind of Freedom in Sha Tin

BEFORE LEAVING PTS we could make a wish list to opt for our choices of posting. My first choice was the Marine Police and my second was the New Territories. A few weeks earlier, Bruce Vogel and Les Bird had kindly taken me out on a police launch. I do not have good sea legs and was ill, but it didn't deter me. However as there were no vacancies in the Marine District none of my intake ended up there so I was posted to the New Territories (NT). The commandant, Peter Webb, interviewed me and I told him I was happy with the posting. I was due to go to Sha Tin which was then a new town. A racecourse had recently been built there. My new quarters were to be in Tai Po Kau. This consisted of a small whitewashed two storey block in a rather elevated wooded position just above the old Tai Po Road. People were telling me how nice these quarters were and how lucky I was. So I decided to drive up in my trusty MG to check it out. I think I was expecting some kind of villa with a nice terrace and pleasant furnishings. I was very disappointed. I met one of the inspectors called Steve who showed me to my room. It was a drab undecorated room with a bathroom.

The bed was bare springs; there were a couple of broken chairs, and no curtains. It was clear the other inspectors had already removed anything useful before my arrival. I was crestfallen, the place looked even worse than my room at PTS. I drove back to PTS that evening feeling very sorry for myself. Over the weekend I packed my suitcase, my Hitachi stereo, and my suits from Sam's and made my way back across Happy Valley, through the Cross-Harbour Tunnel and through Kowloon, to Sha Tin via the Lion Rock Tunnel. I settled in as best I could. I was introduced to the amah named Cheung, an inscrutable old lady who always wore black smock and trousers with black cotton slippers. She used to cook a strange-smelling brownish black soup over a small gas stove on the floor. I did not sleep well. I was due to report to Sha Tin on Monday morning as the new sub-unit commander.

Sha Tin was a modern police station, in a new town, much of it built on land reclaimed from the sea. The police station was surrounded by a high white concrete wall with observation posts or pill boxes built into each corner. Sha Tin only had a couple of housing estates in 1980, and many of the old farms and paddy fields still remained. I was put on shift work. 'A' shift was the morning, 'B' was the afternoon/evening, and 'C' was from midnight to 8am. I worked shifts, fifty-six hours a week minimum, no overtime pay, six days a week. It should have been exhausting, but at the age of twenty-one I didn't really notice it. On each shift I would draw a Smith & Wesson .38 revolver and six rounds of ammunition. I would sign the armoury book and move to the loading/unloading area and place the six rounds in my revolver and then attach a ring on the butt of the gun to a lanyard attached to my Sam Browne belt, and place the revolver in my holster.

My first boss was Chief Inspector Lee Ming Kwai. He kindly took me under his wing and helped mentor me. He was known as Dick Lee, he was six foot four inches tall and very charismatic. He was one of the best bosses I had in my police career. I was happy to see he later rose to become the commissioner. The Hong Kong Police then still deployed, and has retained, foot patrols on beats, signing visiting books on patrol, and it works. This is genuine community policing and not empty phrases and semantics. A police officer on secondment from the UK once asked me: 'Do you have community policing?' The question baffled me, it was the first time I had heard the term. I thought to myself, well who else do we police? As a young inspector I was expected to walk the beat. I also supervised the beat patrols from a dark blue police Land Rover, and had to keep in touch with the report room and any incidents arising.

Due to the large size of the division, I requested to attend a police motorcycle course. After passing the four-week course and gaining my licence, I was able to patrol on a small 175cc Kawasaki police motorcycle which was much more convenient to get around. We had heavy Motorola radios which were very unreliable. Once I was a couple of miles from the station they hardly ever worked properly. On a C shift at about 2am I was on my Kawasaki riding along on one of the newly built highways in Sha Tin which then had virtually no traffic. I noticed that three large, black buffaloes had broken free from their grazing field and were wandering down the middle of the six-lane motorway. A couple of them had metal rings on their noses and wooden stakes hanging on a chain around their necks. I stopped and radioed for backup: 'I need assistance, there are three bulls on the highway,' but there was no way I could get through to the station, all I heard was 'What?', 'Repeat', and lots of static. I decided there was no option but to try to corral them myself. So with my headlamp on full beam, and indicators flashing, I pressed the bike horn, revved the engine and started wheeling the bike around in 180-degree turns trying to frighten them back into the fields. They stared at me as if I was mad, but then remarkably it seemed to work. I suspected my headlamp beam in their eyes had just irritated them. In spite of the animals being rather large, and with quite threatening horns, they slowly started to make their way back to the paddy fields and their adventure came to an end. Later when I returned to the station I told my colleagues about it. But they just laughed; I don't think they believed me.

As Sha Tin had a large number of construction projects, we had a lot of engineers working in the area. Many were granted temporary membership of our officers' mess. Up on the top floor of the station, we had some sleeping quarters and the officers' mess. There was a tradition in many of the stations in the NT to have curry lunch on Fridays. If I was on the daytime A shift, I would usually be commanded by Dick Lee to come up to the mess at about noon: 'Come on young Simon, come up for a curry,' and the drinking would begin. Even thirty-five years later he still calls me 'young Simon' which I find amusing. The two most popular beers were San Miguel and Carlsberg, both brewed in Hong Kong. A new Chinese beer called Tsing Tao was becoming more popular and was my favourite. We used to have some Indian cooks, and also some

Chinese cooks from Shandong who were very good. The curry was usually a choice between mutton and chicken each served with ladles out of large steel containers. There were also large steel pots of boiled rice. Sometimes we would get chapattis, and then there were condiments. These were chopped cucumber, tomatoes, bananas, and onions and of course, mango chutney. I used to really look forward to curry Fridays. I was by far the youngest in the mess and had no old war-horse stories, so spent most of the time eating, drinking, and listening to the jokes and tall tales. I usually did not get out before six in the evening, and after six hours of drinking then climbed into my little MG and drove home to my spartan quarters in Tai Po Kau.

One of the more interesting aspects about Sha Tin District at the time was the village patrol unit or 'VPU'. This was under the control of Sergeant Chan, but a PC Cheng seemed to run a large part of it. PC Cheng would spend the whole week in the villages, sometimes patrolling, and sometimes listening to the villagers' reports and gossip. He would do this whilst sitting at a table in the open air with a report book laid out in front of him; it was quite an idyllic life. The traditional villages pre-dated British occupation but were sparsely inhabited, as a lot of the younger residents had moved to the city or emigrated to the UK. Many of the older Chinese restaurants in the UK were started by the original residents of these traditional villages.

In the villages I went on patrol wearing a blue beret or village police green soft hat. I once found part of an old BOAC air ticket from the 1960s on the floor of one of the houses. It was a one-way ticket to London Airport, before Heathrow was built. A number of the small single-storey village houses still had black-and-white pictures of ancestors on the walls, and personal possessions in drawers and cupboards. There were cups and plates on shelves, and cutlery in the drawers. It was fascinating, a bit like walking into a time capsule, but it was also a bit creepy. I tried to imagine what life had been like back then. How had people felt leaving their ancestral villages and abandoning these personal possessions? It must have been incredibly difficult and sad for them. I hope that they found a better life overseas. It was quite ironic considering I had come over in the opposite direction.

In 1980, an American called Mike lived in a modern Spanish-style villa in one of the villages. He was a very handsome chap who presented the news on TVB each evening. I found out he lived in my division one day when a police file was placed on my desk. It seemed that Mike had a collection of firearms in his house. It's rare for people to keep firearms in Hong Kong and there are strict controls and licensing requirements. What was unusual about this case was that there had been a problem with the last inspection visit. Mike had specific religious beliefs that meant no one wore shoes in his house. The police inspector on the recent visit had refused to remove his shoes and so had not been allowed to enter the house. I was asked to follow up on the case. A few days later I made an appointment by phone, and on the agreed date I travelled over to the village with one of my constables.

It was a warm summer's day and I was in the Royal Hong Kong Police green summer uniform. The house was an ordinary type of Spanish style three-storey villa which is fairly common now in the New Territories and Sai Kung. I walked up a short path with some neat flowers on either side and knocked on the door. A moment later there stood Mike the TV news reader welcoming me with a friendly smile. I said: 'Good morning,' and then I knelt down and without saying anything further removed my shoes. From that moment on Mike could not do enough for me. He took me to the room where the firearms were properly stored in a locked metal gun-case. The house was basic but neat and tidy. I noticed a few Buddhist symbols and pictures on the walls and shelves. After Mike unlocked the case I examined the firearms against my record and ensured all was in order. When I'd satisfied myself that the guns were secure and kept in accordance with the licence I thanked Mike and made my way back to the entrance. He was still thanking me for my 'understanding' as I bent down to lace up my black leather shoes. When I returned to the station I approved the licence renewal. I always preferred a pragmatic approach.

There were still various wild animals in the countryside, but the animal that used to annoy the remaining villagers was the wild boar. When villagers reported their crops had been damaged by wild boar, the police would sometimes organise hunting parties. With Remington shotguns in hand, the party would try to flush out the offending animals. Some of these creatures were large and quite aggressive and it wasn't advisable to get in their way. Naturally there was a benefit of the hunt. If one of the pigs was shot it would be skinned, gutted and roasted on a barbecue. But before that a trophy photograph of the hunters in front of the pig would be taken though. Inside the VPU offices there were a number of framed photos on the walls of policemen carrying shotguns standing behind a giant wild boar they had slain.

The majority of the visitors who stay for two three nights for business or shopping probably don't realise the type of creatures that live on the hillsides. There are still wild deer living on the Peak on Hong Kong Island. In the New Territories, apart from the wild boar there are some quite exotic creatures. There are porcupines, I've never seen one but I've found their quills. Occasionally pangolins are found. There are a wide variety of snakes. I have encountered quite a few when out on hill walks. The most impressive are the Burmese pythons which can grow to a huge size, and the king cobra. Many years later I came face to face with a large king cobra on Lantau Island. I was walking up a dried-up creek when I spotted it. It was only about fifteen feet in front of me. It was sunning itself on top of a large boulder and did not seem impressed by my arrival. It looked down at me, opened its hood and made a move in my direction. I did not wait to see what its intention was; I turned and ran and probably broke some kind of speed record sprinting back down the hill.

CHAPTER VII

The ICAC

WHEN I STARTED OUT in my police career in the late seventies, the force was still reeling from a number of corruption scandals that had occurred a few years earlier. In the first few years I was often asked about this when travelling, the stigma took years to wear off. It had unfortunately cast a shadow over the force, which was a great shame for the majority who were honest and professional. The most famous incident was the Peter Godber case. He had been a chief superintendent who had come under suspicion due to some unusual bank transfers. When he knew that he was under suspicion he requested early retirement. In 1973, shortly before he was due to depart, the police received additional information and he fled the colony using his airport security pass and flew back to the UK via Singapore. Evidence seized from his government quarters included several files, which seemed to be a record of the bribes he had received. Following a long extradition battle he was eventually flown back to Hong Kong in 1975 to face trial, where he was convicted and sentenced to four years imprisonment.

Until 1973, corruption in public service had been largely investigated in-house, and the police had a department investigating corruption. However this case changed public perception and there were growing calls for an independent body to properly investigate cases. During the 1960s and into the 1970s corruption had become endemic in many public services. 'Tea money' was commonly requested for all sorts of assistance. I had heard that there used to be an expression that you could 'ride the train' (take money) 'watch the train go by' (don't take money but say nothing) but you better not try and stand in front of the train! So in 1974 the Independent

Commission against Corruption (ICAC) was formed. In the beginning many of the officers staffing the ICAC were senior police officers
from the UK. The government passed new laws giving the ICAC
extremely wide powers to investigate corruption. By the time I had
arrived in 1979, the ICAC was well established and had already
convicted many current and former public servants. To reduce the
incentive for corruption, a pay review was conducted and civil
service salaries were increased. Although, maybe with a wry glance
backwards, I was told that ICAC actually stood for, 'I can accept cash'.

The police commissioner at the time I joined the police was Roy
Henry, a very experienced officer who had previously served in
several colonies. He was considered a safe pair of hands and proved
so during a time of considerable change. Sir Murray MacLehose
was the governor and ended up being the longest serving governor,
he led Hong Kong for eleven years from 1971 to 1982. MacLehose
was well-liked by the people in Hong Kong and the long and
well-trodden MacLehose Trail in the New Territories was named
in his honour. There is an annual race along its entire length up in
the New Territories which always seemed to be won by the Gurkhas.

According to the *Hong Kong Yearbook,* in 1978 the police force
had 19,000 officers. During the year a total of ninety-one new
expatriates were recruited. In the same year 13,861 people were
arrested for gambling offences, 3,078 were arrested for prostitution
and related offences. There were sixty-three homicides in a population of 4.7 million people which was a low rate compared to many
Western countries. Life expectancy for a male born in Hong Kong
though was only 69.86 years. The population was 98 per cent
Chinese, there were 14,100 British, and 6,200 Americans living in the
colony. Interestingly though by 2012, fifteen years after the Handover
only 91 per cent of Hong Kong citizens were of Chinese descent, and
Filipinas and Indonesians were the biggest expat groups with 168,850
and 165,170 residents respectively. Back in 1978 the first ever methyl-
amphetamine lab in Hong Kong was discovered and made ineffective.
I was pleased though as a young inspector that by the time I joined,
because of the new laws, a modern culture, and improved terms
and conditions, corruption had been almost eradicated, and the
force was a police service ready for the new challenges it faced.

CHAPTER VIII

Vice Squad

A S A SUB-UNIT COMMANDER, I was responsible for all the general management of the junior police officers and the station. Each shift started with a parade and roll call when all the constables and sergeants turned up and were allocated beats, and collected their revolvers and beat radios. This also served as a kind of mini-inspection where the sub-unit commander would check that the junior officers were smartly turned out, that their hair was neat, and the uniform correctly fitted. Generally though the station sergeant would run the show and conduct the briefings. It was here that I learned the most important phrase for a young inspector like myself, which was: 'Carry on sergeant'. These three words spoken with authority were often the only ones I needed. They all knew what to do, but we all had to go through the motions with the inspector. In the report room the duty officer would handle all the cases reported in person by recording them in ink pen in a large hardback log called the Miscellaneous Report Book. He or she would also manage the cells and meals for any people detained.

There was a very strange situation in Sha Tin at this time. Many of the detention cells in the police station which should have been only holding criminals were full of completely innocent people. Although not widely known, many women and children were being held for weeks on end. They had no exercise, or even access to sunlight, even though they had committed no crime. Yet whenever I saw them I could not comprehend how upbeat they seemed. They always smiled when they saw me and we tried to communicate. They were all from Mainland China. They were in a temporary limbo as they were being processed for relocation overseas. Many would eventually be provided sanctuary in the USA. The problem was there seemed to be no secure external housing available for them. Much of the existing secure areas were full of Vietnamese boat people or illegal immigrants already. So these people were crammed into small police cells only designed to hold prisoners overnight. They could not speak English or Cantonese and hardly any of our local Hong Kong officers could speak Putonghua (or Mandarin) back then. I used to get them pots of tea, and extra lunch boxes, and went round the station collecting Chinese magazines and newspapers so they had something to read. I always felt very sad for them and felt the conditions were inhumane. The saving grace was they would move on to a better life, so there was hope for all of them. Interestingly there was never any adverse media coverage about this.

Usually during our first three-year tour of duty we would be placed in the vice squad for six months to a year. This was considered an interesting posting. All the districts had their own vice squad which handled cases involving narcotics, prostitution, and gambling. The only legal gambling was at the Jockey Club, and on the weekly lottery called the Mark Six. The Chinese though love gambling and will bet on almost anything, it is a national pastime but also considered a vice. Many illegal gambling venues would spring up, ranging from small *mahjong* games to larger and more sophisticated illegal horse racing operations. These would be popular because they would offer better odds than the Jockey Club and often offered credit too. In the vice squad we would wear plain clothes and try to blend in with the local people. This was of course not so easy for me.

We were very poorly equipped in the early 1980s. One of my sergeants used his own car and we bought our own pagers to get messages to each other. There were no mobile phones, and police radios were far too bulky to carry on undercover work. Whilst on duty in the special duty squad I was based in the old Tai Po police station near Tai Po market, built in the early 1900s. It stood on a small hill surrounded by tall acacia trees and was quite a pleasant place with its old-style high ceilings, ceiling fans and whitewashed plaster walls. I often tried to eat with the team in the staff canteen. It was okay in the mornings when I could get white bread and luncheon meat with a fried egg on top, and a cup of tea with condensed milk. But the lunches I found difficult. Whatever meat or fish was served seemed to consist of about 90 per cent bone or gristle. I did eat a lot of rice and vegetables and so in spite of the beer I did not seem to put on weight.

In Sha Tin at the time there was not much in the way of prostitution and what there was, was very low key, so most of the time we concentrated on combatting illegal gambling and drugs. The local officers would get tips from paid informers and we would often set up an ambush for a known trafficker. One night we had information regarding a character that lived in an old village house on the outskirts of Tai Po. On doing a local recce we found that the house was unoccupied but also unlocked. We made our way inside and when we didn't find anything incriminating we hid inside in the darkness. After about an hour or so the suspect arrived with his girlfriend. As they walked through the door, we jumped up and cautioned them. They were taken to separate rooms for questioning. My Sergeant Chan was extremely keen and energetic, and quickly located a couple of small straws of suspected No. 3 heroin in the man's jeans pocket. But he was not satisfied and before I knew what was happening, he had told the suspect to remove his jeans and underpants. He told the suspect to bend over forwards, and Sergeant Chan with all the alacrity of experience grabbed the suspect's naked buttocks with his bare hands and pulled them apart as far as he could. As he was doing this he ordered PC Leung to shine a flashlight up the guy's arse. I can authoritatively say that there were no narcotics hidden up there as unfortunately I was in clear line of sight. So with our suspect now replacing his trousers he was arrested for only possessing the two small straws of heroin. Enlightened, but rather disappointed we handcuffed the poor chap and made our way back to the station.

One of the more interesting cases in Tai Po was when we received confidential information about a person called Chong who allegedly ran an opium divan. By 1980 most drug addicts in Hong Kong smoked or injected heroin or 'chased the dragon', which meant heating the drug on a spoon over a flame, and then inhaling the vapours. Opium, which had been traded by British merchants 100 years previously, was now out of fashion and uncommon. The lead took us to the home of a pig farmer a few miles outside Tai Po. We checked the small house and found nothing and of course Chong denied any knowledge of opium, so I decided to have a look outside. There were a few old brick and concrete pigsties but everything looked very overgrown and messy. I noticed there was a remarkable absence of pigs. I got down on my hands and knees and peered into one of the sties at the bottom of the land outside. It had a dirty curtain over the entrance so I decided to crawl inside. The inside of the pigsty was carpeted; the ceiling was only about four feet high. There were some low wooden stools and a narrow single bed. The walls were also covered in carpets. I smelt a familiar aroma. I looked inside an old cigar box and there I saw a ball of black sticky opium wrapped in clear cellophane. Under the bed I found a traditional opium pipe, and other drug paraphernalia. I was elated, an opium divan! Yes, a small one but still an opium divan. I crawled back out and passed the news to the team. To some extent, I felt sorry for the owner. He was over sixty-five years old and told us he had smoked opium all his life. He even showed us a wrinkled bit of brown paper which was held together with yellowed Sellotape. It was a pre-war licence for opium smoking. I don't think he was making any money from it. I wasn't even too convinced about the so-called side effects from opium. The chap seemed to be in rude health. I almost felt sorry for having to arrest him. I remember the magistrate sentencing him rather lightly to a short suspended sentence, and ordering the opium and the pipe to be confiscated. I suspect Chong subsequently continued with his habit.

Some incidents brought home to me strange aspects of the culture and the differences that existed here compared to back home. One day when I was on A shift whilst I was walking through the old Tai Po police station I heard a huge commotion coming from the report room. When I came through the door I saw two uniformed constables struggling to control two old men who were shouting and swearing and waving their arms around. The Cantonese expression that you will hear on every street is *'due lay lo mo'* which translates as 'fuck your mother'. These two old men were shouting this at each other very aggressively. When I asked the duty sergeant what was going on, he said: 'Ah sir, these two old men have been friends for over forty years.' 'It doesn't look like it'! I exclaimed. But it turned out they had met for lunch or *yum cha* that afternoon. It was the first time that they had met in over a year. When it came to paying the bill each of them had demanded to pay. Neither would back down. Both insisted on having the honour of paying. This squabble became an argument, then a stand-up slanging match and finally they started trading punches. At this point the restaurant staff called police, and when the constable arrived they were still swinging at each other. I suggested to the sergeant that they be put in separate cells for an hour to cool off. Sometime later I went down and spoke to them myself with the help of an interpreter. I threatened criminal charges, a court hearing, and a criminal record unless . . . they each apologised to each other in front of me and left together as friends. I'm happy to say that they did eventually agree to this settlement. After an hour cooling their heels in separate cells they were more contrite. They walked out together back down the hill to the market and we never saw them again.

On another occasion I was asked to attend a domestic dispute. A husband and wife had been shouting loudly at each other and it had become quite nasty resulting in neighbours calling police. When we got them back to the station we put them in different rooms and began to question them. It was near to Chinese New Year and the husband had wanted to wash his hair. His wife who was very traditional had reprimanded him and told him he had to wait until after the festival or he would 'wash all his luck away'. He had replied it was all superstition and the two had quickly descended into abuse. I decided to hold them in separate rooms for a while to let them reflect and cool off. I then went back in with a red-tab constable who spoke good English. I first went into the room with the husband. I pretended to get angry. I told him that Chinese New Year was very important. I said that he should respect traditions, that his wife was right and he should not wash his hair. Meanwhile my young constable faithfully translated everything. I then left, and went into the room where his wife was sitting. Again I feigned anger and remonstrated with her for being so traditional. I said that her husband could wash his hair if he wanted, and anyway he was trying to be nice and presentable for the family. Finally I got the couple back together and told them it was 'a final warning, if I see you again I will take both of you to a magistrate.' With that threat I let them go.

They walked out together. They silently climbed into a bus to make their way home. I wondered if they had ever realised what I'd said to them both. I'm pleased to say that I never saw them again so I think it worked.

When I was still in the vice squad I had headed back to Sha Tin one Friday to enjoy the famous curry lunch. During the late afternoon a senior superintendent Atkinson announced that Dick Lee was to be promoted to superintendent. This news was met with genuine warmth as Dick was well liked by everyone in the station. After yet more drinks, Atkinson decided that Dick should treat us to dinner at the Sha Tin Jockey Club. So about eight of us went over to the restaurant and sat at a round table in the Western dining area where poor old Dick was bullied into ordering steak and champagne for all of us. At that time officers from Sha Tin were granted automatic social membership to the Jockey Club and Beas River Club which was a nice perk. After many pints of beer, several glasses of wine, champagne, and more beer I was starting to feel a bit queasy so the steak was very welcome. During the evening Atkinson decided to ask the restaurant manager Jimmy for a 'racing tip' for the Sha Tin race meeting the next day. Jimmy promptly left and returned about ten minutes later. I happened to be sitting next to Atkinson and so although already rather drunk I was able to hear Jimmy bend down and say 'Shamrock' into Atkinson's ear.

The next day I was back on duty in Tai Po, I was slumped over the desk groaning with a mother of a hangover, drinking cups of black coffee and chewing paracetamol like candy. Although mornings were never my best time, I must have looked worse than normal as even my team looked concerned. Suddenly I jumped up. I loudly said: 'Shamrock.' Everyone looked puzzled; they thought I had now gone completely mad. I explained what had happened last night, and asked Sergeant Chan to check the racing pages and see if there was a horse running called Shamrock. Sure enough there was a 'Shamrock' in Race 5. I asked the odds and was told it was on a 6 to 1. Quickly I went round the squad to see how much cash we had and collectively we gathered up about HK$200. One of the young constables was told to go into town and put all the money on Shamrock to win. That afternoon we waited expectantly for the race and listened on the radio. It was all in rapid-fire Cantonese but the expressions on the team's faces said it all. Shamrock romped home by four lengths. What a windfall! Morale was certainly at its highest that weekend. We bought ourselves lunch boxes and stuffed the remaining cash into our pockets. In 1980 the winnings were very welcome indeed. The problem I discovered though, was every week afterwards I was asked for more tips from my secret inside source.

CHAPTER IX

A Bomb in Tai Po

IN THE OLD TAI PO market town there was a small restaurant that served Western food. I used to sometimes walk down when off duty and order a steak with black pepper sauce. It came with crinkle-cut chips and peas, and of course I washed it down with a nice cold Tsing Tao beer. One evening I was sitting by myself when half way through my meal the waiter called Cheung came running up to my table and gabbled something which might have been English: 'Ah sir – balm.' I feebly replied: 'Um pardon?' He continued: 'Ah sir bum! Bam! Balm!' I stared at him with a very confused expression. He became even more agitated and eventually he grabbed my arm and dragged me outside. I was annoyed as I'd only taken two bites from my black-pepper steak. When I got to the doorway, he pointed up the street. I heard screams, and saw people collapsing in the street. There was a lot of smoke and debris, and people stumbling around. I ran up the street to find the Jockey Club betting centre was in flames. I stepped inside the burning building and was able to grab a large red fire extinguisher from the wall. Somehow I pulled out the pin and got it working and aimed the water jet at the people inside with burning clothes and then at the burning paper on the floor.

It later transpired that someone had placed a pipe bomb in the waste paper basket inside the club on a Wednesday evening, a race day, when it was full of punters. Luckily no one had been killed but some had serious burns. Using my scant knowledge of Cantonese I asked some uninjured staff to call for an ambulance. When the situation had become clearer and the fire had been extinguished I tried to take stock of the scene. Meanwhile I did my best to secure the area and stop the staff sweeping the floor and removing evidence. With no mobile phone and no beat radio it was very frustrating because I had to wait for backup from some uniformed officers to help to guard the premises.

I also had to wait for Ron Bagrie, the force bomb disposal officer, to attend the scene. He had to come from his quarters on Hong Kong Island, through the Lion Rock Tunnel and along the old Tai Po Road, so it was almost two hours before he arrived. The first thing he asked was: 'Have you searched the area for further devices?' I hadn't, and the idea that I had been standing there all that time with perhaps another bomb a few feet away did nothing to improve my mood. Next day back at the station I received a verbal 'Well done' from the superintendent. That was it. I didn't even receive a nice comment in my service record.

The next day the incident was on the front page of the *South China Morning Post* and all the other newspapers. The *Post*'s story, written by Tommy Lewis, was headlined BOMB BLAST IN CROWDED BETS CENTRE and went on to say '100 punters battle to flee smoke. A bomb blast rocked a crowded Jockey Club betting centre in Tai Po'. To my knowledge the motive for the bomb attack was never ascertained and no one was ever arrested.

CHAPTER X

Moving into Tsim Sha Tsui

ONE DAY IN OCTOBER 1980, as I was reading police bulletins I noticed that there were some brand-new quarters available. These were on 'quartering officer allocation', which meant that they did not depend on points. Government quarters were allocated usually on a points system. The higher the rank, and the more children you have the more points you get. So as a single probationary inspector my points were basically zero. The place sounded interesting and was in a great location. I had a few hours off, so I climbed into the old MG and drove to the police quartering office in Central. To my surprise I was given a set of keys and allowed to go and check out the new apartments. New World Development had built a block of serviced apartments in Tsim Sha Tsui next to the Intercontinental Hotel on the harbour waterfront. It was part of a complex that included a hotel and a shopping centre. The idea was ahead of its time. In 1980 very few people outside the USA knew what serviced apartments were.

I drove my little MG into the allocated private multi-storey car park. Then I took a lift up to the reception on the fourth floor. It was all very plush with lots of glass and marble. There was a residents' swimming pool, a fully equipped gym, a laundrette, and there was direct covered access to the hotel and the shopping centre. I took the lift to the eleventh floor and entered a studio apartment. The moment I walked in I knew I had to have it. Although small, it was fully equipped; it had a duvet on the bed, a TV, and an electric cooker. There were even cushions on the sofa. The view was over the swimming pool. I was elated; this place was the perfect bachelor pad. I was now twenty-two years old; I was slim, single, horny, and fit for some late nights. I could speak some Cantonese and had money in my pocket. I also had the 'three Cs' that I needed to pick up girls according to a local saying; car, cash, and camera. (Later this became the 'five Cs' when condominium and credit card were added.) I rang the quartering officer and told him I was taking the apartment. He told me 'You have to return the keys and then we will process the paperwork.' 'Too late,' I lied, 'I have already moved in.' He grumbled but did not protest too much. I told him I would dispatch the paperwork in the morning. I ran back to my car and drove as fast as I could back up to Tai Po Kau. It took me no more than twenty minutes to pack before I was back in the car with the soft top down and a very unstable cargo of various pieces of luggage, including grandma's suitcase strapped over the hood. I already knew that I loved the New World Apartments.

I thought I'd died and gone to heaven. There were attractive girls in the administration office, cute girls in the gym, sexy girls in the pool, lovely girls in the laundrette, and smart girls in the hotel, everywhere I looked, wow! I was in the heart of Tsim Sha Tsui. I could walk to bars and restaurants and bring girls back in the evening. I bought one of the first video cassette recorders from a Fortress electrical store and taped music videos to play back when I was 'entertaining'. I had my own phone in the studio apartment, wine in the fridge, and a nice swimming pool view. Soon the phone was ringing each night. I began to meet flight attendants as the New World Hotel next door was popular with crew on lay-over in Hong Kong. I discovered that Gulf Air, Singapore Airlines, and Malaysia Airlines crew all stayed there. Then of course there was Cathay Pacific with its beautiful girls from all over Asia. I quickly found out which clubs and discos the girls frequented. One local girl called Tina lived in the apartment two floors above me. I chatted her up in the laundrette in between putting $2 coins in the washing machine. She was a kept woman, the mistress of a sixty-year-old married multi-millionaire. She had been given a car, the apartment, a wardrobe allowance and spending money. She had everything she could want, but she was bored. So I offered to relieve her boredom. After a few months my social life began to get silly, I was receiving calls from so many girls, I couldn't even remember all their names.

CHAPTER XI

John MacLennan

Until 1991 homosexuality in Hong Kong was a criminal offence. The force had a secretive Special Investigations Unit (SIU), with one of its roles to investigate cases of homosexuality, especially amongst public servants. In 1980 whilst I was still a junior inspector, a news story broke that a young British inspector called John MacLennan had been found shot dead in his police quarters in Ho Man Tin. His service revolver was found near the body. When police went to the scene and investigated they found the front door locked from the inside. There were no signs of any disturbance in the flat and nothing had been stolen. A suicide note was found on the bedside table. Investigating officers concluded that the young inspector had killed himself. The problem was that there were five gunshot wounds on his body, most in his stomach, and many people questioned how it was possible that anyone could shoot themselves that many times.

It later transpired that a senior colleague had tipped MacLennan off that the SIU were going to come to the station the next day to take him in for questioning. There were rumours of clandestine affairs with senior police officers. Some had speculated that there were homosexuals in the highest ranks of the force who were too senior to be arrested. Many journalists refused to believe the incident was suicide and suggested black operations to get rid of MacLennan. Things got worse when a senior inspector called Michael Fulton came forward and said he had been asked to 'set up' MacLennan. As a young inspector I was fascinated by the case, but I was also unnerved by the powers of the SIU.

One English reporter attempted to show it was possible to gain access to the flat via a side window. But in a televised display he struggled to climb up and through the small window. The story remained in the news for a long time, and due to the incredible amount of public interest it was decided that a board of enquiry would be set up to thoroughly investigate all the circumstances. The enquiry was headed by Justice Yang and took over a year to produce its report; it was extremely detailed, hundreds of pages long, and and was highly critical of many areas of the force. I bought a copy of the report and read most of it. Even though I had not known MacLennan, the case upset me. But the conclusion was that MacLennan probably did commit suicide. After this I did not hear much more from the SIU and sometime later the unit was disbanded. In 1991 homosexuality was decriminalised in Hong Kong.

CHAPTER XII

Becoming a Court Prosecutor

TYPHOONS ARE VIRTUALLY an annual occurrence in Hong Kong. The peak season for them is July to September. They sweep in over the North Pacific, often hitting the Philippines or Taiwan before striking Southern China. In September 1983, when I was living in the New World Apartments, a very strong typhoon hit us. It was probably the worst typhoon during all my years in the police. Typhoon Ellen had wind speeds over 200kph and the number ten (hurricane) warning had been raised by the meteorological office. As I had now moved into a harbour-view apartment on the seventeenth floor I had a grandstand view. It was scary. I saw a boat overturned down below me in the harbour and watched as a large plank of wood about eight feet long flew by. Construction workers use bamboo for scaffolding in Hong Kong because it is more flexible than steel and can withstand high winds better. But it was peeling off buildings like a game of Jenga. The bamboo poles were flying around like lethal lances. Fortunately most people were heeding the government's advice to stay indoors.

Most of the fishing boats had got into the typhoon shelters, small harbours protected by concrete storm walls. But as I heard my windows shuddering and vibrating I was worried they would shatter. I made my way down to the management office to get some masking tape which I placed in 'X's across the glass panes. Gusts registered at Stanley that day at speeds of 248kph and the observatory recorded nine inches of rain. It knocked out power lines, and 50,000 people were without power. More than 200 homes were destroyed. Eight people were killed. This was a warning to me about the terrible power of typhoons, and I never took them lightly from that moment on. For the police the only advantage is that there is not much crime during a typhoon, but we were all expected to be available to help with rescues, and the clean up afterwards.

Fortunately my windows survived, and soon after my return to Sha Tin, I learnt I was to be posted to Tsuen Wan Magistrates Court as a prosecutor. This was a plain-clothes position. I was going to have to buy more suits from Sam's! It was an odd arrangement that a young police inspector could be a court prosecutor. I received no additional training. It was assumed that my limited schooling at PTS would suffice. I did not know my way around a court room and was unsure of the proper legal terms. I wasn't even too sure where Tsuen Wan was. When I looked it up on a map I realised that instead of taking a bus, or driving my car, there was a much more fun way to travel over. If I walked out from New World Apartments to the Star Ferry, and went over to Central, I could then walk to an adjacent pier and take a ferry directly to Tsuen Wan. This berthed only about five minutes' walk from the court room. So my daily commute was almost all on water.

Arriving early one Monday morning on my first day, smartly dressed in my shiny new suit and squeaky shoes, I made my way to the prosecutors' office. I had expected a leisurely handover of maybe a week or two to watch and observe while I learnt the ropes. I was in for a rude shock. There was no handover, and no training. As I walked in to see Chris, a court prosecutor who I already knew, another court prosecutor barked: 'You're late,' and thrust a large pile of case files into my arms. 'You're due in Court Three at 0930,' he said before running out of the room. I sat down, feeling rather dizzy.

The court was a rather anonymous building which had probably been built from a standard twentieth-century colonial design. Our prosecutors' office was about 150 square feet, with cream coloured walls, a wooden noticeboard, dark wooden tables and dark wood upright hard-backed chairs. There were some grey steel filing cabinets in a corner and an enormous ceiling fan which blew the case papers everywhere in the summer. I started to read through the case papers: assault, theft, possession of an offensive weapon, nothing looked too serious. But what was I supposed to do exactly?

Having managed to grab a cup of tea, I gathered up the case files and walked to the public area looking for Court Three.

I entered through the large heavy wooden door and looked around. The clerk of the court saw me, and seeing that I looked like a rabbit caught in a car's headlamps realised I must be the new prosecutor. He showed me to my position. I recognised the magistrate's chair on a raised platform with the royal crest and a framed photograph of the Queen on the wall. Then it happened. I was suddenly surrounded by three red-faced angry men, wearing black gowns and waving papers in my face. They were defence counsel for three defendants in one of the cases. They had probably been tipped off it was my first day, but it could also have been my timid and clueless expression. Whatever it was, they smelt blood. The magistrate had not yet entered and they were making full use of the situation. They threatened me, the police, and the commissioner. They said their clients were innocent and evidence had been planted. They warned that there would be huge costs awarded if I proceeded with the case. I must admit I was completely on the back foot. I suggested I would speak to the officer in charge of the case. This seemed to enrage them even more, as they continued to harangue me and shout that enough time had been wasted already. I didn't respond well, my fear was clear to see. I eventually extricated myself and ran back to my office to call the OC case.

Eventually the magistrate walked in from his chambers. He was a tall, slim, dark-haired Englishman surnamed Duffy. We all stood up and made a slight bow. After we sat down, the clerk handed him some papers and then read out the charges for each case in turn. The defendants were asked to take a plea. If they changed their plea to guilty, the magistrate would deal with the case first. He would ask if there was any mitigation, and any previous record before considering sentencing. The majority of the defendants were defended by legal aid counsels on a fixed daily rate. If their clients pleaded guilty, they got to go home early. The wealthier defendants had private counsel who were paid by the hour. They were happy to sit there all day. Those that continued to plead not guilty would be asked whether their witnesses were present and then to wait for a trial to start.

The characters who had engaged the three angry lawyers had been charged with possessing offensive weapons. I looked over at them: they were dark skinned, had tattoos, and were wearing loud gold jewellery. They seemed very self-confident and looked like local triad members. I looked at the case papers again. The evidence was pretty thin and even the OC case did not seem confident when I had spoken to him. I did wonder whether this had been a case that had been brought about to try to send a message to the defendants. Whatever it was I reluctantly agreed to drop the charges and the three pillars of society walked free. Looking at them I thought though it would not be long before I saw them again.

That evening as I made my way back on the ferry I bought a can of cold Carlsberg and sat looking out across the harbour. It was full of cargo ships of every shape and size. As the warmth of the air on the open top deck blew across my face I knew I'd had a bad day. If I did not want to embarrass myself and be known as a pushover I had to learn fast. The next day I asked Chris for advice. Whenever I had some spare time I watched the experienced lawyers at work. One advantage of court work was it was Monday to Friday, no shift work and weekends off. On Saturday I walked down to the venerable Swindon's bookshop in Tsim Sha Tsui. I was looking for books on criminal law, ideally something like – *How to turn an ignorant inspector into a top barrister in ten easy steps* or similar. What I found was far better. I was lucky to find Francis Wellman's *The Art of Cross-Examination* in a paperback edition for HK$25. It was first published in 1903; I devoured all 470 pages in three days. In the absence of any formal training I had to train myself. I was determined never to be bullied and embarrassed again. I imagined I was Francis Wellman prosecuting in a New York court room in 1885 and started to enjoy cross-examination and the whole process more. Next time any jumped-up private lawyer (and there were quite a few) tried to bully me, I would smile and suggest we let the case take its course and respect the magistrate's verdict.

The proceedings were always translated into English and many of the magistrates were British. We therefore had a translator, although as my Cantonese was improving I could sometimes pick up what was being said which gave me a few more seconds' thinking time. At the beginning we had a Shanghainese interpreter called Ying. She was always well turned out and took her job very seriously. Whenever she had any free time she always seemed to be studying. One day we had a nasty case of buggery on a boy under sixteen. I was really surprised to see it in our magistrate's court as such cases were rare and I felt it should be in the district court. The claim was that an Asian security guard in his fifties had lured a local young boy of eleven into his flat with the promise of some sweets and had given him some wine and then assaulted him. It was a tricky case as although there was some physical evidence, and an early complaint, there were no other witnesses, and any evidence at the scene had been cleaned up by the defendant.

I was very carefully questioning the young boy in his evidence, trying to make him feel more comfortable with the surroundings. So I had asked him about this school and his family, and what he liked to do at weekends, slowly leading him to the morning of the alleged attack. During this time Ying was doing her usual professional job of accurately translating. Magistrate Duffy was taking a keen interest, as the case had attracted some attention from the press. Eventually I started asking the victim about the time the defendant spoke to him and how he came to enter the flat. Then I asked how his trousers and pants were removed and how he had been bent over. At this most delicate moment, when I asked the key question: 'Please tell the court what happened next,' the boy responded but I did not catch his reply. Ying turned to the magistrate and loudly exclaimed in English: 'He stuck it up my arse-hole sir.' I looked over to the bench and Duffy seemed to be in slight shock. There was a silence that seemed to last for quite a long time. I bit my lip trying to stifle a smile. Eventually regaining my composure, I replied: 'Quite, and please carry on.' At the end of the case the security guard was convicted and then taken for psychiatric evaluation prior to sentencing.

Duffy and I were on the same ferry heading back to Hong Kong Island that evening. We sat on the open upper deck together enjoying a couple of cold Carlsbergs and debating whether we should suggest to Ying that a more formal way of describing that particular act might be more appropriate in future. Neither of us had the heart to say anything though. Despite the seriousness of the case, Ying's unconventional translation had been a welcome distraction.

After a few months I was more comfortable as a court prosecutor. I certainly did not miss shift work.

Many of the cases involved petty theft, assault or drug possession. For the majority of cases I would approach the cross examination from a quiet and friendly perspective to try to win the trust of the defendant before hopefully asking the killer question. With my lack of experience this only occasionally worked. On one occasion a young chap had been arrested for trafficking heroin. Although Hong Kong law was based closely on English law it had of course evolved and there were several 'presumptions' introduced, so if you had one small packet of white powder or heroin you would likely be charged only with 'possession' of a dangerous drug. But if you were caught with twenty straws of heroin you would be presumed to be 'trafficking'. The police did not have to prove that they saw him actually trying to sell the drugs. The onus was on the defendant to prove that he had them only for his own consumption.

In one case that I was prosecuting, the defendant who had been charged with drug trafficking had claimed he had been standing about two metres inside a narrow alleyway. However he told the court he was able to see everything in the street outside. I showed the court that he could not possibly be telling the truth. He was convicted and sentenced to a term of imprisonment.

My social life was busy too, with my usual nocturnal adventures and rugby at the weekends. But with my lovely downtown apartment and travelling to work on the ferry each day I realised I was using my old MG sports car less and less. So I decided to sell it to another young inspector. I was able to get the same price I bought it for. I didn't really miss it, I was just too busy. One day I got a call from one of my squad mates that the police were coming to town. After momentary confusion I realised that he meant the band 'Police' with lead singer Sting who were then probably the biggest band in the UK. A group of us bought some tickets for the concert which was to be in Tomorrow's World Disco on Hong Kong Island in a few weeks' time.

When the day of the concert arrived five of us turned up in white Royal Hong Kong Police T-shirts. During the show, I noticed a *BBC* Radio 1 DJ called Annie Nightingale in the crowd. We got chatting to her and she asked me if we would like to go backstage after the show and meet the band. I was really excited, and after the show we hung around and were invited into the dressing room. I think we were all very star-struck. The band was really friendly and I remember Sting saying he needed a massage. I thought about suggesting he went to a naughty place in Tsim Sha Tsui where a lovely girl called Rainbow would walk up and down his back. But just then Annie stepped forward and very professionally started massaging Sting's shoulders and back as he sat on a chair. Sting asked us if the band could have our T-shirts to wear at the next concert. We obliged and in return were given a poster each, which was signed by the three band members, and Annie. It had been a memorable evening, and we were all on a high as we left for a few celebratory beers in Wan Chai.

Walking from the ferry pier each day to the court and back was a rather dull journey past industrial buildings and was usually uneventful. One evening though as I made my way out of the court carrying my briefcase and umbrella and looking, I thought, rather businesslike, I saw a crowd gathered on the pavement. There were probably twenty people all trying to look at something. I had not noticed any hawkers in the area so at first I thought it might be a fight. I decided to cross the road and try to get a better view. As I was slightly taller than most people in the crowd I was able to look over and then saw a well-built Chinese man of maybe thirty years of age. He looked quite scruffy and wore a dirty white T-shirt which was covered in blood. I wondered if he had been stabbed but he seemed to be behaving normally and then I realised he was addressing the crowd.

I noticed in his right hand he was holding a snake. It was a live cobra; he was holding it by the neck. It must have been over four feet long and was wriggling furiously. I still did not know what was going on but to my horror he then put the head of the cobra in his mouth. Then in a very violent way he quickly twisted his head to the right about ninety degrees, then opened his mouth and spat. When he held the snake up I saw its neck was now pumping blood everywhere. I could hardly believe my eyes. He had literally bitten the snake's head off. I looked down on the pavement; there were three snakes' heads there. I still wasn't sure what this was all about, then I saw the man take a small knife out of his pocket and with the skill of a practised surgeon he made a small incision in the side of the snake. He then removed a small part of the snake's innards which I later learned was the gall bladder. He placed this in a small glass of strong, dark, Chinese wine; put the glass to his lips and downed it in one. At last I realised what was going on: he was a salesman, and his product was snake wine. He was pickling snakes in wine, and also putting gall bladders in Chinese brandy. The show seemed to be a success, and I saw a number of the punters buying the bottles. They all seemed to be men; I learnt later one of the selling points was that the wine was supposedly an aphrodisiac.

CHAPTER XIII

Life in the Officers' Mess

DURING MY FIRST TOUR of duty I was supposed to continue studying for my 'Standard Two' exams which would enable me to become a confirmed inspector and gain a second silver pip on my shoulder. Of course I did not do anything of the kind. I was having too much fun, and had no inclination to start studying police general orders. I did enjoy reading for pleasure, and one of the most enjoyable books that I read was *Myself a Mandarin* by Austin Coates. The book is a memoir about his life as a special magistrate in the New Territories in the 1950s. I read the book three or four times and still have my copy over thirty years later. It's a fascinating and often humorous account of his work as a colonial civil servant living in a way that now seems as if it occurred hundreds of years ago.

I also travelled around the colony and visited friends at different police stations especially in the New Territories. Some of them lived in the mess too, which I considered to be too close to the job. Although this was a convenient arrangement, if the sergeant had an important case he could easily come up to your quarters and ask for your help even if you were off duty. It was also too easy to nip down to the officers' mess and sign for another beer or find yourself in the mess and become engrossed in conversation with colleagues whilst consuming even more beer. I liked going into a mess to meet my colleagues, and I enjoyed the curry and banter, but I preferred living away from the police politics. Early in my career I made up my mind that there would be two things I would not do: live in a police station mess quarters, or wear a safari suit. My colleagues over forty often wore safari suits but the style never appealed to me.

Many of the officers' messes had a large number of plaques, mementoes, and souvenirs. The old Tai O station on Lantau had photos of officers that had been killed when a Sikh officer went mad. This was alongside photos of a successful tiger hunt, during a time when tigers roamed Lantau. I wonder what happened to all these old photos after 1997. Some of the older more senior officers took mess life seriously and were very rank conscious. There were bar stools in some messes that you could not sit on because 'that's where [a particular senior officer] always sits'.

A story that made me laugh was about a senior superintendent who was a well-known character in the NT. We will call him Rogers. He had a pair of very handsome Dobermans that were his pride and joy and he would often run with them over the hills, terrifying the locals. He had only worked in the NT throughout his twenty-five-year career. He lived in the NT and rarely travelled over to Hong Kong Island. Even though he was quite fit he did enjoy his San Miguel. He also had a favourite bar stool and woe betide anyone who sat on it. The story goes that sometimes he would continue drinking until he would fall asleep on the bar stool, and on more than one occasion rumour had it he had suffered incontinence problems.

One evening after drinking for several hours he rather unsteadily walked out of the mess to the police Land Rover waiting for him in the compound. (Being a senior officer he had his own driver.) In a quite sorry state he climbed in the back seat and told the driver to take him home. But the vehicle did not move. Rogers raised his voice and again told the driver to take him home. Again there was no response. Rogers became angry and started shouting: 'Driver, bloody well drive me home immediately otherwise I will place you on a charge!' It was then that the poor driver emerged from the toilet a few yards away and saw Rogers loudly remonstrating with one of his Dobermans. The dog had climbed into the driver's seat and had its two paws up on the steering wheel. An expat inspector had also happened to walk past and saw what had happened. Instead of trying to explain anything, the driver quietly and gently moved the dog aside and climbed into the driver's seat and drove silently back to Rogers's quarters.

On another occasion I went into East Kowloon to enjoy a special Chinese lunch. The district commander, a very pleasant fellow called Lau, was showing everyone his new pride and joy. It was a large aquarium filled with a variety of tropical fish. It was certainly very impressive and colourful and some of the fish looked exotic and expensive, including those pretty bug-eyed fan-tailed goldfish that are prized by collectors. After a few drinks at the bar, the cook informed us that lunch was ready to be served and we moved into the dining area and took our seats at a large round table. There were about twelve of us, a mixture of expat and local officers. The dishes started to arrive and were delicious. We had steamed fish, prawns, chicken with ginger, black bean sautéed beef and so on. About half way through this feast, we heard a loud splashing from the aquarium which was back near the bar area behind a screen. I said I would get up and investigate.

It was complete carnage. It seems no one had realised that dragonfish had been put in the tank. They are long, sleek silver-coloured powerful predators. It was like putting a couple of hungry sharks in a tank with some small trout. The dragonfish were swimming round the tank biting huge chunks out of the unfortunate ornamental goldfish, which are not exactly designed for speed or evasion. The dragonfish had probably never had such an easy meal. Lumps of goldfish were starting to float on the surface. Meanwhile Ah Lau Sir asked me from behind the screen: 'Simon, what's going on?' Now I will admit at this point I saw a humorous side to this which I know is a bit mean, but when I thought about the cost of the fish and how such a mixture of fish could have been put together it was pretty dumb really. So I had no choice but to call back: 'Sir, your fish are being eaten.' Seconds later he ran over still with a napkin at his neck, and a mouthful of beef with black bean sauce. He looked horrified and I did feel sorry for him. There was nothing we could do except watch the slaughter. A call was made to a guy from the aquarium shop to remove the dragonfish. By the time he arrived a couple of hours later there were no more goldfish to save. It did put a bit of a damper on the rest of the lunch and we were all careful to look sad. The incident was never mentioned again.

At various times in my career I had additional duties connected to mess management. Each mess had a committee and the district commander was usually the chairman. We normally had a cook who was a police constable and had attended some cookery lessons. He often lived in quarters in the station, sometimes with his family. On a couple of occasions I was appointed the mess manager which involved looking after the financial side of the mess. This position often came automatically with a rank and posting. So on taking up a new posting in Kowloon I also had the task of taking over the management of the officers' mess. This usually involved a handover from the outgoing inspector.

Mostly this was straightforward but unfortunately when being handed the accounts from a British inspector called Tim it was rather more problematic. What he gave me was a pile of bills, unpaid chits, final demands, and an overdraft. As a last insult he handed me the petty cash by going into his pockets and handing me a couple of notes and some coins. I was shocked and very upset; I couldn't believe how the mess could have got into such a state. I told him that I wasn't impressed and made sure the other officers knew of our predicament. We had suppliers chasing us for unpaid bills for food, it was embarrassing. Nothing had been managed properly. The price of meals had not been set correctly so we were losing money on every meal. Huge stocks of perishable food had been ordered which had disappeared. I had been told it had been thrown out, but I had my doubts. Alcohol was being sold below cost price. The mess was owed thousands of dollars by inspectors who had long been posted out of the station. I made a number of calls to them, explaining our financial difficulties and that we needed the money. I stopped the mess cook from ordering food, and did it myself. I ensured all stocks were itemised. I raised prices, and asked the bank to extend our overdraft. Gradually things started to improve. After a year it was running properly and we were in credit. When it was my turn to hand over the role I was able to demonstrate a healthy balance sheet with several thousand dollars in the bank. Maybe I was in the wrong profession.

CHAPTER XIV

Police HQ – *Polmil*

OWARDS THE END of my first tour I was transferred to Polmil. This stood for police-military and was a control centre for the colony in the basement of police headquarters (PHQ) in Arsenal St. I was a bit disappointed to be leaving the court but considered this a new challenge and it was only six months before I was due to go on my long vacation leave and collect my gratuity. It was a pretty easy commute across the harbour, and I was back in uniform, but that was fine. We worked longer shifts but had more days off which suited me. It was usually a four days on, two days off system. I was quite nervous as I was in PHQ for the first time and there were of course many senior officers coming in and out during the day. One of those was Bill Boyton, who had a rather fearsome reputation, but by the time I met him he had been promoted to a superintendent and he was perfectly pleasant to me. My first day was actually a night shift, so I reported at 11pm.

It became clear that the senior inspector who was supposed to be training me was not interested in any briefing or training. He was a notorious character called Jim who was more interested in drinking. After a cursory welcome, he said he had to go out, and then disappeared. Meanwhile, the army major in the desk across from me said 'Goodnight' and went off to his bunk for the night. So there I sat, a very young, nervous, ignorant one-pip inspector looking around at the control centre and not knowing what I was supposed to do. There was a television in the middle of the room. There were only two English-language channels, both of which stopped transmission at midnight so that was not of much use. Sometimes I would sit and watch old black and white Hong Kong movies from the 1960s; understanding hardly a word of the dialogue. They all seemed to feature figures from Chinese opera. We also had a female language officer to help with translations and data transmission, but she kept to herself and I hardly saw her. There were no allotted breaks for the inspectors. The military chaps were more fortunate and were allowed to retire to a bunk during the night shift.

So I basically sat in my chair with one eye shut and occasionally answered the phone. Then, at about 5am, Jim suddenly reappeared, in civilian clothes, red eyed, and with a very slurred voice said: 'Have you completed the commissioner's report?' To which I naturally replied, 'What commissioner's report?' He then freaked out. Apparently, as I then learnt, we would receive teleprinter messages with details of all the major cases that had occurred in the last twenty-four hours. The task of the Polmil inspector was to go through all these and then compile a report detailing the most serious cases for the commissioner's attention. There was a guide to what kind of cases that should be included, such as homicides, kidnappings and robberies with firearms. Jim sobered up pretty quickly, helped by several mugs of strong coffee. He wasn't impressed that I had not written it up myself. But then I wasn't impressed that he'd been out on the piss in Wan Chai all night. The report was compiled and typed up just in time for the police motorcycle despatch rider to come in and collect it. The rider would ride up to the Peak to deliver it to the commissioner by hand so he could read it before his driver collected him in his official car and brought him down to PHQ in the morning.

The military chaps in Polmil were mostly pretty good guys and I got on well with them. We talked a lot about the UK and what we missed, and during the day we could watch TV when it was quiet, and quite a few people would come in and out so it was fairly interesting. We had very basic computers on which we could read about cases occurring in the colony. But we still relied a lot on teleprinters and the civilian staff to manually type out reports. We had large black beat radios on our desk and old black telephones which we used to enquire about any new serious cases occurring. One of the military guys that sometimes came in was a helicopter

pilot with the Army Air Corps. He was an older chap called Bob
Morris and we became good friends. He flew Westland Scouts and
offered to take me up with him. I had been up in a Wessex
helicopter whilst I was at PTS.

So on my next day off, I met up with Bob near HMS Tamar on
the Hong Kong Island waterfront. I climbed into the cockpit. It
was great; there were just the two of us and the view from the large
cockpit windows was excellent. We took off and flew over the
harbour heading north. Bob directed the chopper up to the east
over Sai Kung. From the air I could see all the islands and the small
bays. I was amazed at how green and beautiful Hong Kong looked
from the air. He then directed the Scout inland towards the
northern NT and headed to Sek Kong where there was a large army
base. We landed and I climbed out feeling a bit like a VIP and headed
off to the mess for lunch.

The British Army rotated regiments around on tours to Hong
Kong. Each regiment had a different reputation. Which ones were
posted to the colony impacted the number of fights with the US
Navy in Wan Chai. One constant seemed to be the Gurkhas, and
the British officers in the Gurkha regiments seemed to be treated
very well indeed. They had so many of the Nepalese soldiers looking
after them that I wondered if they were even required to pull the
trigger of their own weapon when on the range. The Gurkha
soldiers have a fearsome reputation on the battlefield for good
reason. They are very loyal, but it's probably not a good idea to get
in their way. A few years after I first visited Sek Kong there was a
very nasty incident behind the military confines of the camp.

In Hong Kong there is no sales tax. So it has long been considered
a shoppers' paradise and many items are cheaper than in other
countries. One of the commodities that is sold is '999' gold. This
is in effect 24K pure gold, and superior to the 18K gold commonly
sold in the UK. The pure gold is sold in many shops in Hong Kong
and is sold by weight according to the international gold price. But
in India and Nepal there was a tax on gold imports. Accordingly
smuggling gold into these countries can be quite profitable. Some
of the Gurkhas, it was claimed, had been operating a very profitable
side business of buying gold in Hong Kong and then placing it in

their British Army personal effects when they returned home on leave. By selling the gold in Kathmandu they were able to supplement their pensions.

One British Gurkha officer decided that this illegal activity had to stop and so he ordered that all personal effects were to be thoroughly searched and any gold removed. This did not go down well with the smuggling syndicate. One morning the same British officer reported to his office and sat down at his desk to read some official papers. After reading some reports and sipping his coffee, he opened his desk drawer. That was the last thing he ever did. Someone had placed a hand grenade in the drawer and attached a wire to the pin secured to the rear of the desk. The officer was blown to pieces. Despite all the suspicion surrounding the case no one was ever convicted.

So following our delicious lunch we climbed back in the Scout helicopter and rose up from the landing strip high over the New Territories. This time we headed west towards Tuen Mun, then down over Tsuen Wan and Sham Shui Po and then over the harbour with the hundreds of cargo vessels and various cruise liners and back down to HMS Tamar. What a day it had been. I went up a couple more times with Bob and was very grateful for his friendship and kindness.

One morning when off duty from Polmil and back in my New World apartment I looked out of the window and saw a large group of people on the roof of the Regent Hotel (which later became the Intercontinental). When I looked closer I realised it was the band Spandau Ballet, at the time one of the top international groups. I recognised Tony Hadley and decided to go over and say hello. Going from my apartment to the other block was pretty easy as all the buildings were linked. I made my way to the roof without anyone stopping me. They were filming a video for the song *Highly Strung* (which you can now see on YouTube). When there was a break I went up to Tony Hadley and had my photo taken with him. Later I posted off a couple of prints to my family back in the UK. I think my mother still has a copy.

Back in Polmil and shift work. The evening shifts were quite easy, not much happened and the main job was preparing the commissioner's report in the early morning. I would normally start preparing this at about 5am with help from the female police communications officer. During the morning shifts I would also be requested by the superintendent to assist with administration and prepare for the operations meetings. These meetings were held with both police and military personnel. We had to prepare daily operational reports called MOCOG briefs. There had been newspaper stories of a high demand for Western-style female underwear in China and a business had sprung up in smuggling these items into the Mainland. Inspired by this, one day I decided to write a fake 'MOCOG' brief concerning the smuggling of lingerie into China. This included the news that as the Chinese commune girls were wearing negligees, push-up bras and stockings and suspenders, there had been a reverse flow in immigration, with men from Hong Kong queuing up at the China border to work in the communes. I slipped this into the usual pile of reports to be read over during the meeting which was attended by senior officers including the deputy director of operations. Fortunately my boss at the time was the amenable Neil McCabe, he saw the joke and I avoided any disciplinary issues.

During these meetings senior officers also read through the British Army intelligence reports from the China border the previous day. Along the border there were observation posts manned by the British Army on one side, and the People's Liberation Army (PLA) on the other. The British had recently quietly acquired night-vision goggles and were testing these out for their nocturnal checks across the fence. They would then report any interesting activities by either illegal immigrants (IIs) or the PLA. The British soldiers sometimes saw IIs caught by PLA soldiers being beaten. It was during this time that the Royal Green Jackets reported some nasty incidents over the border near Lok Ma Chau. At the time it was believed that the crack Chinese 42nd Army had been deployed and it seemed they wanted to make their mark. They were using German Shepherd attack dogs. The Green Jackets observed that illegal immigrants were being arrested and handcuffed. They were then released and told to run away but as they did so the dogs would be released. The dogs were observed attacking and savagely biting the unfortunate IIs whose terrified screams could clearly be heard by the shocked young British Army soldiers. It was no doubt designed to be a message to the other young Chinese.

On a late shift one of the British soldiers was peering through his new night-vision goggles on one of the quieter stretches of the border. He was looking across to one of the Chinese military pillboxes when he noticed some activity. It was a moonless night but the goggles were effective and the view was clear. A Chinese soldier emerged holding a small wooden three-legged stool. He looked around carefully before carrying the stool towards a cow that was tethered to a stake in the ground and quietly grazing. The soldier placed the stool at the rear of the cow; then stepped onto the stool and dropped his trousers. However as he aimed to penetrate the cow it was clear that she wasn't so keen on the young soldier and promptly moved out of the way. This resulted in comical scenes where the soldier kept jumping off the stool, re-positioning it and trying again. The cow was not having any of it and kept moving round. Eventually the young soldier gave up and disappeared once more into his pill box. The British squaddie gleefully wrote up his report of the incident which was then sent down to PHQ. I recall this incident created a lot of mirth in the morning meeting. I'm not sure whether this did though justify the large investment in the night-vision goggles.

Within a couple of months of my posting to Polmil, Argentina invaded the Falkland Islands and took over Port Stanley. Margaret Thatcher was now the prime minister and was determined to show her power and restore sovereignty. Parliament was persuaded to declare war and send a task force down to the South Atlantic to recover the islands. It was an interesting time to be in Polmil because the army major sitting alongside me was receiving military communiqués regarding the progress in the fighting. There was no CNN or Sky news, so often we were hearing of events before we saw them reported on TVB. So when the Royal Navy sank the Argentinian ship the *Belgrano*, I knew about it from the military teleprinter before it was reported globally on television. I found this all very exciting. Of course when we later received the news that HMS *Sheffield* had been sunk by Exocet missiles our mood changed considerably. People in the media now often say that this was possibly the last war where military sources were receiving news before the global media. In the 1990s during the Iraq war it was said that CNN were broadcasting news at the same time that the Pentagon was receiving similar reports. By the time of the more recent war in Afghanistan it was said that military sources were watching events on CNN.

Left: Me aged eight in Shropshire, with no idea of the adventures that lay ahead.
Right: My great-grandfather Joseph Roberts in 1888. He served with the army in
Afghanistan in 1879 and later became a policeman in Liverpool. Below: Patrolling the
islands of Mirs Bay in the New Territories as a young inspector in 1980.

Above: My passing out parade at PTS in the summer of 1980.

Below: A view of the Central waterfront from the harbour in the same year.

Above: Aboard a marine launch, 1980.

Below: My first Christmas Day in 1979 at the Dickens Bar. We were trying to be merry but I think we were all missing our families.

Above: Fanling train station in 1980. I sometimes travelled to work in Tai Po on the train.

Below: Police vehicles parked outside the old Tai Po police station in 1980.

Above: Tai Po Kau harbour in 1980. This was very close to my first government quarter.

Below: Tai Po Market Police Station report room in 1980 during my first tour.

Above: In Sha Tin with my MG in 1980. I paid HK$6,000 for it.

Below: On my police motorcycle course in Central in 1980. The bike was a Yamaha 650 twin, a police workhorse at the time.

Top: The Police Casuals rugby team captained by Paul Keylock at the Boundary Street Police Club pitch in 1982.

Left: The MTR not long after it first opened, when you could travel for HK$1.

Bottom: Tsim Sha Tsui bars at night in 1981. I knew the area well.

Above: Flying with Bob Morris in Fanling with the Army Air Corps in 1981. Below: Celebratory drinks in Mongkok Mess when I was promoted to Chief Inspector in 1989.

Above: In China in 1986 during a cycling trip between Macau and Canton.
Below: A street scene in China during my visit in 1981. I saw so many amazing things during the tour.

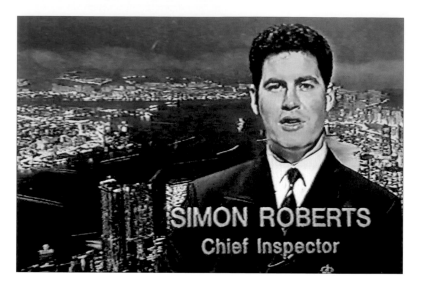

Above: On TV in 1989 as the presenter of the Police Report TV programme. I suspect no-one ever watched it.

Below: Operations Wing staff at PHQ in 1994. I'm on the far left in the middle row.

Above: When I was not playing rugby I played soccer for Dynamos in the Yau Yee League. This was in 1989.

Below: At the Detective Training School in 1987. I actually did well in a final exam for once.

Left: My wedding to
Elizabeth in July 1989.
We are still married more
than 30 years later.

Below: At Goverment
House with the late Sir
David Tang in 1994.

Above: Celebrating a successful case conclusion with the District Crime Squad in Sau Mau Ping in 1987. Below: Trying to be amusing, making a speech as the Course Director at the passing out dinner in 1996.

Above: With John Bicknell in 1998 during the Swimathon. We raised over HK$300,000 for charity in two years.

Below: I met Princess Alexandra at the PTS during her final visit to Hong Kong in 1997. She asked me what my plans were and whether I planned to stay in the police.

Above: About to board a super-fast Cougar Tek in Marine Region in 2001.

Below: In early 2002 I was awarded my long service medal. Here I am with Dom Ziemann and Gari Hopkins. I resigned from the HKP shortly afterwards.

With Lord Wilson, the former governor of Hong Kong, at the UK's National Arboretum at the ceremony to unveil the new Police Memorial in 2018.
Photo courtesy of Andy Lewis Photography

CHAPTER XV

Vacation Leave

FINALLY IT WAS TIME for my first long vacation leave. One of the perks of old colonial service was the long holidays. I received twelve days 'casual leave' each year which I could take in Hong Kong or overseas. In addition vacation leave was accrued through-out the tour of service; this had to be taken overseas. Because of PTS, my first tour was for three years, and so I had accrued about four months paid vacation. I was also given the airfare home and a gratuity which on my first tour amounted to just over HK$40,000. I felt wealthy. It was possible then to buy a small house in England for about HK$170,000. The leave terms for expat officers have changed a lot since then, and gradually more people moved over to annual leave terms. This reduced the actual days of leave accrued but provided a cash allowance each year and you did not have to return to your home country. This was quite generous, so with some clever planning it was possible to effectively get a 'free' holiday each year.

As it was my first long leave I decided to head back to the UK via Asia and chose to visit Sri Lanka. This was partly because it is a beautiful country but more importantly down to the fact that I then had a beautiful Sri Lankan girlfriend called Padma who worked as a flight attendant for Air Lanka. When I arrived, I stayed with her family in Albert Road in Colombo. I was fed on spicy *lamprais*, rice and curry wrapped in a banana leaf. I set out to explore the island by bus and train. This was before the civil war and it was possible to travel all over the country so I was able to go north to Trincomalee where I stayed in a small hut on the beach for less than HK$12 per day. One evening a large number of devout

Hindus walked through the centre of Trincomalee with a number of brightly adorned elephants. The men were chanting, and beating their backs with chains. When I looked more closely I saw many of them had metal skewers piercing their faces, and hooks through their backs. They seemed to be in a trance as they came past me oblivious to any pain. The sounds, smells and sight of this was particularly alien to me even coming from Hong Kong.

The next day in Trincomalee an Italian traveller called Luigi and his girlfriend moved into the next bamboo hut to me on the beach. Luigi decided that he needed something more than a cold beer and so took a Morris Minor taxi into town to buy hashish. He came back later in the evening with a small ball of hash wrapped in waxed paper and proceeded to roll a small spliff. He was happy to share this. We all got pretty high and decided to go for a midnight swim. The beach and sea in Trincomalee is amazing. The beach curves round in a huge golden arc several miles long and the waves wash in from the Indian Ocean with large breakers but the temperature is like a warm bath. I was thrown around by the waves, constantly going under water and hitting my head on the sandy bottom, but surfacing and laughing hysterically.

On my second day on the beach a very attractive Tamil woman of about forty years of age asked Luigi and I if we would like to have a home-cooked dinner that evening. It was her own family commercial enterprise and she was asking a very reasonable price so we agreed. Later we arrived at her house which was a few hundred yards up the beach. We walked in and sat on the floor. The house was very spartan, there seemed to be no kitchen and we wondered what was going to happen. Suddenly a large piece of coconut matting was lifted off the floor and there underneath was a myriad of dishes: fish, rice, curry; it was all delicious. We had a cold beer each to wash it down. At the end of the meal the lady walked outside and dug into the sand to bring out a bottle of arak, which had a label that read 'Army Issue Only' on it. It was presumably contraband. We agreed to buy it and rounded off a very pleasant evening.

After Trincomalee, I travelled to the rock fortress of Sigiriya. This giant rock in the middle of the flat lands of the interior was a virtually impregnable castle with only one narrow path up to the top cut into the side of the sheer rock face. On the summit large bathing pools and drinking water tanks had been dug into the stone. The path up was precarious and I was grateful not to slip, but I was distracted by colourful paintings of beautiful naked ladies on the side of the rock. These paintings were several hundred years old and not protected from the elements, but the colours were still vibrant. From Sigiriya I travelled south by bus and then took a train to Kandy, and from Kandy caught the small train to Nuwara Eliya that winds on a narrow gauge through the tea plantations and hills to the heart of the tea-growing country. This is a famous train journey and one of the most picturesque in the world. I spent the whole journey staring out of the window admiring the incredible views. After all the twists and turns all the time feeling we were about to tip over down one of the valleys we arrived in the tiny little town.

For most of my early trips around Asia I saved money by staying in hostels, travelling on a shoestring. But in Nuwara Eliya I decided to splash out and stay in the Hill Club. It had been built in the 1870s as a private members club for British gentlemen tea planters. When I arrived the place was not yet on the tourist map and there were few visitors. There were fishing rods and hunting trophies on the wall, and everything seemed very dusty. I was pleased to see some English newspapers until I picked one up and realised it was over a year old. The large hardback residents' comments book was still put out and I was thrilled to see it was an original with comments going back to the days of the Empire in the 1950s. It was fascinating to see the grumpy remarks written by the lonely tea planters, such as: 'Coffee at breakfast tepid this morning' or 'Who has removed the copy of the *Times*? It should remain in the lounge'. Dinner was a grand affair but I was inappropriately attired. I was travelling with some cheap old cotton trousers and old polo shirts but discovered I had to wear a jacket and tie after 7pm. One of the friendly waiters went back behind the reception desk and brought out a horribly clashing check-patterned jacket and a garish red tie. I put the tie around my neck around the collar of my polo shirt and put on the rather baggy jacket, and with my cheap cotton trousers I realised I looked ridiculous, but I was compliant! The meal was very pleasant English fare of sliced meat with gravy, roast potatoes and boiled vegetables. I would have much preferred a lovely spicy curry. It was all very genteel and served by extremely polite white-gloved waiters.

All too soon though it was time for me to head back to the UK, catch up with the family and decide what I wanted to do with my life. Rather stupidly I had been enjoying my life so much that I hadn't bothered to take my Standard Two exams. So I was back in the UK with an uncertain future. After a few weeks back in England I realised I wanted to continue in the Hong Kong Police and so I wrote a letter saying I was interested in coming back. To my surprise I was accepted back, even though I was not confirmed in the rank of inspector. This was rather unusual and I knew I had been quite fortunate.

So when my time was up I rented out the small house that I had bought in Shrewsbury with some of my gratuity as a deposit, and made arrangements for my flight back to Hong Kong. Looking back now I suppose this was a pivotal time in my life. If I had not been accepted back in the force I would probably have ended up in a boring English office and this book would never have been written. At the time though I was very excited because it now seemed I might have a future. In fact it got better. When I landed in Hong Kong and called the quartering office I found I had been upgraded to a bigger harbour-view studio flat with a king-size bed on the seventeenth floor of the lovely New World Apartments.

Shortly after returning to the colony and moving in to my new flat I was woken up in the morning by a loud booming noise coming from outside. I thought the place might have been invaded. I jumped out of bed stark naked and threw the curtains open to see an enormous aircraft carrier. It was the USS *Enterprise*, the pride of the US Pacific Fleet slowly cruising along the harbour past my window. There were hundreds of white-uniformed naval personnel standing to attention on the deck in a long line facing me and saluting. Meanwhile another warship was firing a twenty-one-gun salute. I thought this was very kind of them to welcome me back, and hoped it would be a regular occurrence. The US Pacific Fleet was a frequent visitor to the colony and even their nuclear-powered submarines sometimes sailed through the harbour. Sadly though this was the only time I was ever to give the US Navy a naked salute in return.

While that might seem eccentric, there was another police inspector living in the building who put me to shame.

Kurt was of medium height with blonde hair. His family may have been German but he'd grown up in England and spoke with a Home Counties accent. He was a strange chap and there were tales about his behaviour.

Late one evening I was returning home and took the lift up to the fourth-floor lobby. When the lift doors opened it seemed I was inside a snow dome. Millions of tiny glass particles were floating in the air. The carpet was covered in white crystals. Kurt was standing in the middle of this. He seemed stunned. I discovered he had forgotten his apartment keys. He had gone to the management office to borrow a spare set but the office was locked for the night. In his anger and frustration he had shaken the large tempered glass doors violently. In fact he shook them so violently that they had virtually exploded. Security guards were quickly on the scene. They were not happy and Kurt was later told to pay for the replacement doors.

CHAPTER XVI

Police Rugby

I WAS POSTED TO KOWLOON after my long leave and was back in uniform branch as a sub-unit commander, in the same position I had been three years earlier. I knew I had been an idiot in not studying before, and so resolved to collect past exam papers and start to study hard. I decided to examine the questions and exam techniques and endeavour to pass all my exams before my current tour finished. I did genuinely try hard and really got stuck into the books, which needed a lot of discipline when considering all the distractions available. To my surprise I passed all the Standard Two exams, then Standard Three in about eighteen months in three sittings, and even gained a few credit marks. I was able to put two pips on my shoulder and after another year, with five years' service, I would have two pips and a bar, a senior inspector. My salary increased suddenly as there were also generous pay reviews. I was now earning HK$6,000 a month. On my leave days I continued to play rugby for the police team.

Unlike the wild party atmosphere of today's annual Rugby Sevens tournament, at the Football Club in the 1980s families would take a hamper and actually watch the rugby. By the 1990s it was in the new stadium and had become a massive business venture. On the Friday before the event commenced there was always the notorious 'long lunch'. This used to be held in the ballroom at the Furama Hotel. About 300 or more male rugby fans dressed formally in black tie would be eating and drinking from 12 noon. There would always be some famous rugby players on stage to entertain the crowd, and then at about 4pm there would be a charity auction. The auction was quite serious and usually raised a great deal of money for charity. Generous companies would donate luxury prizes and the well-heeled expats would compete to see who had the fattest wallets. It so happened that earlier in the year a sex shop had opened near Lan Kwai Fong. It was called 'Fetish Fashion' and contained a sex dungeon in the basement. At about 4.30pm, four young ladies in black leather bondage gear walked on stage. The reaction from the 300 young rugby fans in the audience can be imagined. Then the master of ceremonies took the microphone and announced the prize, which was for four lucky chaps to spend a night in the dungeon with the four young ladies on stage. The 'big swinging Richards' working for the international merchant banks went into a frenzy. I was in the audience and made sure I kept my arms by my side. The bidding went mad. I recall the winning bid was around HK$300,000. The winners were merchant bankers. The atmosphere was electric. I just hope they got their money's worth!

Back to police rugby. In the early 1980s when I played we had four teams: the Police 1st team, then the Wanderers, the Saracens and the Casuals. I never played for the first team simply because I was never very good. I occasionally played for the Wanderers and the Saracens, but mostly for the Casuals under the sterling leadership of the always jovial Paul Keylock. There were many expats in Hong Kong at the time and a lot of armed forces personnel. So we would find ourselves playing the Royal Green Jackets, or the Flying Kukris or possibly the Football Club or the Kowloon Cricket Club. The pace of the game was fast, the pitches were hard and I often got cuts, bruises and sprains. Most of the cuts became septic and I was always dabbing TCP and other antiseptic into the wounds. But there was the promise of jugs of cold beer at the bar in our Boundary Street club bar after the game.

At the time the Police Rugby 1st team was captained by Bruce Vogel. Bruce had attended the same grammar school as me, but we had not been in the same year. He had joined the force a few years before me. Bruce was well over six feet tall, had sandy-coloured wavy hair and he was as strong as an ox. He was also a devoted family man who was happily married to his childhood sweetheart. He was often referred to as a gentle giant. As well as being the police captain he was also a regular international in the Hong Kong national side. He had also enjoyed a successful start to his police career and after serving in the Marine Region he was quickly promoted to chief inspector and then superintendent. I had been out on Marine Police launches with Bruce and had visited his family in his married quarters and I really looked up to and respected him. In the early 1980s the Police Rugby Club's greatest rivals were the Hong Kong Football Club team.

The Football Club team were based on Hong Kong Island next to the Happy Valley Racecourse. They had a stadium which could seat a few thousand people which also served as the venue for the annual Rugby Sevens tournament before it became the huge event it is today. I remember watching one of the matches between these two sides. The police team was a mishmash of different shapes and sizes and often assorted kit. When the Football Club team ran on all the players looked like Adonises. All similar sized, immaculately turned out, all tanned, blond, with chiselled jaws and determination. All these encounters were full-blooded, no-holds-barred type games. What I remember though is that the police invariably won, especially when Bruce was leading from the front. Everyone looked up to Bruce and everyone seemed to love him. But Bruce had a secret, one that was to have tragic consequences. A few years after I had watched him, Bruce was again leading his beloved police team in a frenetic encounter on a warm afternoon on the Football Club pitch. During the game near the middle of the pitch with Bruce in his usual head-down position driving forward, giving no quarter, he suddenly collapsed. Players on both sides stopped and came to his assistance and administered first aid. An ambulance was quickly summoned but despite everyone's best efforts Bruce never regained consciousness and he died that day out on the rugby pitch playing the game he loved. It transpired later that Bruce had been to see a doctor who had told him that he had a heart defect and suggested he should stop playing rugby. Despite this Bruce decided that he would keep playing and leading the team. The tragedy was felt right across the colony and all the clubs raised a glass that week to Bruce. When it came for the time to see him off it was standing room only in St John's Cathedral with people standing at the entrance outside waiting to pay their respects.

But life as always went on and the club tried to pick itself up although it was impossible to fill Bruce's boots. One of the popular events each season was the overseas rugby tours. The rugby tours seemed to be one of two types: either they were reasonably serious, on official tours to places like Canada or Australia, or less serious tours to places like Bangkok or Angeles City in the Philippines. Thailand and the Philippines are not known to be centres of rugby excellence so most of the matches in these places were against other expatriate sporting clubs, so they tended to be less serious. These unofficial tours were extremely popular and it was amazing to see how many part-time rugby players suddenly made themselves available when they knew of a tour to Bangkok or Angeles.

When our plane had taken off the captain or tour manager would stand up on the aircraft and address the squad: 'Lads, I need to remind you of the Kai Tak rules. Enjoy the tour, enjoy the rugby, play hard, play fair and enjoy the R&R, but remember, what happens on tour stays on tour.' Bangkok is now well known for its attractions in Pat Pong and Soi Cowboy. Angeles was maybe less well known. There was a large US Air Force base there and a bar industry had grown nearby to ensure the US servicemen did not get too lonely. Most of us from that era are grateful that photographic evidence does not exist of the worst excesses of those tours several decades ago.

An official police rugby tour to Canada with a large squad had been successful in winning most of the matches. On the official tours the overseas hospitality was excellent and we were usually treated with a great deal of generosity. On a tour of Australia in 1985 we were taken out on the town in Kings Cross in Sydney, a notorious red light district. The Australian police detectives did not let us buy any drinks in the visits to the bars. But then I noticed that they didn't seem to be paying for any either. Back in Canada the squad had been invited at the end of the tour to a formal reception in the governor's mansion in British Columbia. The lads were all very smart with their matching blazers with the police crest, crisp white shirts, and rugby club ties. The evening was very grand, with white-gloved waiters in tailored waistcoats serving canapés and elegant wines. The illuminated manicured lawns, grand foyer, and pianist created a wonderfully cultured atmosphere as the governor and his guests mingled with the tour party. As the evening wore on the tour party took advantage of the vintage wines and other free drinks.

It came time for the governor to say a few words of appreciation and for the tour manager to reciprocate; everything was very civilised and convivial. Then rather unexpectedly the governor said that he had heard about the famous tradition of rugby songs and asked whether the group would sing a rugby song for his guests. This left the tour group rather nonplussed as most of the rugby songs involved renditions of doing things to young maidens. Then someone had an idea. They stood together shoulder to shoulder and to the tune of *Amazing Grace,* sang *'Due lay lo mo / Due lay lo mo / Due lay lo mo; chau hai.'* It was reminiscent of a top-level Welsh male voice choir, while still being highly obscene Cantonese invective.

The rugby squad took a bow whilst the governor thanked the group profusely for the lovely hymn. The next day the tour party boarded a Cathay Pacific plane back from Vancouver on the long flight back across the Pacific to Hong Kong. However a couple of weeks' later things changed for the worse. A letter arrived on the police commissioner's desk. It seemed that amongst the governor's staff that night there had been a waiter originally from Hong Kong. He had not been so amused by our version of *Amazing Grace* and had told colleagues what had actually been sung. This had then filtered back to the governor who understandably was less than impressed. The commissioner in turn summoned the tour manager to his office and gave him a massive dressing down. He warned future rugby tours were now under threat. I suppose it was to be expected. I must confess though I did find it funny and had a lot of respect for those guys.

CHAPTER XVII

At the Emergency Control Centre

Later in my tour of duty I was seconded to the Kowloon Emergency Command and Control Centre. This was a uniformed position and required shift work, but I worked fewer night shifts and had more time off to enjoy the pleasures of Hong Kong. The location in Kowloon was also closer to my apartment. The work was easier too as we had a nice air-conditioned environment and plenty of other staff to help out with the majority of calls. So although the centre handled the 999 emergency calls I would only be needed when it was a very serious case, or when the caller spoke English. There was a well-known character called Khan, an ex-Auxiliary Police officer, who called us almost every day. Usually he called the emergency number to report minor traffic violations. Sometimes he sent faxes through with numerous foul-mouthed insults against the commissioner of police and all the British officers, calling us 'bloody pig bastards sons of whores' and so on. We filed these away. The local officers did not like to speak to him so when he called I usually handled him. I tried to be polite but at the same time to end the call as soon as possible. I think he had been subject to disciplinary action during his career and held a long-standing grudge against British officers.

We also had a European lady caller named Claire who lived in Kadoorie Avenue. I think she might have been divorced and she seemed to be looking after her son who she was continuously worried about. When she called she always asked to speak to a British officer. Then she would explain that her son had gone out of the house and she wanted someone to find him. Initially I was concerned until I found out her son was eighteen years old. She would always request that a British inspector go to her house to see her. I usually said that I would send Inspector Wong. At which point she lost interest, until the next day when she would try again. The strangest call I dealt with was from a young American chap called Andy who called up to see if we knew if anyone could fix his radio. I was given the call, and thought it was an odd request but as he was quiet and polite and sounded normal I advised a couple of places he might go. However he then went on to explain that the problem was that a microchip had been planted in his brain by the CIA and it was interfering with his radio reception. I should have ended the call then but it was a slow evening. After rambling on about the microchip he abruptly said that he had a very small penis, and 'even though I work out a lot and am very fit, my penis never gets any bigger.' I replied 'I'm sorry to hear about that but I'm not sure it's something the Royal Hong Kong Police can help with.' I don't think it was a joke as he sounded very serious and appeared to be alone. He then continued with a story about how he was being followed by secret agents wherever he went. He spoke quietly and seriously throughout all of this. Well at least it made my shift time go quicker.

During my first tour in Polmil I had become friends with another inspector called Dave. Dave was an interesting character. His favourite place outside work was the Chin Chin Bar in the old Hyatt Hotel. The Hyatt was then located towards the south of Tsim Sha Tsui. Dave was always a very sociable chap and he used to love chatting to the female American tourists, especially the older ones. A pretty young woman of maybe twenty-five years of age would walk past, Dave would ignore her. But if an American woman aged sixty or over came in, Dave would get up and talk to her. During his evening soirées in the Chin Chin Bar he met an American gentleman called Bill. Bill had some very interesting connections with the movie industry back in the United States and he seemed to know a lot of people. One day Dave called me to ask what my shift pattern was that week. I told him my roster and Dave said: 'Okay I've got something interesting for you next Wednesday.'

It seemed that Bill was also involved with the Macau Trotting Club, then recently created (in 1980). In spite of the Chinese love of gambling, the sport had not been very popular so the owners decided to spice things up by bringing over some beautiful ladies from America to create new interest in the club. In fact Dave told me that movie stars including ex-Bond girl Jane Seymour, Morgan Fairchild, Miss Universe, and Miss USA were visiting Hong Kong to create publicity for the new venture. Bill had been concerned about security and knowing Dave was in the police had asked him for help. We didn't get paid, we did it as a favour on our day off. This was before the security industry had become licensed and close protection made available from reputable companies. This sounded like it could be an interesting day so I replied: 'Yes, I think I might be able to help you escort some movie stars and beauty queens around Hong Kong.'

On the Wednesday I put on a smart white shirt and blue tie and my Ray-Ban aviator sunglasses and went out into Kowloon to meet our lovely VIPs. After our introductions we took the ladies out shopping, visited a few traditional medicine shops and then went to a famous restaurant for a very nice *dim sum* lunch. I remember Jane Seymour mentioning that her father was a doctor and the conversation was friendly and I tried to be a good host. I was supposed to be a bodyguard for the group so I smiled and tried not to say too much.

Morgan Fairchild was lovely and very friendly. She told me that if I ever went to the States I should go and visit her. Sadly I never did. It was interesting that in spite of the four gorgeous women walking around Kowloon there was not much interest from the local people. Maybe they thought they were just tourists. There really wasn't any 'bodyguarding' needed but I suppose it kept up appearances. I would have really liked to have guarded Morgan's body a bit closer though. Towards the end of the day a press conference had been arranged at the Intercontinental Hotel in Tsim Sha Tsui. This was a bit tricky because although I wasn't being paid, I did not want to be seen. So I tried to be inconspicuous which was a little difficult as I was wearing aviator sunglasses inside a window-less room and was next to the lovely ladies.

There was a very large press corps present with TV and radio and of course all the local newspapers. I tried to move over to the left of the group to stay out of camera shot. Everything went well, there were no embarrassing questions, the girls all flounced and pouted and at the end of it Bill seemed very pleased. I was not required later in the evening so when the group were safely back in their hotel I said my goodbyes and returned to my apartment. I was also very pleased with the day although I was not able to tell anyone about it. The next day the *Hong Kong Standard* had a picture on the front page of Jane Seymour with yours truly very clearly standing at her side. Remarkably though no one recognised me and I kept that story a secret for years. In spite of this publicity drive, horse trotting never did become a success in Macau and in 1989 it changed ownership and became the current Jockey Club. Dave sadly died a few years after our personal protection adventure; he suffered a massive heart attack and collapsed sitting on a bar stool in his beloved Chin Chin Bar. He was only in his thirties. His funeral was held in St John's cathedral with several hundred friends and colleagues in attendance.

CHAPTER XVIII

CID *Detective*

SOME MONTHS LATER while posted to East Kowloon I was summoned to a progress report meeting with the district commander, Chief Superintendent Douglas Lau. I was still trying to stay out of trouble. I was pretty happy with my role and had few ambitions. My annual reports were okay, very middle of the road with no criticisms, but then not many compliments either. To my surprise, Lau said that he thought that I would be suitable as a detective. This came as a bit of a shock. Me, CID material? I knew that some guys had gone to CID and were stuck in divisional crime squads for years. I didn't want that. I suspected that it wasn't actually that he thought I would make a good detective – it was more likely that he was simply short of detective inspectors. So I replied that I would be okay to move over to CID but only if I was able to attend the Detective Training School (DTS) as soon as possible and then move into the more senior district crime squad (DCS). Lau agreed to this, and he kept his promise.

So after a few months of kicking my heels in the divisional crime squad working shifts and handling minor theft and assault cases, I was sent on the next available DTS course. In the 1970s the CID school had been at PTS, but in the 1980s the school moved to some old colonial buildings that used to belong to the Royal Air Force at Ping Shek near Kai Tak Airport. The senior staff officer was a chap called Babbington. The course took twelve weeks and I enjoyed it. The hours were nine to five, it was plain clothes, and I was gaining new skills and qualifications. I don't remember it as being particularly high tech in terms of the teaching. It was all rather traditional but we had a decent group of twenty-six inspectors on the course and I was paired up with a very friendly Eurasian female inspector called May for the joint project so I had no complaints. We had many practical exercises. These included mannequins splattered in ketchup lying on the floor with a hidden murder weapon and so on. At the end of the course there was a long written exam and other practical assessments. Commander Lau had said he would put me in the DCS if I came back with a good report, so I decided I would try to pass. However given my poor results with previous exams I was still rather nervous. When I was told that I had scored 76 per cent and had the fourth-highest mark in the intake I was the most surprised of anyone.

I remember feeling proud of my result. It was a far cry from scraping a pass at Police Training School a few years before. Perhaps it made me think about my future too. A few months later in line with my new serious persona, I also decided to move onto the 'permanent and pensionable' establishment. This was a big decision but thirty years later looking back it was one of the best decisions I ever made. I became a member of Her Majesty's Overseas Civil Service and have the papers to prove it.

I returned to my district in East Kowloon in good spirits knowing that I was now a qualified detective. Chief Superintendent Lau was good to his word and within a short space of time I was put in charge of the district crime squad. I was still a senior inspector. My salary jumped again to about HK$9,000 a month. I received my 'two pips and a bar' on my shoulder. The next possible promotion was to chief inspector. That would mean passing a promotion board as I had now passed all my professional exams, so further promotion was on merit. At around this time the government had gone through a major pay review for the civil service. This resulted in a huge pay increase for police ranks but especially senior inspectors. So I felt quite flush for a few months until I found different ways to spend my money. I had quite a nice corner office in one of the newer stations. It opened into a large open-plan office where my team of six junior officers sat under the watch of my second in command, a formidable station sergeant called Leung. This was to be my district crime squad and they were an excellent team.

Staff Sergeant Leung was a large-built man with three daughters, who with his wife ran a restaurant business on the side. The station sergeants were sometimes referred to as the 'tigers' as it was felt they actually held the power and made all the decisions, which was true to some extent. I wanted to get to know my team so I spoke to them first as a group, and then individually. I also had to read through all the current case files and prioritise future investigations. Team harmony and morale is very important as we had to work long hours together in close proximity on very tough and stressful cases.

Apart from a love of gambling the other thing that is important in keeping a Hong Kong Police detective team working is food. When working long hours I could get by with regular cups of coffee and tea, but this does not work with local officers. At first when I heard grumblings about being hungry I would say: 'Let's carry on and do a few more hours and see what we can uncover,' but I soon realised it was actually much more productive to stop completely. At night the mess was closed so we would usually send for a takeaway. One of the lads would be nominated to collect the food, and orders were taken. I would often choose Singapore noodles or fried rice. Usually we would buy cans of soft drink to wash it down. As the officer in charge, I would often put my hand in my pocket and pull out HK$100 to cover the cost. It was common to do this and I never made expense claims. These meals were referred to as 'late night snacks', or *siu yeh*. One of the detective constables would return, carrying the thin polystyrene boxes in white plastic bags with the freshly cooked rice and noodles steaming away. I must admit it tasted delicious and it had a miraculous effect on the team. Everyone was rejuvenated and could then carry on for several more hours.

Reading through some of the older case files was interesting. In one case a female bank employee had stolen one million Hong Kong dollars from a large bank HQ by simply wearing a large down-filled jacket. This bank had spent a fortune on the latest high-tech security devices to prevent robberies. Yet this employee had simply walked into the vault and picked up bundles of high-denomination notes and put them into large pockets she had sewn into the coat. It was only after checking bank records of all the employees that unusual spending was noticed and she was arrested. In another case that was never solved, a middle-aged man had run away with a younger woman who had actually been boarding with the family. He had stolen a large sum of money from his employer in what was clearly a well-planned inside job. Records indicated that they had flown to Peru, but in spite of the help of Interpol and the Peruvian police no arrests were made.

In the 1980s in Kowloon there were still squatter villages on the hillsides. These were mainly inhabited by recent immigrants from China or people who had never registered for social housing. These communities were often on the edge of existing towns. Their homes were temporary structures made of scavenged wood and other materials. Some of the huts had electricity which was often illegally tapped. Cooking was via LPG gas stoves which was not safe in such a flammable environment. We used to occasionally patrol the squatter villages but mostly they took care of themselves and we usually only met the inhabitants when they reported cases to us. It's difficult to calculate how many people lived in these squatters' huts but it was certainly in the tens if not hundreds of thousands. The government continually tried to clear the squatters' villages and move them into approved housing. In 1978, more than 30,000 people were re-housed in 159 clearance operations. There were often terrible fires and sometimes residents perished. Often the cause was down to cooking fires; this put a constant burden on government authorities.

One day a mother brought her daughter to the station to report a case. The mother was in her early thirties and was living in one of the squatter huts on the hillside behind the station. The woman surnamed Kwan had a nine-year-old daughter called May. Kwan worked outside in the nearby town as a waitress in a restaurant. Her husband had walked out a year before and never returned. With no unemployment benefits, she had no choice but to go out to work if she wanted to put food on the table. Kwan had come over to Hong Kong as an illegal immigrant from South China as had millions of other Hong Kong residents. She had no family in Hong Kong, her parents and two sisters were still in China. When she had to work she usually left May with a kind fifty-five-year-old lady who lived in one of the nearby huts. However the 'aunty' was away and with no one else available Kwan had left May in the care of another neighbour, a retired tailor called Yung who was in his early sixties and lived alone.

After her shift ended Kwan had returned to the squatter village and picked May up from Yung's hut. She noticed May's eyes were red and she was very quiet, but hadn't thought much about it. However when she returned home and bathed May she noticed bruises on her thighs and then May complained that her vagina was painful. Shocked, she asked May what had happened. May again fell silent and whispered that Yung had done some bad things. Her mother was now becoming increasingly alarmed and asked May what things. The daughter then revealed that Yung had told May to sit on his lap to watch television and that after stroking her hair and kissing her, he had put his hand between her legs and pressed his fingers into her. Then he had taken his penis out and rubbed it on her private parts.

So Kwan had come down to the station to report the case. As it was a possible rape or attempted rape the duty officer had decided to pass the case to my district crime squad. We sent a female police officer to accompany the pair to hospital to have the girl examined to determine if there was any evidence of penetration. Samples and swabs and photographs would also be taken and we wanted to collect clothes, especially panties and other clothes that might have come into contact with Yung. Meanwhile some of our team members went up to the village on the hillside to locate Yung. Not surprisingly he had moved on and was not waiting around to be arrested. But I had a good team; they worked tirelessly, energised by more lunchboxes. The next day Yung was picked up whilst staying over with relatives. We now had to wait for the forensic and medical reports to come back. Meanwhile one of our specially trained female police officers started to take a statement from the little girl.

We obtained a useful medical report which did support the girl's claims of an assault, but evidence of penetration was undetermined. There was redness and soreness around the vagina but the hymen had not been damaged. This meant we might be able to proceed with charges of attempted rape but probably not rape. Meanwhile the forensic evidence was not as promising. It seemed there were no traces of sperm, hair or any other traces on the clothing. Later when we asked the mother about this, she admitted she had laundered all the clothes before bringing them in! This was a blow to our case because matching up some samples with the accused would have made it very difficult for the defence.

In the evening Yung was led into our offices for questioning. He was around five feet nine inches tall, quite slim, his shoulders slightly stooped. He had a long face, a hooked nose, and thinning grey hair. He was not a particularly handsome chap and I suspected his family may have had northern Chinese origins. Staff Sergeant Leung decided to lead the questioning. The questions went on for some hours and even though my Cantonese was limited it was clear that the questioning was robust and that Leung was getting frustrated. The problem was that without forensic evidence the case was hard to prove. We had an early complaint which was useful, we had medical evidence and we could show that the little girl was with Yung, but in court it could be her testimony against his. But although Yung looked fairly pathetic he was not stupid.

We knew he was guilty, and he knew we knew. He looked and behaved like a guilty man but he was not about to confess. The questioning was getting nowhere and Leung was getting more and more upset. I was sitting some distance away and listening to the exchange. Just before midnight I went up to the mess to sign chits for some Coca-Colas and Fantas for the team. When I came down I heard shouting and someone crying for help. As I walked into the main office there was no one there, but the shouting got louder. Still holding the plastic carrier bag with the cans of sodas I looked around to see Leung next to a window. He was leaning out of the window and I realised he had picked Yung up and was holding him upside-down by the ankles out of the fourth-floor window. Leung was red in the face shaking the guy's ankles and screaming at Yung to confess. Poor old Yung was obviously terrified for his life and was begging to be brought back inside. I put the bag of drinks down and walked up to Leung and putting a hand on his shoulder I said gently but firmly that he should bring Yung back into the room.

I had never seen Leung like that before. I suspected he had lost his temper because he was the father of three girls of his own and maybe he was imagining this horrible man abusing one of his girls. We never talked about it again, and Yung never made an official complaint. All along Yung agreed that he did look after the girl that day but had not indecently touched her. He had no criminal record and I suspected he had assaulted the girl, but perhaps it was that he had simply taken that one opportunity. I didn't think he was a serial offender. The case papers went to the Crown Prosecution Service for consideration of charges. Yung was bailed and told to return in two weeks. When we got the case papers back, we opened them up and read that the government lawyer recommended no charges due to insufficient evidence. We were all very disappointed. Yung did report back on his bail and after giving him dire warnings about his behaviour, he was released.

CHAPTER XIX

The Drugs Bust

INEVITABLY IN OUR LINE of work, long hours were required. Most of the time we did not earn overtime pay, so I made a note of the extra hours and I would sometimes give one or two of the team a day off in lieu when things were quiet. Of course we would often work late into the night as we were looking for people when they were at home. I went out with my Sergeant Chan and a couple of the team one evening looking for a suspect linked to a homicide case. Staff Sergeant Leung was having the evening off. The addresses we had were in Sham Shui Po in West Kowloon so we climbed into our unmarked Mitsubishi saloon car at about 9pm and drove across from our station in East Kowloon. In CID I carried a Smith & Wesson .38 special, which was a snub-nosed version of the revolver I had carried in uniform branch.

Many of us bought our own leather holsters. Some detectives used a leg or shoulder holster but I preferred a simple one that I could put on my belt under a jacket or shirt out of sight. Once we had arrived in Sham Shui Po we parked up in a dark side street. There were around six addresses to be checked that night, and all seemed to be in dingy old tenement blocks. These had no lifts so there was a lot of climbing up and down stairs. Inside there were exposed pipes and electric cables in the corridors. The floors, walls and ceilings were constructed from the same drab, grey cement. The front doors had padlocked metal gates. Some rooms had red papers with various fortuitous slogans stuck on the walls. There were often little pots with incense sticks burning outside the metal gates. There would be the sounds of chatter, noises from televisions, the clatter of chopsticks and *mahjong* tiles, and the occasional cry of a child drifting through the narrow low-ceilinged corridors.

After the third address I told my team we would just check one more and then have a break and maybe grab some iced drinks to cool down as the weather was still warm. The summer months and especially July and August are hot, the humidity level can be over 90 per cent, and people perspire standing still. When I had been out on uniformed patrol it sometimes felt like I was wearing a damp electric blanket over my head. The heat, humidity, and pollution combined made breathing itself very difficult to endure. In West Kowloon that night it seemed someone had sucked all the oxygen out of the atmosphere and replaced it with damp, grey, fetid gas. I suspected smoking cigarettes might have been a healthier option.

So with the promise of some refreshing cold drinks in our mind we made our way into one more building. We were on the second floor, and as we were making our way up, Sergeant Chan noticed a young man. He was in his early twenties, wearing a plain white T-shirt and blue jeans walking down the stairs towards us. He looked pretty normal to me but there was something about him that made Chan suspicious. Perhaps it was his facial expression, something about his eyes. Whatever it was, Chan stopped him on the middle of the stairs.

Chan spoke quietly; he identified himself and asked the young guy for some ID. Everyone has to carry their Hong Kong identity card at all times. This used to be a laminated card with a name, photo and identity number. They were frequently forged and such were in great demand amongst illegal immigrants. When Chan was checking the ID he was also looking at this person. The ID card claimed his name was Mak. Chan noticed the chap seemed to be breathing quickly, and appeared very nervous. Chan even placed his hand over the man's chest and felt his heart beat which pounded faster. He asked him if he was carrying anything, Mak said no, but after a caution Chan started checking his pockets and almost immediately found ten straws that looked like heroin. I had mixed feelings about this now as we were looking for a homicide suspect but now had to deal with a drug possession case. The team and I were all standing close by, there was nowhere Mak could go. Chan continued to question him. Next some keys were found. With Chan still holding the ID card and the straws, Mak was asked about the keys. Mak admitted they were for a small room one floor up.

So while Chan stayed with Mak I took one of my detective constables and went up to see if we were being told the truth. We came to the room mentioned and I took the bunch of keys and opened the padlock on the door. I slid the metal gate aside and then opened the wooden door behind. The room was tiny; it was maybe ten feet by about eight feet. It contained a single bed, a wooden wardrobe, a small wooden stool, and a wash basin. It looked empty of any possessions; there were no clothes in the wardrobe, no pictures, and no personal items at all. As my colleague stood by the door, I decided to bend down and look under the bed to find a number of plastic shopping bags. I pulled one out, it felt heavy. I looked inside – wow! I saw several large bags containing what I was almost certain were the grey granules of 'No. 3' heroin. My heart started racing. This now looked like a real case.

I told my detective constable to go down and bring everyone up to the room. I didn't want to handle the bags directly because of fingerprints. This was a significant find and bigger than anything I'd dealt with before. We brought Mak into the room and he admitted they were his. We called back to the station and told them the news. After sealing the room and with the straws and bags and Mak safely in our possession we made our way back down the stairs to our car. By the time we got back to the station it was after 11pm and we were all really tired so it was agreed to put Mak in the cells downstairs and we would order *siu yeh* and some cold drinks to re-energise ourselves.

Whilst waiting for our food we took fingerprints from Mak and then from the bags. There was 3.6 kilos of heroin, quite a haul. I telephoned our Narcotics Bureau; I was hoping they would take the case off us. I had plenty of cases to keep me busy, and didn't really need another drugs case. I left a message with their duty officer who would pass the news to an inspector by pager as it was now almost midnight. About half an hour later we received a return call. To my disappointment they weren't interested in taking the case. I never found out why, they had handled smaller cases before.

This meant that I was going to be the 'oc case' and I would have to start putting the evidence together. So we brought Mak back from the cells and started taking a statement under caution from him. Meanwhile we began labelling the exhibits and writing our own statements about what happened. I would have to put a file together and send it off to the legal department for counsel's advice. When the advice came back it surprised me: he had recommended the case go to the High Court. So it had been a good night's work, but we still had to find our homicide suspect.

CHAPTER XX

Hong Kong's Biggest Robbery

WHILST I WAS ON DUTY one afternoon in 1991, I was called out to an armed robbery. An armoured car belonging to the security firm Guardforce had collected a load of cash from Kai Tak Airport and was due to deliver it to a local bank. The van was well protected with two armed guards carrying Remington shotguns. This vehicle was holding over HK$190 million, or around US$22 million. The mastermind of the robbery was a notorious and dangerous criminal called Cheung Tze-keung, or more commonly known as 'Big Spender'. He apparently gained his nickname by betting large sums at the gambling tables in the Macau casinos. Cheung and two accomplices were heavily armed. They had surprised and overpowered the guards who had no answer to the superior firepower. Cheung's gang were able to load the bags of cash into a waiting vehicle and escape. It was all over in less than a couple of minutes, and no shots had been fired. I was called out to the scene and was one of the first officers to arrive. The Guardforce van was still there with its rear doors open, some empty bags lying around and two very nervous and dazed guards sitting on the edge of the road with their shotguns propped up alongside them.

When the uniformed officers arrived, a cordon was put around the scene so that forensics officers could examine the area without evidence being disturbed. Meanwhile the press was also there and tried to enter the area when they thought we weren't looking. As word spread more reporters arrived and then radio and TV crews; the press throng was looking more like a small army. The multi-million dollar robbery would be front-page news. Some of our own Police Public Relations Bureau people then arrived to try to keep the press under control. But after about an hour the reporters were getting very restless: they wanted a story. The PPRB lady approached me and asked me to speak to them.

I reluctantly agreed, and when I was fairly confident that I had enough information I went to talk to the press, who numbered at least thirty people by this time. As I stepped forward the reporters pressed in, thrusting a mass of microphones in my face, and then the television lights were switched on blinding me. I started to speak, trying to regain my composure. That night it was all over the evening TV news with yours truly looking like a rabbit in a car's headlamps. I was quoted in all the morning papers. Back in the office I even received a call from the *New York Times*. I was convinced it was someone taking the piss at first. Gradually I realised it was a genuine call. The money stolen had come from the Bank of New York.

Big Spender was eventually caught and convicted of robbery. As expected, he had an accomplice on the inside who had been informing him of the guard van's movements and contents. However he then got off on appeal on a legal technicality. However Cheung became even greedier and a few years later devised a scheme to kidnap Victor Li, the son of Hong Kong billionaire Li Ka-shing. It is believed a ransom was paid, and although no one knows for sure outside the Li family, rumours suggest an amount of around US$120 million may have been handed over. Victor was released and the family beefed up their own private security. Some of the new private protection force included ex-Hong Kong Police officers.

Buoyed by this success he and his gang planned another audacious kidnapping, this time of Walter Kwok of Sun Hung Kai Properties. It is claimed he managed to extract US$80 million for Kwok's safe release. So in these two cases alone he probably escaped with around US$200 million! By this time he was attracting a lot of attention in both Hong Kong and China. Some reports suggested that Hong Kong's richest tycoons were even expressing concerns to Beijing. Big Spender's luck eventually ran out one day during a large armed raid in Guangzhou just over the border. A heavily armed contingent of the Public Security Bureau raided his hideout. Police also arrested thirty-two accomplices, and seized eleven luxury cars, US$5 million in cash, plus firearms, grenades and explosives. When he went to trial the police escort resembled an army on the march with armoured cars and police in bulletproof vests. The trial was closed to the public and press. Cheung was convicted of multiple charges. He was sentenced to death and executed by firing squad. Two movies were made based on his exploits: *Operation Billionaires* in 1998 and *Big Spender* in 1999.

CHAPTER XXI

Death in Service

I WENT THROUGH A BAD TIME in the mid-1980s when a number of my friends and colleagues passed away. In the mid-1980s apart from Bruce Vogel, I had a friend who died from a motorcycle accident in Admiralty on the way back home from a seafood dinner on Lamma Island. Another friend, Andrew Churton, died on Special Duty Unit selection during an exercise in the hills of the New Territories. Andrew was a lovely young man who lived near me. I remember speaking to him before he went away on the selection process; he was so excited, and looking forward to it. It was a terrible and unnecessary tragedy as he died of dehydration. I was extremely upset, and his death had a huge impact on all his friends and colleagues.

Another inspector was cut up by boat propellers after he fell in the water on the south side of Hong Kong. It was reported that the 'dead man's handle' had not been fitted to the outboard motor, and the boat turned around and struck him. I seemed to be spending a lot of time in St John's Cathedral. Hepatitis was also quite common in Hong Kong. For hepatitis B, infection rates in the UK are around 0.3 per cent of the population, whereas in Hong Kong the rate is 12 per cent. Many liver cancer sufferers are hepatitis carriers. I saw local colleagues die of liver cancer. By the time it's diagnosed the tumour is too big and it's too late to treat. I had a colleague, a detective constable in my team named Kwan. He was thirty-eight years old, a teetotal non-smoker, a keen hill-walker and a devoted family man. His wife was thirty-four years old; they had two young daughters aged six and eight. He lived in police married quarters in Kowloon. Like most liver cancer victims, he had been diagnosed late. Most liver cancer victims in Hong Kong were dead within a year, and many within weeks. There were no specialist government hospices available and when his situation deteriorated he was simply admitted to a regular public hospital and placed in a general ward with everyone else. My colleagues from the team and I visited him regularly. It was not easy. There was no treatment. He knew he was dying.

Sometimes his wife and daughters were there when we visited. Kwan was very concerned for the welfare of his young family. When an officer died his family could only retain police quarters for six months. One day I went to visit, and tears started streaming down his face. He cried quietly maintaining his dignity. He asked me to leave; I did so, wiping a tear from my eye as I left the ward. The next morning I learnt he had died during the night. He had been so brave. The mood in the office was very sombre, no one spoke. Arrangements were made by the family for a traditional funeral with burnt offerings, mourners in white shrouds, and Buddhist prayers. The service was held in a funeral parlour on Hong Kong Island.

We all had gone around the police station and collected a large sum to donate to the family. There was still the tricky issue of housing. When I returned to my office I started making telephone calls and writing memos to the Housing Department. I was quite emotional about the whole situation. I was determined to resolve the issue and ensure Kwan's family were looked after. Fortunately my intervention and persistence seemed to work. Personnel Wing at Police HQ helped a lot too. Mrs Kwan and her daughters were granted new government housing and were able to move into a reasonable public housing flat in Ho Man Tin, not far from their old police quarters. I went to visit them, in their new home. I was relieved that at least they now had a decent place to rebuild their lives.

CHAPTER XXII

The Snake Catcher

U NUSUALLY FOR SUCH A SMALL, densely populated area, Hong Kong has a wide variety of snakes. These include two large ones: the Burmese Python which can grow to twenty feet in length and the King Cobra which reaches ten feet. I recall seeing a brave police team go into a village on Lantau and use poles with wire nooses to catch an eight-foot-long python. I saw many snakes in the countryside. I'm not normally afraid of them except the time I was out on a hill walk near Discovery Bay when I looked up and saw a very large black King Cobra stretched out above me on a large boulder, just watching me. I turned tail and ran back down the creek.

One of the more strange tasks for colleagues in the uniform branch was to call out a snake catcher when we had reports of a snake being seen in a public area. Most of these reports came from people living in the squatter villages on the hillsides. I used to wonder if some of the villagers were in cahoots with the snake catcher. He seemed to be called out to the same area quite regularly and always seemed to catch the same type of snake.

So one afternoon in the station when the snake catcher came in for his fee I decided to ask to see the evidence. He was a rather plump man in his mid-fifties, with a round jolly face, crooked brown teeth, and very short-cropped grey hair. He always wore an old grubby sleeveless vest, the same nylon shorts, and rubber slippers. Over his shoulder he carried a large brown hessian sack which appeared to be writhing with snakes. His fee for catching a snake was HK$100. He came into my office chuckling through stained uneven teeth, looking for his reward.

One of the uniformed junior officers from the report room was with him. I was feeling mischievous. 'Show me the snake you caught,' I cheekily asked. Our snake catcher did not hesitate; he swung the sack round, reached down into the sack, and caught a large dark-grey rat snake by the neck. He then lifted the four-foot-long and apparently well-nourished snake up into the air. I'm not sure what it was, perhaps suddenly coming out of darkness and having its head thrust up towards a bright neon ceiling light, but something spooked the snake. As it was being held up on display it suddenly crapped half-digested rat entrails over my pristine office carpet. What the fuck! The stench was unbearable. Think of the worst smell ever and multiply it by ten. The young constable and I keeled over, retching and gasping for air. We were desperate to get out of the office but the snake catcher was in the doorway. There was nothing for it, we rudely pushed past him, and the large pooing snake, and ran, whilst holding our hands over our faces in a vain attempt to mask the appalling odour. As we escaped I told the constable to pay the man out of our petty cash. I ran up the stairs to the changing rooms to shower. The smell in my office lingered for months afterwards. No matter what we did and how many times we cleaned and disinfected it, the smell never went away. I never again asked the snake catcher to take a snake out of his bag, and paid him immediately without complaint.

CHAPTER XXIII

Moving out of
New World Apartments

ONE MORNING SITTING in my office, I received a government memo that ruined my day, my week, my month, even my year. It was from the quartering office stating that the New World Apartments were to be handed back, and all government tenants would be moved out into traditional government quarters. I was really depressed; I did not want to move anywhere else. I called the quartering office and asked what I had to do. Initially I was told that I could stay until the end of my tour but that soon changed and I was told that I would have to move out earlier. I was offered a flat on Hong Kong Island.

I arranged a recce of the proposed new flat a couple of days later and couldn't believe my eyes. The block was in a terrible state and when I entered the flat it got worse. The flat was tiny and in an awful condition. It was filthy dirty, and had broken furniture. The place was covered in dust and mouse droppings. Broken discoloured venetian blinds hung from the window frames. It was on the first floor but was facing another building and had no natural light. The whole interior design and shape of the flat was strange, it had no bedroom and a bed had been pushed into an alcove. I made a note of the long list of deficiencies and went back to my office to type up my reply. I said it was unfit for human habitation and refused to move. I was then told that I could apply for alternative accommodation using the normal process of the points system.

Although I was still unhappy I eventually moved into a larger flat in Beacon Hill Road in Kowloon Tong. When moving into a different flat we were allowed a redecoration and I decided to brighten the place up. I requested each room to be painted in a different colour. So my lounge was bright yellow, one bedroom was green, one was blue, the kitchen was orange. It was my little pathetic attempt at rebellion, but I think it did cheer the place up. Another issue I had to face was purchasing new furniture and curtains and cushions. I slept in a bedroom at the rear of the flat next to the old amah's room. It was not New World Apartments but I would have to get used to it.

One night a few months after moving in, I woke suddenly in the early hours when it was still quite dark. I had felt a presence in the bedroom. I woke, and sat half-up in my bed. I saw a silhouette at the entrance to my bedroom. It looked like a middle-aged or elderly woman in black garments. I did not feel scared, the air did not go cold, and as quickly as she appeared, she disappeared. The atmosphere was calm, I had no goose-bumps. I got out of bed and looked around the flat. There was no one there. Whatever it was seemed benign. The next day I received a call from my father telling me my grandmother had just died. Some weeks later a redirected letter with £50 cash arrived from her in which she predicted that she would not live much longer. I always used to visit her when I was back in the UK. We usually went out for lunch together. She told me in her last letter that she would have loved to visit Hong Kong but she knew she never would. I don't know what I saw, but I never saw it again, and I still have my grandmother's last letter. I don't read it often as it makes me feel so sad.

In order to cheer myself up I bought a secondhand Nissan 280ZX coupe. It was black, with dark-gold alloy wheels. It had an automatic gear box, and air-conditioning and was very fast, I loved it. I paid HK$16,000 for it to a wealthy young Hong Kong guy who was going to the USA to study. I thought it was a bargain. I once drove it late one night through the Aberdeen Tunnel at 100 mph. I really didn't realise the speed until I glanced down at the speedo and realised it was in miles and not kilometres per hour.

Living in Beacon Hill Road was very different from Tsim Sha Tsui. It was a pleasant area but did not have the same attractions as the city centre. One morning I heard someone shouting outside in the street. I looked out from the balcony and saw a local man with a black bicycle and two large stainless steel buckets on the road below. He was the *dou foo* seller. Customers had to take their own bowls down to him. He would scoop pieces of white bean curd into your bowl and then pour a sweet syrup over them. It was delicious. Whenever I saw him I would grab a large bowl and try to get the lift down to the ground floor before he moved on. I liked to go back up to the flat and eat the sweet bean curd when it was still warm. What a treat!

The Beacon Hill Road flats had a design fault. One day I heard from a colleague that someone had been watching my nocturnal activities. At that time I was going out with Linda, an aerobics instructor. We were both very healthy and energetic. I had been rather mean with curtains and thinking the bedroom was not overlooked I had not had them fully fitted. It transpired that a colleague's wife had realised that if she stood in the amah's room at the back of her flat and looked out of the corner of the window, she could see into my bedroom. Soon tales of my activities were being shared around the neighbours and colleagues. The following day I went into the China Products department store in Yau Ma Tei and purchased some new curtains. I never told Linda. Thankfully Facebook was not around then.

Linda and I decided to have a weekend in Macau. Macau was then a Portuguese colony and had been for 400 years since the time of Vasco da Gama. We joined another couple, Chris and his Kiwi girlfriend Jennifer. Instead of the jetfoil, which skated over the water at speeds of about forty knots and cut the journey time to about one hour, we took the slow ferry, which was much more romantic. We checked into two rooms at the old Bela Vista Hotel. I'm sure at some point the hotel did have a *bella vista* (good view) but new developments had ruined it sadly. Macau in 1985 was still a very quaint and picturesque place though. The main place for gambling then was the Lisboa Hotel. The room was lovely, it was spacious with whitewashed walls and high ceiling, with a ceiling fan, and it all seemed very colonial. The problem was that when I jumped on the bed, the mattress folded up in two. We could not have much fun on such an unstable soft surface, so we had to make do with other locations.

The following day we all went over to the beautiful Pousada de São Tiago Hotel for lunch. This hotel was quite posh in comparison to our Bela Vista, and the traditional Portuguese cuisine was delicious. We enjoyed spicy prawns, African chicken, and egg tarts, all washed down with lovely Portuguese wine. Having ate and drank our fill we decided that it was time for a spot of sightseeing. As we made our way across the lobby to the main entrance I noticed a huge black guy dressed in a black T-shirt and track pants come through the doors towards us. He was followed by a familiar-looking couple. It was Madonna and Sean Penn; they were in town filming *Shanghai Surprise*. Madonna was wearing a dark blue pea coat, she had no make-up and her hair was scraped back in a pony-tail. She was wearing blue jeans and simple cotton sneakers. I remember she seemed tiny, and her expression suggested she did not want to talk to anyone. Sean Penn had a similar serious look. Maybe filming had not gone well? Later when I saw the movie I suspected the entire shoot had not gone well. The one thing about Madonna though that stood out to me was her jeans had holes in the knee. I wondered why she couldn't afford a new pair. It was at least two years later before I realised that she was ahead of a new fashion trend.

CHAPTER XXIV

Adventure Sports

I HAD BECOME KEEN on sport as a teenager at school. I attended a rugby-playing school and enjoyed playing soccer at weekends too. Some of my police colleagues were super fit and into ultra-marathons and triathlons, but that was not for me. The Hong Kong Police were generous with giving time off for sports, and some chaps took full advantage. I thought that a day off for playing golf or to go sailing seemed extremely benevolent. There were also overseas tours with additional time off. We had some excellent sportsmen from the police who represented Hong Kong at international level, and even some such as Mike Watson and Mike Field who represented Hong Kong at the Olympics. When I came to Hong Kong, apart from rugby, I played soccer for the Dynamos, and later for Hearts. The highlight was when we were captained by Peter Barnes and came top of the Yau Yee League Division C in 1991. I usually played full back. I was never very good but it was fun, and at least I made up the numbers. But I was also interested in trying more exciting pursuits.

When I was at school, aged sixteen, I had been in the RAF Air Cadets. I had applied for, and been selected to attend, a glider piloting course near Liverpool. This consisted of three weeks' full-time tuition followed by three solo flights. I was a reasonable student but I remember being very nervous indeed on my first solo flight. There was a winch lift up to about 1,000 feet and then a cable release. I survived it all, and still enjoy the thrill of going up in a glider whenever I can although I have to be with a qualified pilot as I no longer have a valid licence.

I once also did a bungee jump near Queenstown, New Zealand from Skippers Canyon Bridge. I was terrified. I had to hobble along a short wooden plank with my ankles bound, almost 300 feet up. I screamed like a little girl on the way down. I also took up scuba diving, and it still is one of my favourite sports. I have completed over 120 logged dives around the world and always carry my PADI licence when I'm travelling. I joined the British Sub Aqua Club in Hong Kong and went on a few overseas trips with them. One of my favourite dive locations is the Philippines. We were once diving in Puerto Galera doing a drift dive at Kilema down to eighty feet. I was buddied with Paul who was an experienced diver. When we were at about sixty feet he started sending hand signals and I realised he had no air left. I was surprised, but fortunately I had plenty left in my tank. I swam over and handed him my spare yellow octopus breathing apparatus which he gratefully accepted. We linked arms and made a slow controlled ascent to the surface.

One thing I had wanted to do since I was a teenager was a parachute jump. When I was eighteen my parents had paid for a private course at a small air base near Hereford in England. I had driven over to there three times in my little Fiat 124 to complete my jumps but was thwarted by bad weather every time. Then it was too late as I was on my way to Hong Kong.

When I had been up in Shek Kong with Bob one afternoon in his army helicopter I learned that there was a parachute club next to the air force base. I decided to sign up and start the training at weekends.

The cost of the course and the jumps was only about HK$200 which seemed reasonable. The training was very similar to that which I'd received a few years earlier in Hereford. We would be jumping out of a small Cessna 182 aircraft on a static line from 2,500 feet using a canopy GQ aeroconical parachute. Once we had completed the classroom training and learned all about parachutes and manoeuvring, we climbed up on platforms to practise jumping and landing safely. We were taught to fold our body up and roll to avoid any broken bones. My instructor was a young chap called Andy Sinclair who did an excellent job in coaching us.

There were four of us on the course including a young English-woman. Mary had been very enthusiastic during the course and completed her training with ease. When the big day arrived and we were all kitted up we made our way to the Cessna and took our assigned positions. It was a small aircraft and it could only carry the four of us with the pilot and our instructor.

It was a partially cloudy April day. The wind speed was favourable and I was both excited and nervous about the jump. We were seated in the aircraft in the order we were going to jump: Mary first, then me and then the other two students. With a static line the parachute is linked to a hook inside the aircraft, so the parachute deploys as soon as the person jumps out, without any free fall.

We had to climb out of the aircraft in the series of steps we had been taught. First, place a hand on the door, then one foot on the step, then the other hand on a strut, then another foot out of the aircraft, then another hand on the top of the wing. Finally we would have both hands on top of the wing and both feet outside the aircraft, facing forwards, but looking sideways at our instructor and waiting for the order to jump.

We were up to altitude and approaching the jump zone. The side of the aircraft was open so the wind was strong and very noisy. Mary began to step out after the hook was attached. She stepped out of the aircraft but made the mistake of looking down. She suddenly looked terrified and shouted: 'No, no!' as the instructor screamed at her to jump.

She was halfway out and her parachute had been attached. The drop zone in Shek Kong was very small and there was no room for error. Reluctantly the instructor pulled her back in to the aircraft before detaching her hook to her parachute and making sure she was strapped safely into her seat. The aircraft had to go round again for another circuit. So whilst the pilot was manoeuvring, I shuffled into position for my jump. This was not easy as Mary was still in the seat next to the door, so I had to attach the hook and climb around her. I then had to clamber over to the exit and go through the same routine of hand-foot-hand-foot until I was standing outside the aircraft travelling at 100 mph, whilst holding the wing and trying not to get blown off.

The red-faced and wide-eyed instructor yelled at me: 'Jump! Jump!' He didn't want another refusal.

This was the moment I had waited for since I'd been eighteen. I launched myself off the back of the wing and arched my body, but as I did so the parachute was already deploying and seemed to be pulling me back up, although this was just an illusion, I was simply falling more slowly. As I looked up to the white parachute I noticed the lines had twisted. With the training I'd received I was able to pull the guide lines and move my body to get the parachute back to normal. It was then that I looked down.

What I hadn't appreciated was how small the landing site in Shek Kong was. From 2,000 feet it seemed to be the size of a postage stamp. I decided not to manoeuvre at all but rely on the good judgement of the instructor until I was down to about 1,000 feet. This turned out to be a good move as when I looked more closely I saw many hazards, such as barbed-wire fences and steel pylons, next to the landing site.

The last 200 feet flashed past and suddenly the ground was rushing up to me. At about ten feet I pulled hard on the chute with both hands to stall it, but I still landed quite heavily and rolled my right ankle. But I had survived my first parachute jump. I was elated. I asked a friendly club member to take a photo with me on the ground holding my chute. I completed two more jumps and was presented with a certificate which is now framed and proudly displayed on my wall. I was told after I had jumped that the Shek Kong landing area was one of the smallest in the world permitted for first-student jumps. Sadly the club closed before the handover in 1997.

CHAPTER XXV

The Sex Trade

BACK TO MY POLICE WORK. Hong Kong is well known for its sex industry and has never really hidden the trade. In 1978, 3,078 people were charged with prostitution and related offences in Hong Kong. In 2014 over 4,000 people from Mainland China alone were arrested for prostitution offences. Much of this business was controlled or protected by the triads, and the largest societies were the 14K and Sun Yee On. In my later career, the Sun Yee On seemed to be the most influential and better organised. In the earlier twentieth century, triad initiation ceremonies were quite elaborate affairs, but when I was serving it was believed that this had been compressed to avoid interruption and discovery by the police. There was a lot of street-level activity and members would often have tattoos of dragons or similar to mark themselves as triads. Arrests were usually of low-level street fighters but rarely the big bosses who controlled them. Like most organised crime a lot of the funds were laundered through business fronts. Many of the most senior triad bosses appeared in public as respectable millionaires, though with rumours about shady backgrounds. I would take my team to conduct raids on establishments controlled by triads and made arrests, but mostly to disrupt their business interests. Territories and businesses were divided up so that if we were in a particular street in Yau Ma Tei we would know it was 14K territory. Apart from protection or 'tea-money', triads would make money through illegal gambling, narcotics, and the sex industry.

The sex industry evolved over the years. Prostitution itself was not an offence but soliciting and living off the earnings of prostitution was illegal. In the 1960s and early '70s, tea dances were popular.

These were large rooms that played popular old-style dance tunes. There were 'ladies' present who would dance with customers for a fee. The male customers would buy tickets that would allow them to dance for a period of time with the lady of their choice. If they liked the lady they could buy more tickets. If they wanted to take the liaison further they could pay a separate larger fee and buy the lady out for an hour or two. There were also numerous 'one-woman brothels'. These were one-bedroom apartments where the woman lived and worked. Sometimes a small yellow sign indicated the address, or there were cards outside stuck to walls or in telephone boxes. The women would look through a spyhole in the door before deciding whether to let a customer in. The women had a certain amount of independence but still suffered the occasional robbery, and abuse at the hands of their pimps.

There were also a few brothels that provided a number of girls. These were illegal and the owners knew that these would be targeted by police. They would be well protected and passwords would be needed to enter. In Kowloon Tong there were several large villas that had been converted to 'love-motels', like the famous Lui-Lui Motel. These were registered businesses. Garish neon signs on top of the roof indicated the type of business. Rooms were rented by the hour. They were comfortable and functional with small bowls of condoms by the bedside, and twenty-four-hour pornographic movies on the TV. They were popular with young couples who lived in shared bedrooms in public housing estates as a way of enjoying some privacy. When cars entered the car park, a metal plate would be placed over the number plate to ensure discretion. There were always a lot of Mercedes in the car park which suggested that many of the clients were wealthy businessmen enjoying a dalliance with their secretary or a secret girlfriend.

The bars in Wan Chai provided thrills. They were mostly a rip-off and catered for Western businessmen with too much money and no idea how to approach a regular local girl. In the late 1970s the Wan Chai bars still had Chinese girls, and still looked the same as during the Vietnam War when they catered for thousands of troops enjoying R & R. Later in the 1980s these bars were staffed by girls from the Philippines and Thailand. In Kowloon there was the 'Bottoms Up' bar which was unusual in that it sometimes featured topless European women. This bar became famous when it appeared in the movie *The Man with the Golden Gun* starring Roger Moore as James Bond. Another famous place in Tsim Sha Tsui was 'Red Lips' which I suspected to be a retirement home for tired prostitutes. It looked like the kind of place where after a lifetime of working on their backs the ladies would congregate before finally retiring to the great brothel in the sky. For young off-duty inspectors it was a rite of passage to go to Red Lips at least once. The decor was almost as tired as the ladies who worked there. The seats were red plastic upholstered benches, but the beer was cheap and the music was mostly cheesy old pop tunes. There was a lady there called Josephine who could recite Shakespeare. That was a surreal experience, getting drunk in Kowloon with an old Chinese lady quoting passages from *King Lear.*

Massage parlours and saunas were often a front for vice establishments. They were usually rather ornate and actually did have good facilities such as hot tubs, plunge pools, and steam rooms. Once finished with that part of the facility customers would move to a large lounge where assistants would ask patrons what kind of massage they required. The masseurs had numbers and regular customers would request a particular girl by her number. For a new customer the massage might seem a bit reserved. The owners were always nervous of an undercover officer testing the place to see if other services were offered. For regular customers the gloves were off. In fact everything else was off as well. 'Happy endings' were normal, and for regular customers a full sex service was available at the right price.

I know the police raided these establishments but I cannot recall a case where one was closed down by the authorities. I always felt that the girls worked there from choice. Some sectors of the community state loudly that no woman would choose to work in the sex industry, and that they must all be coerced. I accept that some women are coerced or threatened, but equally there are many that are not. The story of Brooke Magnanti who wrote under the pseudonym Belle de Jour was a good example. She is a beautiful, well-educated, intelligent woman who realised she could earn a lot of money by providing an escort service in London. She used the money to further her education. She caused further controversy when she claimed she actually enjoyed the work.

Of course there were girls in Hong Kong who became drug addicts and to pay for it became prostitutes. There were also women who became indebted to triads who then were threatened and entered the sex industry to pay off their debts. One trick the triads used was to send out their younger members to scout for impressionable girls in fast-food restaurants and amusement games centres, especially girls who might be estranged from their families. Once the triad had selected a target he would look after her, buy her meals and drinks, take her to movies and spend as much time as possible with her. He would seduce her, hold her hand and act like a lovestruck boyfriend. Everything seemed perfect until one night he would suddenly appear fearful and scared. Naturally his sweetheart would ask him what was wrong and reluctantly he would tell her his terrible story.

His mother had become seriously ill with a rare illness and needed specialised treatment or expensive medicine from the USA. He had used all his savings buying medicine, and then had resorted to taking a loan with a loan shark. With interest this debt had now grown to a massive sum and the triads had threatened to 'chop him to pieces'. Some of his triad friends would arrive on the scene and start to push him around and abuse him. The girl by this time would be frightened and worried that her beau would be seriously wounded or even killed. When the gang had left the 'boyfriend' would talk about 'us' and 'we' to make the girl feel it was her problem too. Reluctantly he would suggest a way that she might save his life. She could sleep with men for money and after a few days the debt could be paid. Of course, before long she would be servicing ten men a day in dingy flats. She would be introduced to heroin to dull the pain, and would enter a downward spiral from which there was no escape. It was a really nasty trick that destroyed many young girls' lives.

As Hong Kong became wealthier in the 1980s more luxurious nightclubs began to appear, especially in Tsim Sha Tsui East, another area that had been reclaimed from the sea. Few expats ventured here unless they were a guest of a wealthy local businessman. Most of the customers in the 1980s seemed to be wealthy Hong Kong businessmen, senior triad members, and latterly businessmen from the Mainland. One of the biggest and most popular clubs was Club Volvo which later had to change its name following complaints from the Swedish car maker. Club Volvo had a model Rolls-Royce car inside the club which was used to ferry top clients to the private rooms. The interior was extremely ornate with mock Greek statues, Venetian columns, large palm trees, fountains, gold-plated chandeliers, and thick luxury carpets. There were numerous private rooms with large cream-leather sofas, glass-topped tables and large-screen televisions. On entering a room with your friends or colleagues, bowls of expensive fresh fruit would be laid on the table and guests would be given a karaoke menu.

The most popular drink in such clubs was French cognac. There was no three-star brandy or even VSOP in the place. The cheapest brandy was Martell Cordon Bleu. But the most common drink was Hennessy XO which was about HK$1,500 a bottle even in 1985. Some customers even ordered the Louis XIV which was several thousand Hong Kong dollars a bottle. In the 1990s the fashion moved to French red wine, with bottles of Louis Latour and Chateau Margaux consumed, sometimes mixed with Coca-Cola. Very attractive young Hong Kong girls, dressed in *cheung sams*, with perfect hair and make-up would then start to filter into the room and a mama-san would introduce the girls. The mama-san would then leave but come back about twenty minutes later. If anyone didn't like a girl they would say so and the girl would be quietly replaced. The drinks flowed and the singing became worse. The girls laughed and poured drinks and flirted. I went there once when invited by a businessman friend of a friend. I was quite reserved though, as I was still a serving officer and did not want to become compromised. It was of course possible to buy the girls out for the night. The credit card bills must have been crazy.

Across the Pearl River estuary to the west of Hong Kong was the old Portuguese colony of Macau. Unlike Hong Kong, Macau has a legal casino industry; the most famous of these was the Lisboa. Ferries and hydrofoils took gamblers across the waters. The old ferries were wonderful. It was possible to reserve a private cabin and the journey took hours, so it actually felt like going on a foreign adventure. The gambling industry attracted the sex industry, and in the Macau Ferry Terminal there were posters advertising 'sauna tours' which was a euphemism for a more intimate form of service.

In 1994 a well-known Hong Kong lawyer called Gary Alderdice met a blond twenty-year-old Russian callgirl. Natalya was based in Macau and worked in one of the nightclubs. Alderdice fell in love with the young Russian beauty and bought her out of the club. Over the next few months he spent a fortune buying her out night after night. He eventually checked into the Westin Resort in Macau with her and stayed there for over a month. He was madly in love with her. The nightclub was unhappy about their loss of revenue and threatened to rescind her visa and send her back to Russia. The couple decided to go together to Vladivostok and buy her contract. So Alderdice withdrew a sum believed to be US$150,000 in cash which was placed in a briefcase and they made their way to Russia to meet the gang members.

They checked into a hotel room and at the agreed time there was a knock on the door and four gangsters walked in. As Alderdice was talking and proffered the briefcase full of cash, one of the gangsters pulled out an automatic pistol and shot him through the eye, killing him instantly, according to reports. Natalya was raped and tortured and eventually shot dead. The incident certainly sent a strong message to any other girls thinking of leaving the business. It certainly sent shock waves through the Hong Kong legal fraternity where Alderdice had been a well-loved and respected lawyer.

In my official role, we continuously raided vice premises. Mostly these were on the opposite end of the price scale from Club Volvo. When we entered we would get the proprietor to switch on the lights and tell everyone to stand up and take out their identity cards. The ID cards would then be called in via radio and immigration and police databases were checked to see if the ID cards were genuine, or if the person was wanted for any offences. After the earlier 'tea dances' such cheaper establishments had descended into a more perfunctory type of business. These were called *yue dan dongs*, literally 'fish ball stalls', after the street stalls where hawkers sold the deep fried steaming snack so loved by Hongkongers. The fish balls are slightly smaller than a ping pong ball and are served on thin wooden skewers, usually smothered with chilli sauce. The idea was that the girls in these vice establishments were teenage schoolgirls whose small breasts resembled fish balls.

In fact this was almost certainly a rumour spread by the owners to attract punters, who seemed to be all local Hongkongers. The interiors of these premises were furnished with high-back benches, often covered in red leatherette, just large enough for two people. On entering, the customer bought tickets which enabled him a certain number of minutes with a 'girl'. They were shown to a numbered private bench by a hostess with a small pen torch; as the places were virtually pitch dark. This helped conceal the fact that most of the girls were in fact rather mature ladies who would probably not be able to work in classier clubs.

The customer and the girl would sit down together on the bench in the twilight making small talk and fumbling with each other under their clothing. If sufficient tickets were bought, the customer would get a hand-job and a 'happy ending'. But when the lights went up it was amusing to see the customer realising that the 'girl' he thought he was with was not young at all. The smell of semen was never quite masked by the burning of joss sticks and the industrial air conditioners. In one of these establishments in Kowloon, I realised with horror that some idiot had decided to furnish the place with fitted carpets. As I walked across the room, past the strategically placed tissue boxes and toilet rolls, I realised that my black leather police-issue shoes were squelching on the floor, and sticking to the carpet. I tried holding my breath and very thoroughly wiped my feet on the way out.

CHAPTER XXVI

Expat Life

THE LONGER I LIVED and worked in Hong Kong the more I realised that there was certainly an expat pecking order. Police officers were middle class, as we were British and had reasonably good salaries. But we were looked down upon by the fat cats in the banks. At the top end were the 'Jardine-Johnnies' and the 'Swire boys' with their amazing salaries, bonuses, and housing allowances. When I occasionally met or became friendly with a young chap who worked in a merchant bank I could not believe the huge apartments they lived in. These guys bought Porsches and yachts, had the best club memberships, and spent weekends golfing and sailing. Police might aspire to the Football Club or the Kowloon Cricket Club. Otherwise we would make do with the Police Officers' Club in Causeway Bay. If I was ever at a party with different social groups it was made pretty obvious that I was not one of the 'boys', and the women made it clear what they aspired for too.

In my early years many people still believed the police were totally corrupt and it took a long time for this view to change. For that reason many police chose to socialise only with other police and their families. Personally I tried to avoid this, as I felt that when police are together they all talked shop, and when anyone was promoted there was inevitably a certain amount of jealousy. I tried to make friends outside the force. So I still avoided police messes after work. But I still played rugby and had a good circle of close police friends. One of the places I enjoyed visiting was the Mariners' Club in Tsim Sha Tsui, mainly for the outdoor swimming pool.

In the evening I liked the China Fleet Club for the black pepper steak and chips which was always served with peas and diced carrots and tasty black pepper gravy. The China Fleet Club was popular with servicemen and had a small number of souvenir and tailor shops. The British Army had regiments on rotation in the colony and some had better reputations than others. The squaddies from the Parachute Regiment, with their red berets certainly lived up to their fearsome reputation. There was a popular watering hole in Central called the Bull and Bear which was designed to cater for the 'suits' from the office towers nearby. To the chagrin of the infamous matriarch, the indomitable Phyllis, it also often attracted British squaddies. The attraction was probably the old English atmosphere and more importantly the nice traditional warm British ales served. In the early to mid-eighties there were not many British-themed pubs and most of the beers served were cold lagers. The majority of the military guys were perfectly well behaved, but some certainly played up after a few beers.

After a number of incidents in which fighting and drunkenness disturbed the convivial atmosphere in the Bull and Bear, Phyllis decided to ban all military men from the pub. I heard the final straw was when someone decided to go to the toilet and do a 'number two' in an ashtray which was then placed back on a table. She placed a notice on the door saying British servicemen were not allowed. With my close-cropped hair I was also stopped from entering until I showed my police warrant card. For much of the time the soldiers were confined to barracks in Stanley or Fanling, but on their evenings out they made up for lost time. We also had regular visits from the US Navy's Pacific Fleet. Their aircraft carriers, cruisers, and submarines would often come into our harbour in an amazing show of strength. A single aircraft carrier would have a complement of over 6,000, the population of a small town.

I was invited on the USS *Enterprise* by a friend of a US officer in 1985. We had dinner in the ward room. The whole ship was incredible. We went below deck and saw the Phantom fighter jets, and the giant lifts that carried them up to launch. I also saw the huge electronic maps showing all ship movements in the South China Sea. The ship seemed big enough to have its own ecosystem;

we felt we could have declared war on the world. When the US sailors went on R&R in Wan Chai it seemed they were taking over the whole city. They were followed by large numbers of white uniformed military police (MPs) who carried truncheons and often tried in vain to break up the inevitable fights. One problem the US sailors faced was that all their ships, unlike the British ones, were dry. Their tolerance to alcohol seemed pretty low to me. A couple of beers and they tended to get very merry indeed. I recall a time when the British Parachute Regiment were in town at the same time as the US Pacific Fleet. Lockhart Road and all the bars resembled a huge battleground. The poor old MPs on both sides were cracking skulls with seemingly no effect. The Paras were often smaller than their US counterparts but more than made up for their lack of stature in naked aggression. The MPs would try to drag their wayward troops off to the nearby military vans and then back to the barracks or ship, but some ended up in the police cells in Wan Chai. We tried to leave these patrols to the MPs though, they had their own efficient ways of enforcing discipline.

A lot of the expat police officers enjoyed a good curry, and of course there was always the ordering of a vindaloo to test your manliness. I had never eaten a proper curry before coming out to Hong Kong. The first time I bit into a baby green Thai chilli I thought I would need an ambulance. Over time I built up a tolerance and although I still cannot quite stretch to a vindaloo, I can eat, and certainly enjoy, spicy Asian food. After our rugby games it was common to head for a popular curry house and of course everything was ordered with extra chillies. Over in Kowloon there is a famous building called Chungking Mansions in Tsim Sha Tsui. This was built in the early 1960s, and consists of five blocks. It was initially intended as a grand residence for wealthy Hongkongers. By the 1980s it had been taken over by travellers from Africa and South Asia. It offered all types of goods and services, and always had an interesting clientele including friendly women hanging around the entrance. Any non-Chinese person walking past then, and now, will be made all manner of offers.

Chungking Mansions is well known on the backpacker circuit for cheap accommodation. When the cheapest regular hotel prices are often over HK$1,000 a night, this is a welcome alternative for those on their first Asian adventures. But today, with very low approval ratings, it's perhaps best to read the reviews on Tripadvisor first. The thing that I often visited Chungking Mansions for was the curries. On the upper floors there are various 'messes' which were supposedly private clubs. They do this to avoid licensing laws. Membership was instant and free as soon as you walked in. My favourite, which is still going strong today, was the Taj Mahal Mess in Block B. The food was simple and tasty and for HK$20 or HK$30 I could get a chicken curry, rice and chapatti plus a large bottle of chilled Tsing Tao beer. I took my cousin Stuart there when he visited from Canada. We both ate and drank our fill, and we could never believe how small the bill was.

In the streets nearby and near the Star Ferry were some hard-core street sleepers. When Hong Kong charities talk about helping street sleepers now, they seem to be concentrating on those people who have recently lost jobs and are temporarily suffering tough times. I look at the pictures of some of the current street sleepers and they don't look like the ones I knew. The old-school street sleepers had been living rough for years. Their clothes were black strips of material hanging off their bodies, their shoes were bundles of rags, their skin the colour of teak. They had long, black matted hair down their backs resembling Rastafarian dreadlocks. Everyone gave them a wide berth. They lived all year in doorways and underpasses with cardboard boxes and plastic bags for bedding. I always thought they looked quite scary. It seemed the social services rarely troubled them and if I saw one when I was patrolling I ignored them. They never bothered us and we never bothered them. They might have a red plastic cup to collect a few coins and some restaurants used to give them leftover food.

There were also some White Russians still surviving on the mean streets of Kowloon in the 1980s. Anti-Bolshevik Russian refugees had left Russia after the 1917 revolution and some started to arrive in Hong Kong, via China, in the 1950s.

When I lived in Tsim Sha Tsui I often saw two women walking together. They were known as the 'famous sisters' and would often walk the streets, waving their arms about and mumbling together. They looked Caucasian and most people assumed they were White Russians. They moved between Central and Tsim Sha Tsui. There were lots of rumours about them. They had very long, wild, curly grey hair often falling in front of their faces. I would try to avoid their gaze when I saw them. They often ranted or mumbled; unintelligibly, at least to me. Some people said that they had been wealthy traders or merchants but had fallen on hard times and never recovered. I never saw them in any premises; they seemed to live only out on the street. There were silly rumours that they still carried gems and occasionally paid for goods or favours with a diamond taken out from secret pockets in their skirts.

In addition to the watering holes of Wan Chai, a new entertainment area began to develop in Central in a small road on a slope called Lan Kwai Fong. It was all started by two enterprising chaps called Gordon Huthart and Allan Zeman, who opened Disco Disco and the California club. Disco Disco was notorious for its 'Boys' Night Out' on Thursdays, catering for a gay clientele despite homosexual acts then being criminal offences. Gradually more bars and restaurants opened and the area became a popular expat hang out. This was a welcome change from the seedy girly bars of Wan Chai and was popular with the wealthier expats working in Central. Some of the more Westernised local people also began to spend evenings there. One way to enjoy Lan Kwai Fong without the crazy prices was to buy beers from the nearby 7-Eleven and then mingle with the milling crowds in the street.

In 1993, in the early hours of January 1st when the street was packed with partygoers celebrating the New Year, a tragedy occurred. No one knows exactly how it happened or how it started. The place became far too crowded in such a narrow space. The steep street was wet with rain and spilled beer. Someone slipped and fell and someone fell over them and suddenly the party had an atmosphere of terror. Screams from the young people rang out as they started falling. The crush became unbearable and people were trampled. People started pushing in an attempt to get away and hysteria took over. By the time police and emergency services restored order some twenty-one young partygoers had died. There was an inquest into the tragedy and now at Christmas and New Year the area is heavily patrolled by police and areas are divided by mills barriers to prevent overcrowding. Today it is still a popular haunt for night owls.

Possibly in response to the increased popularity of Lan Kwai Fong, Wan Chai started to change and although the girly bars remained, regular bars and pubs opened nearby creating a more cosmopolitan scene. Gradually in the mid-1980s Chinese girls in the bars were replaced with girls from the Philippines, Thailand and Indonesia. New bars came and went on a regular basis and new ones like Carnegie's with live bands opened up. Wan Chai never lost its notorious reputation completely though. Years' later new bars opened up with more imaginative ways to attract punters. One of these featured a 'dentist's chair'. This had an original old style dentist's chair in the middle of the bar. Here for a fee, you could recline in the chair and have bottles of tequila and vodka poured down your throat. It was in this bar that Paul Gascoigne and the England soccer team got into trouble. They had gone there to celebrate Gazza's birthday after a lacklustre performance against a Hong Kong select team. The lovely English lads followed this up by going straight from the bar to the airport for the midnight flight to London. According to reports they upset fellow passengers and trashed the Business Class cabin on Cathay Pacific causing considerable damage. I believe several players were banned from the airline afterwards. Wan Chai though was still a venue where you could sit in a bar from one morning to the next. Some superstars went straight from the bar, to the Hilton Hotel for breakfast, and then to the office and bragged about it for years afterwards.

Another thing Hong Kong is famous for is festivals. So with Chinese New Year and other traditional festivals, plus Western ones, it's a good place to enjoy a lot of public holidays. For many expats the festivals were a bit of a mystery but most enjoyed the colours, the noise and the pageantry. Some expats who had lived in Hong Kong for many years called themselves 'Old China Hands' and considered themselves an expert in all things Chinese. Some really did have a good knowledge of the history of the region but a lot seemed to be more expert on talking about themselves and drinking. I also found the instant pundits amusing. These were people who had lived in Hong Kong for two or three years and had read a couple of books, and 'Hey Presto' they suddenly became an expert on Sino-Western relations, and would pontificate to anyone in earshot. For the rest of us the days off work during the festivals were welcomed, and if it was Chinese New Year I enjoyed the Lion Dances and the fireworks in the harbour. Sales of fireworks to the public were banned, because of fears that the gunpowder could be turned into bombs, following the riots in 1967 when supporters of Chairman Mao turned firecrackers into improvised explosive devices. I still saw strips of firecrackers being lit in the New Territories villages but they were not tolerated in the urban areas. To appease the population the government decided to hold one giant firework display in the harbour each New Year. Even during the 1990s over HK$1 million was spent each year on the spectacular displays. The fireworks are launched from barges providing a fantastic view for people in Kowloon and on the Island.

The other colourful event I enjoyed was the Dragon Boat festival. The races started around 1976 with races between fishermen and some visiting Japanese. This is now a massive annual event with races held all over the Territory. I even participated in a series of races in Discovery Bay one year and our boat came second in the final. There is one main international tournament with about ten countries competing, and it has become immensely popular with residents and visitors. Other festivals are perhaps less well known and confined more to local residents. On Ching Ming thousands of people make their way to burial sites all over Hong Kong to sweep their ancestors' graves. Families gather on hillsides, sweep the graves, burn joss sticks, and proffer tangerines and burn heavenly money and other offerings. I was always impressed by this piety and thought it should be something we could teach our young people in the West. The Mid-Autumn festival is when the shops are full of mooncakes. Traditionally these are square cakes of short-crust pastry, not too sweet, filled with bean paste and a large hard-boiled egg, representing the moon, in the middle. I was never too keen on these and was happy when bakeries started making smaller, sweeter varieties without the egg.

In most police stations and especially in the CID offices there would be a small shrine. This would be a tall, open cupboard or altar, normally red and gold with a large shelf and a porcelain statue of 'Kwan Dai'. He always looked very fierce and was usually holding a long scimitar or spear. A small pot with a couple of burning joss-sticks would be placed in front of it. Kwan Dai was the police protector and the person we prayed to when we were requesting safety or help in solving an investigation. Perversely, the triads prayed to exactly the same deity, so I used to sometimes wonder where His loyalties really lay.

Sometimes if someone was having some bad luck, he would also *bai san*, pray, to Kwan Dai. If the bad luck continued or became really serious a *fung shui* master might be called in. The *fung shui* guys were really expensive though, costing several thousand dollars for a single consultation. Usually after getting a *fung shui* master in, it meant moving your desk around and buying a large fish tank. When someone was promoted in the station a 'Bai Kwan Dai' would be arranged. These were elaborate affairs often involving a Taoist priest. Long tables would be set out in front of the altar with all manner of foodstuffs but always including at least two small, whole roasted suckling pigs. These were roasted so that the skin was sweet and crispy. The most senior officers and the person being promoted would be invited to make the first cut of the pig. After holding joss-sticks and kow-towing to Kwan Dai, a large sharp steel chopper would be handed over. In one violent swoop the blade would come down and the little piggy would be split in half, to much applause from the officers present. The crispy pig and roasted chickens would then all be chopped into small pieces and everyone would tuck into the greasy meal, using our hands eating off paper plates. Of course bottles of cold San Miguel would be available to wash it down.

Roast suckling pig was pedestrian compared to some of the dishes I tried in my early years in Hong Kong. The cooked food stalls, or *dai pai dongs,* in the streets of Kowloon served up all sorts of delicacies. Amongst these were fried intestines, congealed pig blood, '100-year-old' eggs, and smelly bean curd. The hawker stalls that sold these were mostly unlicensed and would have look-outs posted to warn them if there were any government officers planning raids. A girl I knew, called Durga, was buying some spicy fishballs from a hawker when the chap suddenly fled after receiving a warning of a raid. Durga was upset because she hadn't paid. A crazy scene ensued with a fleeing hawker and his fishballs scattering pedestrians, chased by a young Nepalese lady waving cash shouting *'Pang-yau, pang-yau!'* (it means 'friend' and was the only Cantonese she knew) followed rapidly by two government inspectors from Urban Services. The stalls usually had an LPG canister perched underneath, and gas stove, with a wok and boiling oil above it. I never really took to this kind of food and suspected that it was probably not the healthiest option. I did quite enjoy congee or rice porridge, especially with thin slices of fish in it. The other winter dish I enjoyed was snake soup. Each winter the Temple Street night market in Yau Ma Tei had excellent snake-soup stalls. It was a thick broth with thin slices of snake, with some chicken, mushrooms, ginger and vinegar and pepper. I thought it was delicious and as it is considered a 'warm' food, ideal for a chilly winter evening. The Hong Kong markets were tame in comparison to those over the border though. The markets in Canton were more like zoos. There is a saying in China that the Cantonese people will eat anything with four legs except a table. In 1981 in the Canton market I saw live cats, pangolins, rabbits, turtles, salamanders, and even dogs in cages, and others already skinned, hanging by the mouth from butchers' hooks.

Hong Kong people at birth were given names consisting usually of three characters, the first the family name and then two for the given name. So a girl might be given the name Law May-wan. Law would be the family name and May-wan the given name. The given name would usually have a meaning such as 'beautiful cloud'. In secondary school it was common to adopt a Westernised name as well. Sometimes this was given to them by a teacher but often they would choose the names themselves. Perhaps to proclaim their individuality Hongkongers often devised unusual names which many Westerners found amusing. The Hong Kong Chinese have a great sense of humour and will make puns out of almost anything. I had a civilian colleague surnamed Yue who gave himself the Western name Simon. The joke was that Yue also means 'fish' in Cantonese, and Simon sounds like Salmon. So he was always known as Salmon Fish. Biblical and historical names were common. In the training school, amongst the locals we had an Angel, a Samson, and a Satan. I knew a guy called Hitler Wong. There were quite a few guys called Jesus. I came across a senior female civil servant with the surname Kok which was quite common. Unfortunately though, she had given herself the first name 'Ophelia'. I imagined us meeting: 'Hello, I'm Simon. What's your name?' 'Ophelia Kok.' 'Well thanks, maybe later.'

Naturally some Western names seemed funny to the locals too. When we joined the police we were all given Chinese names. Mine was so complicated I had it changed to something easier. But before I did so I made sure I checked carefully for any comical connotations. You need to be careful, Cantonese people are very inventive. If your name can be twisted to something funny it will be.

I eventually moved out to a nicer place in Ede Road in Kowloon Tong. I thought it was time to spend some money and started buying some small pieces of furniture and covers for the sofas. I avoided the single quarters at Ho Man Tin and the Hermitage. These were one- and two-bedroomed flats, and were quite convenient and self-contained. But the percentage of single police inspectors was quite high and so were the chances of bumping into colleagues after work. A lot of guys appreciated the restaurant and bar and the availability of part-time maids. The Hermitage was conveniently located in the lower Mid-Levels for the guys who worked on Hong Kong Island.

One day a very nasty incident occurred in the Hermitage government quarters between two British inspectors. It seems that a mature Thai lady had been working as a domestic helper for some of the residents. She was apparently also providing sexual services. The inspectors, named Dallas and Davidson, each felt they should have exclusive access to her favours. There was a confrontation and a knife was used. Following a terrible struggle resulting in the walls being covered in blood, Inspector Dallas lay dead. The other had numerous knife wounds. Davidson claimed he was attacked first and had acted in self defence. Crown Counsel however decided he should be charged, and he appeared on trial at the High Court. Justice Barnes presided. Surprisingly after the hearing the jury found him not guilty of either murder or manslaughter.

The Shangri-La was a notorious police officers' quarters in Kowloon Tong. This place was once a very nice detached villa surrounded by gardens, but it had been converted to house single British police inspectors. There was a shared kitchen and a large communal living room with several double bedrooms leading off the main lounge. The parties here made the movie *Animal House* look like a kindergarten tea party. There was a story about one of the residents bringing a lady back from an infamous bar for some R&R. God knows how much he'd had to drink before he thought this was a good idea. After they had both disappeared into one of the bedrooms, two other colleagues returned from a night on the town. These two had also enjoyed a very liquid evening and wanted some more fun. They spotted the lady's clothes lying over the back of the sofa. Then they found a plastic disc and decided to have an impromptu game in the expansive living area. The game became quite boisterous as they jumped over sofas and threw the disc back and forth. Possibly because of the noise, the lady came out of the bedroom and was shocked to find the two drunken young inspectors playing Frisbee with her breast prosthesis.

CHAPTER XXVII

The Drugs Trade

MOST PEOPLE WITH EVEN scant knowledge of the history of Hong Kong are aware of the opium trade and the fact that some of the traditional *hong*s or trading companies made huge profits from the drug. The government also gained significant income – in 1918 alone, the Hong Kong government took revenue of HK$8 million from licences and taxes associated with opium, a sum that amounted to over 40 per cent of total revenue that year. Opium remained legal until 1945. In the UK in the nineteenth century, opium was a popular recreational drug and was even added to some babies' medicines. I'm sure it effectively kept them quiet. I remembered the elderly Tai Po pig farmer we had arrested for possession of a small amount of opium. The opium was black and sticky and had a musty, smoky smell a little like truffles.

Heroin is synthesised from opium and is several times stronger. It was sold by the German company Bayer from the 1890s as a 'non-addictive morphine substitute' for the treatment of migraines and menstrual cramps. The tradename was coined as it made the user feel 'heroic'. As its addictive qualities became clear it was banned in many countries from the 1920s.

Gradually after the war, heroin replaced opium among Hong Kong addicts. Most opium poppies were grown in the 'Golden Triangle', an area on the borders of Northern Burma, China, Thailand and Laos. The narcotic came from there via different overland routes then by plane or ship into the targeted countries. My copy of the *Hong Kong Yearbook* for 1979 states that, 'the main method of importation of drugs was by air through Kai Tak Airport'. I don't know who said this but I very much doubt it was correct. There is no doubt that narcotics are smuggled in suitcases and by air cargo, but the chances of a random body search or a search of baggage, or by drug-sniffing dogs, means that detection is always a possibility. Meanwhile, there are thousands of vessels entering and leaving Hong Kong port and the opportunity for concealment is much better, as are the chances of smuggling much larger quantities. Drugs can be hidden in shipping containers or trans-shipped to smaller vessels when nearing Hong Kong.

When I had served in Tai Po I had travelled by police launch to a small island called Tung Ping Chau up in Mirs Bay near China. Its permanent population was three elderly residents. In the early 1990s a massive haul of several tons of heroin was washed up on the beach there. The drugs were sealed in watertight black plastic bin bags and then wrapped in fishing nets. It was one of the largest hauls of narcotics police had ever seen and it certainly surprised the handful of day-trippers sunning themselves that afternoon. It seemed that fishing boats were sailing out to the edge of territorial waters to meet a larger 'mother' ship from south-east Asia that would transfer the narcotics to the fishing boat. The bags would be placed in the fishing nets and weighted with lead or rocks so that they sank below the surface. The fishing boat could then sail back to the colony with its nets running behind as if it was trawling for fish. Once it was near a pre-determined cove it would handoff its cargo to smaller dinghies or *sampan*s which would carry it onshore. It could then be transferred to an anonymous white van or small truck into the city. Unfortunately for the crime syndicate this particular cargo had somehow become dislodged and had washed up on the beach of the remote island.

In the 1970s and '80s the type of heroin seen on the streets was referred to as 'No. 3' heroin. This had the appearance of grey coffee granules. A popular method of holding and carrying it was in clear plastic drinking straws, the ends heat-sealed using a lighter. The usual seizures had a purity of about 20–30 per cent.

In Hong Kong a popular way of taking the drug was 'chasing the dragon'. The addicts would take a few granules of the drug and place them in a spoon or on tin foil then use a cigarette lighter to heat up the narcotic. When heated, the granules liquefied and gave off a vapour which the addicts inhaled through some rolled-up paper or a drinking straw. They thought the vapours looked like a dragon's tail, hence 'chasing the dragon'.

Injecting the drug was also popular and sharing of needles was commonplace. This became very risky when the Aids epidemic swept across the world in the mid-1980s. The government methadone clinics started to give out free disposable needles to stop its spread. I came across many heroin addicts over the course of my police career. In spite of their emaciated form, they still seemed to be able to run pretty fast. When early in my career one suspected addict in possession of drugs was spotted by my team, he ran off across the rooftops of several buildings, leaping from one to another like a jack rabbit. I couldn't believe how agile and quick he was.

The only dangerous drugs or narcotics I personally came across were opium and heroin. In Hong Kong today, cannabis, ketamine and methamphetamine ('ice') have become more popular amongst the younger generation and cocaine amongst the wealthier locals and expats. There was though another, more insidious, narcotic. When I was serving in Kowloon in CID I was called to the scene of a suspected homicide. On arrival at the small government flat in one of the newer blocks in Kwun Tong I found that Brian, the chief inspector crime, was already at the scene. The area had been cordoned off and we were waiting for a pathologist and official photographers. We could clearly see into the kitchen and dining area in the flat through the open front door but did not want to disturb the crime scene. On the tiled floor lay a young woman on her side, maybe in her mid-thirties. The floor was covered in blood, vomit and phlegm. The flat was rather untidy and on the dining table in the kitchen was an open lunch box containing rice and barbecue pork which was apparently untouched. The rest of the interior was unremarkable.

I looked at the woman on the floor. Her eyes were still open, she appeared to be looking towards me. Her face and hair were covered in dark congealing blood; we surmised that she had met a violent death at the hands of an intruder. Once the photographer had come and taken numerous pictures, and the pathologist arrived, Brian and I entered the flat. We examined the body together with the pathologist at the scene, before the body was removed to the mortuary for a post-mortem. We could find no injuries on the body whatsoever. The cause of death was a mystery. We started looking around the flat to see if there were any clues. We found the woman's handbag, identity card and purse which seemed to be all intact. Some shelves had been disturbed and some items were on the floor indicating a possible struggle.

On checking cupboards we found numerous bottles of cough medicine. We noted a number of prescriptions from various doctors. On completing all our checks at the scene, the body was removed and we waited for the results of the post-mortem and the toxi-cologist's report. The cause of death was concluded to be an overdose of codeine. The young woman had developed an addiction to codeine, a common ingredient in many prescription cough medicines. Over a period of time she started consuming more and more of the drug. She was visiting different private doctors to request the cough medicine. The morning of her death she had not eaten anything. After consuming increasing quantities of the cough medicine to achieve the same high, her body had at last given up. She had tried to vomit but with nothing in her stomach, she only retched up blood and phlegm. In her final death throes she had spun around knocking down shelves before collapsing and dying. This was the first such case I'd ever encountered.

In the 1970s over 80 per cent of all drug addicts were addicted to heroin. Even in 1978 the illegal heroin trade was considered by the government to be worth a staggering HK$380 million. In the 1990s there was an influx of higher-grade heroin. This was as a result of bumper harvests in the Golden Triangle on the Burmese border. The purity and strength rose considerably from 'No. 3' to be classified as 'No. 4', a fine white powder with a purity of over 60 per cent. Suddenly we were finding dead bodies of drug addicts all over the city, and for a few months the situation became very serious. The addicts were injecting the same quantities of the new purer narcotic as previously, but they did not have the tolerance and so suffered overdoses. This situation received very little media attention; after all they were only drug addicts. Eventually through social services, charities, methadone clinics, and the police, the word was spread that addicts should be careful of this new stronger drug, and lower their dosage accordingly. In the police station we would sometimes have drug addicts in the cells that went through a cold turkey withdrawal. They would start shivering and shaking and hyper-ventilating and sometimes vomiting. I had little sympathy for these people who had brought the situation upon themselves and caused everyone so much trouble. As the withdrawal symptoms became more serious I would have to send a police officer to escort them to a government clinic for a small plastic cup of methadone to settle them down before their court appearance.

Later in my career I was required to oversee the disposal of the seized stocks of narcotics. At regular intervals the narcotics disposal team would arrange disposal of drugs seized by police, and after the court case had been completed. Firstly I had to go down to one of the impregnable police strong rooms in Police HQ. Every bag and exhibit, no matter how small had to be checked off a ledger. They were then placed into wooden drums. The drums were loaded onto police trucks inside the walled compound of PHQ. There was a heavy escort of police motorcycles, and Land Rovers carrying police armed with shotguns. I sat in the front of the lead vehicle. I felt like the general at the head of an invading army.

Once the paperwork had been cross-checked and all the drugs had been loaded, the steel gates to PHQ slid open and our escort was directed out onto the street. We put on our sirens and lights and the motorcycles went ahead to clear the way. We were headed across the harbour to the Wong Tai Sin incinerator. Once there my officers carrying shotguns formed an armed guard around the perimeter. The numbered drums were carried off individually and placed in the incinerator and destroyed by the fire. It would have made the biggest spliff in the world. I watched the flames, and I saw the smoke licking out from the tall chimney. As I watched, I wondered if any of the local residents in the nearby apartment blocks might have become a little high. I felt a bit strange to be responsible for destroying something worth over HK$200 million.

CHAPTER XXVIII

The Case of the Human Soul

HONG KONG HOMICIDES always seem to be unusual. In London it seems that the majority of homicides are related to youth gangs, or a dispute outside a nightclub where one person pulls out a knife and fatally stabs someone. In the US, most homicides seem to be from gun-shot wounds, often a result of an argument outside a gas station or in a domestic dispute. In Hong Kong homicides are rarer, and tend to be either very gruesome or very imaginative, or both. I always thought the pathologists must have an interesting life. I saw the pathologists' catalogue once on a familiarisation visit to Police HQ. These large hardback volumes are full of photographs of bodies with short descriptions underneath. I guess pathologists around the world must swap details with each other, a bit like schoolboys used to swap picture playing cards. And now I can share some interesting cases I came across during my time in the police.

I was at home in my Kowloon government flat on a Sunday morning in August, 1989. It was a day that felt as if a heavy woollen blanket soaked in warm water had been put over my shoulders whilst I was sitting in a sauna. Blinking my eyes exerted sufficient energy to sweat. It was a day when flies sit down and give up hope; a day when the cicada beetles sound like pneumatic drills. It was on days like this that I rued those last two beers the night before. Never again Gunga Din, I promised myself. I was looking forward to a relaxing morning sitting in front of the air-conditioner, or under a ceiling fan with a chilled glass of orange juice, a black coffee, the Sunday papers and my favourite chair. Then the black Bakelite phone in the hall rang.

I picked it up to hear the gruff tones of the duty officer, Sergeant Chan. A life in the force and two packs of cigarettes a day had given him the type of world-weary been-there-done-that type of mono-tone that Dirty Harry would have been proud of. 'What's the problem, Sergeant Chan?' I asked, knowing that to ring the inspector on a Sunday morning, it must be something unusual. 'Well sir,' he replied, 'we've found a human soul.' Understandably somewhat taken aback by this ecclesiastical tone I asked for details. I was told that a couple of constables had been alerted by some early-morning walkers who had found a 'human soul' on a hillside in Kowloon.

This one I can't miss, I told myself. In view of the time of year I made certain provisions before leaving. I covered my exposed skin in factor-50 sunscreen, then sprayed myself with mosquito repel-lent, and then poured some *pak fa yau* – whiteflower embrocation – over a tissue and stuck it in my pocket.

About fifteen minutes later a blue police Land Rover arrived to pick me up. In another twenty minutes I was at the scene. A few uniformed officers in their green uniforms and a couple of junior CID guys were standing listlessly on the hillside near the road constantly mopping their brows and lazily brushing flies away from their face. One of the constables waved me to follow him up a well-worn path through the low scrub. The area was popular with early-morning walkers, and had many small pagodas and family temples dotted around with small urns and incense sticks.

There were only a few tall trees, and most of the scrub did not extend more than a couple of metres tall so the pagodas gave welcome shelter from the elements. I was led along the path which extended parallel to the road below and opposite one of the huge public housing estates. This one consisted of drab blocks twenty storeys high, made of grey concrete, with bamboo poles covered in laundry hanging out of the windows. It looked the same as hundreds of others in the city. Within seconds I was perspiring in the heat and was glad I'd applied mosquito repellent.

About eighty metres along the path the constable stopped. Another stood guarding the path. There was nothing to be seen.

Seeing my perplexed expression, the first constable pointed down. There on the path lay a very large banana leaf. 'Underneath the leaf, sir' the constable said, and I carefully bent down and lifted up a corner of the leaf with my pen, and got a whiff of something nasty. There under the leaf sitting on the path was a neatly severed foot. Just the foot, this was the 'human sole'. By the size and shape it was certainly from a female. The bone at the ankle had been shattered rather than sawn, and the flesh had tooth marks. But these looked like pointed carnivore tooth marks so I ruled out cannibalism. This was later confirmed when the hill walkers who found it told us they had seen some wild dogs pick it up and carry it a short distance before abandoning it.

I walked back to the assorted group of officers I had first met; it was now mid-morning, the temperature was above 85° Fahrenheit, with humidity to match. I asked what action had been taken so far. I was told that police dogs had been called; they had attended the scene and had already departed having found nothing. Also they added they were now waiting for the Tactical Unit to come and sweep the area for clues. The news that the police dogs had found nothing did not surprise me. The dogs were great for morale and public relations, but generally ineffective in my experience for genuine police work. The pro-canine lobby will jump up and tell you about how highly trained they are, but when was the last time you heard of a story where Fido or Rex solved the case? I had many experiences when the dogs would come in with their handlers, wag their tails and slobber, and that was just the handlers. The dogs would pad up and down, do a couple of circuits, then get back in the van and disappear.

Once, during a sweep of a Vietnamese refugee camp in the old RAF base at Kai Tak I found a shoe-box under a bunk bed. When I opened it we found a plastic bag with white powder in it. The Vietnamese told us it was washing powder, but it didn't smell like it, and in reality we do not follow the traditional Hollywood example of dipping our wet finger in as if it was a bag of sugar and taking a long suck of our fingers followed by the statement 'That's good shit'. No, we relied on our tried and trusted canine allies. So to make it fair we put the box back under the bed and walked Fido in from the end of the corridor – nothing. Okay, next we put the box in the corridor. Nothing. So next we opened the box, still nothing. We ended up holding the bag under his nose, still not a sign of recognition. I sent the bag to the lab. Results came back twenty-four hours later: ten ounces of No. 4 heroin.

Meanwhile back with the human soul, we were still waiting for the tactical unit to arrive and sweep the area. I decided to have a sniff around myself. As it turned out 'a sniff around' was most apt. I started by going up the hill passing the morning walkers with their jogging suits and little towels round their necks. Past the small semi-circular graves with the joss sticks and small urns. After about fifteen minutes I was at the top of the hill, which was only 150 metres or so above the road. I stood still to catch my breath. There was a great view over the sprawling tenement blocks and Kai Tak Airport with the 747s making their final approach over Kowloon City. I then noticed a disused quarry at the same level as the road, about 150 metres from where we had been standing. I made my way slowly back down the hill. I nodded as I walked past where my colleagues were still standing and chatting and made my way towards the base of the quarry. The area was very overgrown with tall grass, scrub, small trees, and with some large boulders scattered amongst the vegetation. It was still bloody hot; I paused and mopped my brow with a tissue.

I'd come to recognise the smell of decomposing human flesh from my many trips to the morgue to witness post-mortems. It was the worst smell in the world (apart from snake shit) and the reason I'd brought the *pak fa yau*. I climbed on top of one of the boulders; it was about a metre tall and two metres long. I sniffed deeply. I moved towards the rock face of the quarry. Again I stopped and stood on a different boulder. The long grass, up to a metre tall, obscured my view. Now I was sure. My heart started pounding, sweat was pouring down my face and neck. I edged closer again. Certainly something, then I lost it, perhaps the wind direction changed; I stood motionless and then turned my head in a different direction. I must have resembled a police dog more than a police officer.

Suddenly I saw a splash of colour under a small tree. I moved closer. In the trees, there! A broken body, twisted, shattered limbs, torn clothes. Face unrecognisable, I stood transfixed. By this time my heart rate must have doubled. Decomposition had commenced, the summer heat accelerating the process. Maggots already infested her face. I turned and ran quickly back to my colleagues. I shouted to them: 'I've found her, I've found the body!' They all looked at me, disbelieving at first, but they realised from my expression I wasn't joking. Then they followed me to the scene and started to cordon off the area. I became strangely elated. Of all the large peer group I had been the one to go off, try to do something different, and succeed.

We were all convinced that we were looking at a very nasty rape and murder. The forensic people arrived and started taking photos and samples from the body and surroundings. As we were discussing the case, a young constable came up to me and said quietly in my ear: 'Sir, do you think she might have jumped?' He had a point. Looking again at the shattered limbs, the injuries, the position of the body, its location under the cliff of the quarry, it just might be a suicide.

It was later confirmed to be a suicide case; the poor woman had jumped from the top of the quarry. Further checks found her shoes still on the top of the quarry. It's a strange fact that most people who commit suicide by jumping from height in Hong Kong remove their shoes first. Subsequently the case took a poignant turn as the woman was identified as the wife of a serving police officer. It was confirmed she had suffered emotional problems for several years. Despite my brief elation at the discovery, I suffered nightmares afterwards. For several nights after I would suddenly see her face staring at me with the teeth and eye balls appearing through the writhing maggots, until finally the memories faded.

CHAPTER XXIX

A Very Strange Case

ONE OF THE MOST UNUSUAL cases during my time in Kowloon East CID occurred in Amoy Gardens, later to gain notoriety for being one of the centres of the SARS outbreak that killed so many people in 2003. In the 1960s and '70s Kowloon East had been an industrial area full of sweat shops producing the cheap garments, toys, and plastic flowers that Hong Kong had become famous for. In the 1990s, as the economy became more service orientated, the factories were gradually replaced with housing complexes. Amoy Gardens is a middle-class private estate consisting of blocks of about twenty stories high, divided into small apartments. This area to the north-east of Kai Tak Airport was popular as prices were cheaper than downtown Kowloon or Hong Kong Island. But it still had good MTR and bus links.

My colleague received a call one day from a concerned mother who had not seen her seventeen-year-old son for almost three days. It was not a missing person case however. She knew exactly where he was. He'd had an argument with his mother and had run to his bedroom and locked himself in. Since that time he had not emerged, and no sounds had been heard. He had not been to the bathroom, and had not eaten or drunk anything for almost seventy-two hours.

When Sergeant Wong and Constable Cheung turned up at the scene they expected it to be a routine domestic dispute. 'Domestics' were one of the most common police reports and as the colony became more affluent, such reports seemed to become more frequent. The demand for housing and lack of space meant that families consisting of eight or more could be living in an apartment of only 400 square feet. The problem of personal space was resolved by hanging curtains from rails on the ceiling to create small temporary sleeping cubicles.

Amoy Gardens however was a private apartment complex and although the apartments were small, it was clean and well managed. When Sergeant Wong arrived he noticed that the boy's bedroom door was locked. The apartment was about 600 square feet with one bathroom and two bedrooms. The teenager was an only child. The boy did not respond to Sergeant Wong's demands to open the door. Following a short discussion with the mother it was agreed that the door would need to be forced open. A couple of hefty kicks and a shoulder charge managed to do it. As the door swung open, there was that smell again, the nasty stink of decomposing human flesh. Backup was requested immediately from Ngau Tau Kok station.

The lad was lying face down on his bed. He had rope tied around his wrists behind him, that was linked to a rope around his ankles which were bent behind his back, and also to a loop around his throat. There was more. Stuck in his anus was a length of white plastic pipe about seven inches long and a two inches in diameter. In his mouth was a banana which had by now turned brown. He was wearing a white schoolgirl's dress. On his feet he had short white cotton bobby socks, and a pair of black schoolgirl patent leather shoes two sizes too small. Pinned to his chest was a home-made laminated school identity card containing a real photo of a schoolgirl.

The officers stood there, stunned for several moments trying to make sense of probably the most bizarre sight to ever confront them. The mother stood standing at the door, in shock; she broke down sobbing and had to be comforted by a female constable. There was nothing anyone could do, the boy was obviously dead, no question of resuscitation. The usual radio messages and phone calls were made. It looked like some kind of sadomasochistic homicide, and would probably need to be referred up to a regional crime squad. The specialists arrived, and fingerprints and photographs were taken at the scene. A post-mortem was booked at the Kowloon mortuary for the next day.

The Kowloon public mortuary is a depressing, dingy place, and behind its closed doors often resembles a little shop of horrors. The mortuary attendants sometimes appeared as eccentric, as the reality of seeing bodies cut open every day would demand. After the usual exhaustive examination it was shown that there were no injuries to the body, other than the marks caused by the ropes.

The pathologist surmised that the cause of death was suffocation caused by the banana becoming lodged in the teenager's throat. This led to further enquiries. The bedroom door had been locked from the inside. No one had entered the room before the body had been found. The fingerprints had shown only the marks of the parents and the victim. Then came another surprise, analysis of the knots in the ropes had shown them to be probably self-tied. Finally, a quantity of pornographic magazines had been recovered hidden under the bed. These had contained images of sadomasochistic scenes involving young schoolgirls. With the agreement of the pathologist we classified the cause of death as accidental, due to asphyxiation as a result of auto-eroticism. Such cases are extremely rare in Chinese society. In fact it was the only case I heard of in Hong Kong in over twenty years. The family were naturally shocked but they did not appeal our conclusion. It is debatable how much his mother actually knew about her son's private habits. It is easy to argue that in such a small flat she must have known what he had been doing in his bedroom. But as I had seen in other cases it was not always the case. Still I did feel sorry for the mother losing her only son in such horrible circumstances.

CHAPTER XXX

A Nasty Murder in Kai Tak

VIETNAMESE REFUGEES had started arriving in Hong Kong via small boats in the late 1970s. The first arrivals were ethnic Chinese, and many of them were doctors, accountants, and engineers by trade. Following the Viet Cong victory, the Chinese minority were seen as American collaborators, and treated harshly by the new regime. They were comparatively wealthy and began to pay large sums of money to boat owners and criminal gangs to be smuggled out of the country.

The trickle became a flood. A large ship called the *Skyluck* entered Hong Kong harbour with 2,651 refugees on board in February 1979. The ship's captain was believed to have been involved in the smuggling racket and was arrested. By 1980 there were 38,000 Vietnamese in various camps in the colony. The United Nations High Commissioner for Refugees (UNHCR) became involved as permanent homes were sought for these 'boat people'. Many of the initial arrivals were taken in by various countries including the USA, Canada, Australia, and France. A camp was built on the site of an old RAF air base next to Kai Tak Airport.

As word reached Vietnam that people were being resettled in the USA, the demographic of arrivals changed. There were more ethnic Vietnamese, and they did not have the educational background of the initial refugees. Unsurprisingly, countries started to be more wary about giving refugee status to these new arrivals. As resettlement slowed, the camps filled up. Kai Tak was on my patch and I had to conduct patrols there often.

Outside the camp was a busy road and a bus stop. Some Vietnamese men would hang around the bus stop, waiting until a woman was about to board a bus. They would then suddenly snatch her necklace or a handbag and run. The entrance to the camp was less than 100 metres away and they knew once they were inside they could disappear. So we set up covert observation posts with binoculars and police radios in buildings opposite the camp. One or two younger officers would go to the bus stop, posing as prospective bus passengers. The idea was to catch the thieves in the act. It sometimes resulted in a chase to the camp gate. The operations had limited success though because the robbers became skilled at profiling out the likely police officers.

The camp was made up of old corrugated iron-roofed huts. Inside there were long corridors and dormitories with wooden bunk beds. There were huts for single male, single female, and married accommodation. There was electricity and water, and shared bathroom blocks separated into male and female facilities. There was a UNHCR office near the camp entrance headed up by a long-suffering and exasperated chap named Wong. I shared his frustration as it always seemed that the residents did little to help themselves, or keep the place clean and tidy. In addition there was a lot of petty crime and squabbles to deal with.

On one of my first visits I introduced myself to Mr Wong and he showed me around. After going through the old huts and seeing the bunk beds and the communal showers he said he had something to show me. We went through a wooden door into a room that was more luxurious than my government quarters. The large room was carpeted, it even had wallpaper. There was an air conditioner, and expensive lighting. On one side of the room was a king-size four-poster bed. On the other side there was a large colour television, hi-fi, and VCR. I thought that whoever lived in this place must be controlling every racket in the camp. Mr Wong told me it belonged to Pham Van Ngoc, the 'King of Kai Tak'.

A couple of months later, I was still in CID and running the district crime squad. It was the eve of Chinese New Year, a five-day holiday. That evening around ten o'clock I received a call from the station and was told to report to the Kai Tak camp. There I found some senior local officers already at the scene, including District Commander Douglas Lau. They were understandably unhappy at having their family New Year dinners disrupted. I was told there had been a homicide and I was to take over the case. My team members started to arrive. It was a cool February evening and as we walked around we heard accounts of what had happened. I went to the scene of the murder which was at the back of the camp on open ground. The victim's body had already been removed and was in the mortuary, which was rather annoying. Few witnesses were coming forward but gradually we started to piece together a rough picture of what had occurred. It seems the victim was named Tan. Tan was a bit of a thug and had been drinking beer since the early afternoon. After becoming quite merry he decided, fatefully, that he should try to muscle into a card game being run by Pham and his cronies. At first Pham did not agree to allow Tan to his table, but eventually had reluctantly agreed. However as the game progressed the atmosphere became uglier. Tan started losing money and began to swear, the swearing led to abuse, and then threats.

A fight broke out and Tan, realising he was outnumbered, turned and ran out of the small hut. He was hotly pursued by Pham and his gang. Exactly what happened next was still unclear, but it had resulted in one chap in the morgue. Meanwhile our chief suspect had disappeared. I discussed the case with my team. We knew there must have been plenty of eyewitnesses, but everyone was afraid of Pham. I talked to an Indian security guard who had been posted nearby. Even he said he had seen nothing. So we had an outdoor murder scene with no dead body, virtually no witnesses, and no murder weapon. Once we had done all we could at the scene we left for the station. We had some *siu yeh,* the trusty rice and noodles, and compared notes. It was the early hours of the morning. The team went home. I slept behind my desk in a sleeping bag that I kept for such occasions. In a few hours I would have to report to the Kowloon Public Mortuary.

I'm always amused by the American cop shows when the family go to identify the body. The mortuary rooms are always spotless, the attendants immaculate. The body is in a stainless-steel drawer at waist height, covered with a clean white sheet up to the neck. The deceased always looks serene, as if sleeping. My reality was far away from this fantasy. Kowloon Public Mortuary was an old building even in the 1980s. It had a small public waiting room, and double doors leading into a large area with the stone slabs for the bodies, and ceiling fans, with extractors in the walls to dilute the smell of death. I had some *pak fa yau* oil on some tissues in my pocket to try to mask the odours. In addition to the large room where the dissections took place there was also a cold storage room where bodies were placed which were unidentified, or stored during long weekends, or public holidays. The room quickly filled up, and what I saw was horrifying: a large pile of bodies stacked one on top of the other. Many were the bloated bodies of suspected illegal immigrants that had been pulled from the sea.

I thought back to my first visit to a mortuary. It was during our familiarisation at Police Training School. We were shown a body that was in a state of rigor mortis. The pathologist had asked our group to feel the body, and even invited anyone to try to bend the deceased's arm. A couple of the British lads actually stepped forward and took up the challenge, wrestling the stiff body which was a bit too much for the rest of us.

I saw a young European couple sitting in the waiting room sobbing quietly. When I entered the main large room I saw the tiny body of a nine-month-old Caucasian baby waiting to be examined. On another slab was the mangled body of a local man aged about sixty who had jumped out a window on the fifteenth floor of a Kowloon housing block. But I was there to see Tan. He lay on the third slab. He hardly looked dead. He was tall for a Vietnamese, maybe five feet ten inches tall. He was tanned and muscular. He had short black hair and large tattoos on his arms and chest. His flesh still seemed slightly warm. The pathologist, named Chung, and I looked at him. We were both rather puzzled. There were no obvious signs of a violent death. No stab or chop wounds, no blunt object traumas. There were some very small red marks over his body but they did not look significant. So with that the examination started. Chung took a sharp scalpel and made an incision in the area of the throat and ran the cut down to Tan's groin. We were both in for a shock. As he cut the body open we both shouted 'Wah' and leapt backwards. As the incision had passed the gut a tidal wave of frothy grey liquid and rice came gushing out of the stomach over the slab and onto the floor.

Once the flow had subsided we stepped forward again sloshing on the puddles of liquid. So now we knew what his last meal had been, a bowl of rice porridge, and about six pints of San Miguel beer. With the incision made, the gut was opened and internal organs examined and removed. Then the rib cage was opened with a pair of very strong pliers and the heart and lungs examined. Finally the scalpel made a circular incision around the head at the height of the forehead, the face was then peeled off down to the mouth exposing the facial muscles and eyeballs. A large saw was then produced and the top of the skull was cut off and removed to expose the brain which was also examined and removed. Through all of this, Chung's expert eye was making sense of everything and he was talking and explaining his actions.

He reminded me of the small red marks on the body. He then pointed out similar marks to Tan's internal organs. They matched the shape, size, and location of the external marks. Something small, sharp, and narrow had passed through Tan's body and punctured most of his internal organs. His lungs, spleen, liver, and stomach had all been punctured causing massive internal bleeding. There were in total about eight puncture wounds. By the look of the injuries whatever it was must have passed right through him back to front, and front to back. Chung gave me his preliminary conclusions. I thanked him, and made my way back in our CID saloon car to my quarters. The first thing I needed to do was remove all my clothes, and throw them into a washing machine. I made my way to the bathroom, jumped into a very hot shower and stood under it for a long time and then I washed my hair and changed into a fresh set of clothes. Even then the smell of death seemed to stay with me for a couple of days. And years later, as I wrote this, it suddenly came back to me. I don't think I ever did remove the taint of digested beer from my shoes.

Once I had felt at least partly refreshed and slightly cleaner I drove back to the station to share the initial news from the post-mortem with my team. At least now I had an idea what kind of murder weapon we were looking for. This coincided with another visit to the camp by my Sergeant Chan and during another search in daylight he and the team had found some items they thought might be connected to our case. They had collected a number of blood-stained narrow aluminium pipes. These were water pipes with a diameter of about one centimetre. The pipes were all about a metre long. What was significant was that one end had been filed down to the sharpness of a razor blade.

The Vietnamese in the Hong Kong camps were incredibly imaginative when it came to making home-made weapons. It seemed they could manufacture deadly weapons out of almost anything. We regularly searched the camp looking for drugs and weapons. Some of the weapons hauls were amazing. Any piece of metal could be sharpened and improvised into an implement to maim or kill. There were often small floods in the camps because gangs would rip out the narrow water pipes to turn them into lethal lances. The pipes we found in grass near the murder scene matched the description of what the pathologist had deduced as the weapon. We collected the blood samples and the results came back as a blood-type match with the deceased. We sent them away for further analysis to see if it was possible to get any fingerprints or other microscopic evidence from them. Meanwhile we continued to try to build a picture of what had happened that night of the murder. The narrow sharpened lances were easy to hide. When placed behind other pipes or along the floor they would be almost invisible. We believed they were hidden in the same room where Tan and Pham and the others were playing cards. When the dispute became violent and Tan tried to escape it would have been easy for the gang to pick them up and give chase. When they caught him they could have run him through with the sharpened lances which could have gone through him like butter. They left hardly any marks, and there was not much blood lost, but as Tan continued to run he would be bleeding to death internally.

We continued to make enquiries and gather evidence. I started to check Pham's record. What I found shocked me. I discovered he had been implicated in two earlier murders in the same camp. The first case had been concluded as inconclusive due to lack of evidence and Pham had been on bail but not been charged. The second case was more robust and Pham had been charged, but after a court hearing, he had been acquitted. So this was the third homicide in which Pham had been a suspect. No wonder he had enjoyed such power in Kai Tak camp. As I was digesting this I was told that Pham had just voluntarily come into the station to give a statement. I walked downstairs to prepare an interview room. If Pham was indeed prepared to give a statement then I would need an interpreter and a communications officer to make notes and then I would have to get a written statement in Vietnamese with an approved English translation.

When everything was ready I made my way down to the small, bare, white-walled interview room. I was disappointed to see that the interpreter was a very young and rather timid-looking Vietnamese woman. Pham was seated on one of the straight-back wooden chairs and a plain wooden table was placed in front of him. The interpreter and I sat down opposite. Pham was in his early thirties and very unremarkable looking, around five feet eight inches tall, slim build, with short black hair fairly neat and parted on one side. As we started talking though my view changed. When I looked at him, his eyes were black and expressionless. As the interview progressed it seemed I was not getting anywhere. Pham confirmed his identity, he said he was in the camp on the evening of the murder. He said that he had seen the deceased once or twice, but had not seen him on the night in question. He claimed he had no knowledge of the attack. When I pressed him that people had placed him at the scene and told him he was a prime suspect his face darkened. He stared back at me and said: 'I have been tortured in the Vietnam war and nothing you can do will make me talk.' This guy had all the hallmarks of a psychopath.

Pham was released on bail. The interview had not been a success but at least I now knew what I was dealing with. I became more determined to take this case through to a conclusion. My hardworking team and I started building a case. We had a couple of lucky breaks. Ironically the Indian security guard's claim that he had not seen anything actually helped me as it contrasted with Pham's account of where he had been and what he had done. My team of local junior officers were great; they worked really hard, and put in a lot of extra unpaid hours. I think they ended up hating Pham as much as I did. We all wanted to see this guy put in prison for a long time. I compiled statements and exhibits and started to put a detailed case file together. The case file had to go up to the crown prosecutor in a set format and with information cross-referenced just so. A badly formed case file would attract the scorn of the legal counsel and some sarcastic comment in the minutes on return.

I was fortunate that in this case I did not get bollocked and the remarks were fairly positive. I was invited for a meeting in the legal department to discuss the case. So on the appointed day I went over to Central District. I turned up in shirt and tie to meet the legal counsel, an expat government lawyer named Jenkins. I was able to satisfactorily answer his questions and he said he would send the case up the chain for another opinion.

A few days later the word came back. They had decided that there was a prima facie case against Pham and that he should be tried in the High Court for murder.

This was a result in itself and the whole team were elated after all the long, long hours and stress of the case. I now had to arrange for Pham to return on bail so he could be formally charged. There is often a preliminary hearing in murder cases with a review of evidence. In this instance, Pham was not put into custody, but bail conditions were tightened. I had to ensure that everything was prepared exactly as the crown prosecutor wanted it for the date of the trial. All the statements, exhibits, and photographs had to be chronologically arranged and the summonses to witnesses sent out. We helped with transport too, to make sure witnesses arrived on time. When the first day of the trial arrived I was very nervous. I put on a smart dark blue suit, with a white shirt and blue tie. I gathered up my papers and made my way across the harbour to the new High Court building not too far away from the Conrad Hotel.

As it was a murder trial in the High Court a jury had to be decided upon. Fortunately the jury selection was agreed upon quite easily. The be-wigged judge was the very able Justice Barnes. As the officer in charge, I was a key witness too, and was called to give evidence on oath about the case and the investigation. Fortunately this was where my experience as a court prosecutor several years earlier stood me in good stead. When it came to the turn of the defence counsel to cross examine me he did not make much impression, and I made sure that I faced the jury when I gave my answers. Much of the evidence was circumstantial but it seemed that the case was going okay. I noticed that as Pham stood in the dock, his gang members sat up in the public gallery. The case evidence only took two days. Pham decided not to give evidence. His defence was simply a complete denial of being anywhere near the scene. When the case concluded at the end of the second day Justice Barnes summed up and the jury were asked to retire to consider their verdict. By this time it was about 7pm.

None of us were sure if the jury would need to be put up in hotel rooms overnight. Pham was sent to the cells underneath the court building. The crown prosecutor Jenkins and I and a couple of my team went to a local café for something to eat and a cup of coffee. We would be signalled by pager if there was news. Later we went back to the court room. It was now about 10pm so I told my remaining team members to go home. It began to look as though there would not be a verdict that night. Then suddenly we got news from the clerk of the court that the jury had come to an agreement and verdict. So just after 11pm Pham was brought back up from the cells. Justice Barnes asked the jury if they had reached a verdict. 'We have, your honour,' the head juror replied. There was a pause that seemed like an hour, and then: 'We the jury find the defendant guilty of murder.' I looked at Pham; he stood expressionless in the dock. Third time lucky, for me but not for Pham, I thought to myself. I saw Justice Barnes reach down and pick up a black cloth from under his raised bench and place it on top of his head. He turned to Pham and said: 'I hereby find you guilty of murder, and sentence you to death.' However, all in the court knew that the governor would commute this to life imprisonment, as had been policy since 1967.

All the stress, hard work, and tension seemed suddenly released. I fought to maintain a solemn expression. Inside I was elated. I went forward and shook hands with Jenkins and thanked him for his support. It was then that I looked up and realised that Pham's gang were still in the public area glowering down at me. My team had all gone home. I was unarmed – as firearms were not allowed in courtrooms, before coming to court I had returned my Colt .38 to the armoury. My euphoria suddenly changed to concern. I was alone, it was almost midnight, and there were six very pissed-off Vietnamese gang members probably thinking that I should be the one sentenced to death. Once all the formalities had been completed I decided to slide quietly out to the MTR in Central and take the train back across the harbour to Kowloon. The next day I took my team for *yum cha*, a delicious lunch of assorted *dim sum* to say thanks for all their hard work.

The issues with the Vietnamese boat people did not go away and they continued to arrive in Hong Kong. But there was little doubt that arrivals after 1980/81 were more economic migrants rather than genuine refugees. The estimate of the total number of arrivals varies from about 150,000 to 200,000. The majority were settled in third-party countries. The most popular choice was the USA. I heard of cases of the migrants being offered resettlement in countries such as Norway, and refusing. Some were allowed to stay in Hong Kong and a few were even forcibly repatriated to Vietnam. We still had issues with criminality and disturbances but the worst by far occurred in a section of the Sek Kong camp where about 800 Vietnamese were waiting to be voluntarily repatriated back to Vietnam.

This was a closed camp and held migrants from both North and South Vietnam. Earlier in the day there had been a dispute about the use of hot water. The arguments between two factions broke out again in the evening and became much more serious. The gangs both had stashes of home-made weapons and used them to good effect. The disturbance became a full-scale riot and 400 additional police were called up to try to break up the fighting. As the camp held families and women and small children it was a terrifying situation. More Vietnamese from an adjoining section of the camp even broke a fence down and joined the fighting. The police started losing control in spite of firing thirty-three rounds of tear gas to try to subdue the violence. As this was happening a group from the South chased another group from the North into one of the accommodation huts. The Northerners who thought they were going to be chopped to death barricaded themselves in. The group from the South became frustrated, so they set fire to the hut instead. In the inferno, twenty-four of the migrants burned to death. It took fire-fighters ninety minutes to put the fire out. The grisly task of trying to identify the charred bodies took a long time afterwards.

As for our own local camp at Kai Tak, life returned to a kind of normality only briefly. In spite of Jenkins telling me that our case was water-tight, Pham appealed the conviction. Incredibly, the conviction was overturned. I was stunned. Pham was released from prison and of course quickly returned to his luxurious quarters in the camp. He immediately resumed running his drugs, gambling, and prostitution business. The prostitution part was a new line, as he discovered there was a ready market for fresh young Vietnamese girls in the Kowloon brothels.

Pham seemed untouchable. He had been implicated in three murders and got off every time. He was invincible. His very presence around the camp instilled fear. He started spending more time in the bright lights of Kowloon. He also started drinking more and coming back to the camp inebriated after swigging fancy cognac in the smart Kowloon nightclubs.

He had made plenty of enemies, but he had such an aura no one dared speak ill of him, let alone challenge him. But the murder victim, Tan, had a younger brother named Huy. In the twelve months since his elder brother's murder he had quietly watched the swaggering Pham striding around the camp showing no remorse for his victims and treating all his country people like dirt.

Huy hatched a plan and plotted a day of reckoning. One day, following his normal routine, Pham walked out of the camp for some high class recreation in the bright lights of the city. He made his way to his favourite club where he smoked foreign cigarettes, drank French cognac, and cavorted with Chinese call girls. At around 2.30am he took a taxi back to the camp entrance and after paying the fare, paused and lit a cigarette, then walked towards the tall metal gates and the steel wire fence.

When he was crossing the road and was about twelve feet from the entrance, a dark figure quietly slipped out of the shadows behind him. Without warning a heavy, razor-sharp meat cleaver chopped down on Pham's neck. It sliced down to the bone. As Pham stumbled forward, blood spurting out of the wound, more and more blows rained down on his head, his neck, and his back. Pham lay face down in a widening pool of dark blood. Huy threw down the meat cleaver and ran. Pham died on the spot from the injuries and massive blood loss.

There was no need for an experienced pathologist to determine the cause of death. No one mourned, there was no funeral. There was no celebration either, but there was a kind of relief amongst the Vietnamese that this character was no longer in their midst. I had by now moved on to another posting and I contacted the CID inspector in charge of this new homicide case. He was an experienced and smart local inspector named Chung. I went over to his office. We had a cup of tea, and went through the case papers together and I looked at the photographs of Pham's body. When we started talking about suspects, Chung said he knew who had killed Pham. He told me it was Tan's younger brother. I replied: 'Well, I suppose you are going to throw every resource at the case to ensure he is brought to justice.' Chung looked back at me and smiled. 'Of course,' he replied rather sarcastically. For many people, justice had already been served that night.

CHAPTER XXXI

Chief Inspector

I HAD BEEN A SENIOR INSPECTOR for four years, and for more than two of those years I had served in tough CID postings. It was 1989, I had a steady performance record, but not spectacular. I still had a bit of a reputation for being outspoken, but I was trying to control it. I had been recommended for promotion to chief inspector in the previous year and this year had been recommended again with a strong recommendation from my district commander. I had made it to the board interview stage. Everyone tries to prepare for promotion boards. And everyone says they don't. I read the latest force pronouncements and considered both local and international policing issues. I'm never sure this actually helps, but I suppose it made me feel as if I had done something. I made an effort to look fairly competent, and smartened up my appearance before I made my way to Police HQ on the fateful day. After a short wait of about twenty minutes I was told to enter the interview room to be grilled by the board. I opened the door and marched smartly up to the promotion board. The three senior officers were sitting behind a long dark wood table, with various papers scattered in front of them. The board chairman was an expat named Williams. It turned out to be the strangest interview I've ever had.

I was asked to sit down. It seemed the board had no idea who I was. Was it a trick to try to unnerve me? They got my name wrong, and my posting, and most of everything else. They thought I was called Rogers and worked in a different district. It was becoming embarrassing, and Williams in good humour eventually said: 'Well, tell us something about yourself.' So I reverted to my roots and spent ten minutes talking about my childhood and formative years in England. I left out the part about my Fiat 124 car getting stuck in a field. The questions then moved to some current policing issues which were in the news and easily answered. About thirty minutes after I sat down, the process came to an end. It was all very amicable, if rather unusual. I never knew if the mix-up was intentional and had been some kind of tactic. A few weeks later to my great surprise, I was informed in a letter that I had been successful. I was to be promoted to chief inspector. I sometimes wonder if there actually had been another more able candidate out there who should have been promoted instead of me.

CHAPTER XXXII

Illegal Immigrants

IT WAS COMMON FOR DETECTIVES to be posted back to uniform upon promotion. Depending on vacancies and the request of the officer a move back to plain clothes could be offered at a later time. After promotion I was initially posted back to Kowloon as an Assistant Divisional Commander. After a year I had the opportunity to go to a staff position in Police HQ as the officer in charge of the Anti-Illegal Immigration Control Centre (AIICC). This was part of the Operations Department under the command of Assistant Commissioner Brian Wigley. My section had two parts, a working office collecting data on methods used by immigrants to enter Hong Kong in the Police HQ itself, and a repatriation centre up in the New Territories near the Chinese border in a place called San Uk Ling. I enjoyed this arrangement because it gave me some flexibility about my movements and I could spend at least one day a week up at the repatriation centre. San Uk Ling was in the closed area of the northern New Territories. This was a restricted area that required special passes to enter. This was designed to create a buffer zone between the border and the rest of the colony.

The immigration centre at San Uk Ling was comprised of offices run by the Immigration Department, the police offices run by my team, and another, more secret, section run by British intelligence. Naturally, I often visited this section to try to see what was going on. The Immigration Department people were really an administrative unit for the physical repatriation of the illegal immigrants (IIs) back to China. My team were involved with interviewing the IIs before they went back to determine how they had crossed the border. For example, where they had crossed, whether they had paid anyone –

the 'snakeheads' – to help them. Where had they lived in Hong Kong, and whether they had found work? All of this information would be correlated and the data placed in regular reports and briefings which could be used for our patrols to assist us with deploying our own manpower. After being in the unit for about six months I wrote a staff paper regarding our processing of the IIs.

I still have a copy of the Chiefs of Staff paper. It is five pages long and recommends changing the escorting process of the IIs to make it more cost effective by changing the teams and deployment, allowing eight officers to return to front-line duties. The notional savings amounted to HK$1.2 million. The recommendations were accepted by Brian Wigley and adopted by the Operations Department which gave me a lot of satisfaction.

The guys in the British military intelligence office were looking for different information. I was amazed to discover they all spoke and wrote Chinese fluently. Their tuition had been in Mandarin, not Cantonese. They had been selected for their linguistics ability and sent away for a whole year to do nothing except perfect their Chinese language skills. I was impressed. They were all very modest and did not give much away. I think their posting was fairly easy and I'm not sure how much genuine intelligence of value they gleaned. I suspect they were more interested in the occasional Chinese military defector that came through their offices. As China opened up more, and the date crept closer to the Handover, they told me they were more interested in the rare times that they had someone from North Korea come through San Uk Ling. I recall one day when they had a young man who had crossed the border from North Korea into China and then gone overland into Hong Kong. They were all very excited and looking forward to obtaining some information about what was happening behind the walls of that secretive regime.

Illegal immigration from China created enormous social problems for the Hong Kong government. As Hong Kong's economy boomed in the 1970s, China was still very much a closed society and subject to the various upheavals created by Mao's different programmes and purges. When he died and Deng Xiaoping started the long road to reforming the economy with his 'four modernisations', China was still an economic backwater. The temptations for the rural poor, especially in nearby Canton, to cross into the bright lights of the colony were hard to resist.

From 1974 Hong Kong had the 'touch base' policy. I suspected that whoever dreamt this up was probably a fan of baseball. It meant that if an II crossed over the border and 'touched base' – reached the urban area – he or she would be eligible for a Hong Kong identity card and the right to live and work in the colony. Perhaps the rationale for the policy was that if a person could evade all of the patrols, checks and road blocks, and make their way all the way into the city without being caught, then they were probably smart and fit enough to contribute to Hong Kong society.

The term 'illegal immigrant' or 'II' is more general than 'refugee' or 'asylum seeker'. The UNHCR has a sensible approach to the definitions of displaced people. The IIs that I and the police dealt with in Hong Kong would now be called economic migrants. They were simply Chinese people in search of a better life. I could not blame them. If I had been a young man working on a farm in Canton I would have probably done the same. In 1980 though, due to the vast numbers of IIs, the 'touch base' policy was scrapped. From that year on, all IIs wherever arrested were held in police cells and then bussed through holding centres up to San Uk Ling to be placed in trucks and sent back over the border to China. In the eighties we heard stories that the people being returned were sent to labour camps for re-education. However as the numbers in-creased and the costs for the labour camps grew, I understand the Chinese government abandoned this idea and simply fined the returnees instead. The Hong Kong government really had no choice but to close the door. The population of China at the time was almost a billion, whereas the population in the colony was just over 5 million.

The story and plight of the Chinese IIs though is not well known outside of China. When I was still at PTS one of my cohort had a friend in the Army Air Corps. One Saturday he was taken up in a Scout helicopter and came back with some shocking photographs. His friend had taken him over the east of the colony, around the small islands and creeks north of Sai Kung. Washed up on the tiny beaches in these hidden coves were scores of dead bodies. He had not counted how many he had seen, there were too many. I don't recall this ever being reported on the TV news. Once on a leadership exercise out of PTS a few months after I arrived, we were near Shek O Beach on Hong Kong Island. A body washed up on the beach and we all assumed that it was an II.

There were various methods that the IIs used to try to get into Hong Kong but for the young men and women, swimming across Deep Bay or Mirs Bay was a popular and cheap option. This was generally during the summer months when the weather and sea temperature was warmer. Very often a truck's inner tube would be inflated as a buoyancy aid.

Another type of flotation device was made by placing inflated condoms inside a specially tailored cotton vest. The IIs would wait for favourable conditions and tides and trust that currents carried them in the right direction. The problem was that many of them could not swim and had never even been in a swimming pool before, let alone the sea. If the conditions changed or they were hit by waves, or the inner tube or flotation device burst they would drown. The other danger was from sharks. The South China Sea is home to the tiger shark. After the Great White, the tiger shark is one of the largest and most dangerous predators in the water. They are migratory and they soon realised there was easy pickings in Mirs Bay in the summer. The sightings of sharks increased. The news tended to keep Hong Kong beachgoers out of the water especially in the early evenings, the sharks' favourite feeding time.

Many IIs had tried to cross the Sham Chun River as it was narrow and appeared to offer the most direct route to Hong Kong. As the colony developed though, the river became more polluted, and the risks of poisoning possibly outweighed the advantages of the speed of the crossing. It was also in this area that the Chinese authorities concentrated more of their security forces. The Chinese police and army had no qualms about shooting their own people who tried to flee the Motherland. They also had fierce dogs that were trained to chase the people crossing the border. Meanwhile on the British side the Hong Kong government decided to build a new border fence along thirty-two kilometres of the land border. The new fence was a formidable barrier. It was over twenty feet high and built of extruded steel, not chain link so it was virtually impossible to cut and was topped with several strands of razor wire. When anyone tried to climb the fence, motion sensors would silently alert nearby Gurkha patrols.

There were also lookout towers located all along the fence and army patrols hiding in ambush in the undergrowth. The Gurkhas were issued with BMX bikes in order to reach the scene quickly. It looked quite comical when you saw a little guy in full combat fatigues pedalling furiously on a BMX bike along the border road. But they were practical and effective and a lot quicker than trying to run along the perimeter. In spite of all the seemingly impregnable defences the IIs were still able to climb over it. Most of the people attempting the crossing were young, fit individuals and they would have shared information and tactics amongst themselves. A common method for getting over the fence was using a fork and spoon. The II would carry a fork in one hand and a spoon in the other and place some sacking over their shoulder. To make footholds they would poke a fork through the fence and step up, then a spoon slightly higher and so on until they got to the top. Then they would throw the sacking over the razor wire and pull themselves over it without cutting themselves too badly. I heard that someone had been observed doing this, and was timed crossing over the fence in less than ninety seconds.

The people who had more money would pay snakeheads to assist them with the crossing. Probably the most convenient method of getting into Hong Kong except via a false passport was to come in by fishing boat. But as the boats were regularly stopped by the Marine Police the risks were high and the fishing boat owner faced imprisonment. Some people tried to come in on the cross-border train and many succeeded. But the areas around the stations were well secured and the trains were subject to regular patrols. Those that managed to swim across or climb the fence still had to get into the urban areas and find friends or relatives to help them. On the main routes in the New Territories and Sai Kung regular road blocks were mounted to stop and search vehicles, especially public light buses. Many were easy to spot due to their Mainland-style clothing and haircuts.

One II decided to disguise his haircut by wearing a Beatles wig. It was easily spotted by the wise old Sergeant Tsang walking down the bus, who as he walked past simply lifted the wig, then tapped the II on the shoulder and casually said: 'You're nicked, out you get.' Some IIs invested in a fake identity card before crossing. In the 1970s and early '80s the HKID card had a photo and an ID number laminated by two sheets of plastic. They were easily forged. The officers patrolling had no direct links with Immigration to verify the ID so they asked questions to see what the person knew about the colony. We would ask, 'How much is a ticket on the lower deck of the Star Ferry?' or 'What is the name of the famous hotel with a rotating restaurant?' or 'What is the name of a Japanese depart-ment store in Causeway Bay?' Together with their own suspicions such questions would normally be enough to satisfy the officer that the person was an II even when they were holding a HKID.

Up at San Uk Ling we saw many interesting cases. Collecting all the information about the routes and methods the IIs used was a full-time job. One day the team told me about an interesting interview. Most locals had 'red books'. These were not the thoughts of Chairman Mao, but a HSBC savings book. Each time a deposit or withdrawal was made the book would be updated by the teller. Many people carried them all the time. That day the team had interviewed a very pretty nineteen-year-old woman, who was orig-inally from Shanghai. I went to see her myself and she was indeed attractive. That was not what was interesting though. On checking her belongings she was found to be carrying a savings book showing a balance of over HK$1 million. This was incredible at a time when the average wage was HK$8–10,000 per month. Most people would have needed to work for over ten years to earn, let alone save, that much.

When my team had asked her how she had such a large sum of money she openly admitted she had worked as a prostitute. We still did not know how she had managed to open a bank account as an illegal immigrant. We assumed she had used a false identity card. We had no powers to take the book away from her and decided to let her keep it. We expected that in a month or two she would be back over in Hong Kong working again. But there was one thing troubling me. If prostitution was legal, which it was, why were prostitutes not paying tax? When I was back in the office I raised the issue. It obviously struck a nerve as I was asked to meet various legal counsel. I was even called before the Secretary for Security, Regina Ip to discuss the issue. Eventually this did generate a change in policy. The law was changed by the Legislative Council. This brought prostitutes and the earnings of prostitution under the government tax regime, which only seemed fair to me.

During the making of the BBC TV series *Hong Kong Beat* in the 1970s, the film crew moved around different parts of the colony. They followed the Emergency Unit and other busy police districts trying to film any juicy cases they could find. They also spent time up at the border and with the Marine Police. The BBC crew spent a whole night out on the water hoping to film IIs swimming across the bay. One officer on the launch with the film crew told me that for the whole night the sea was calm and there was absolutely nothing going on. So shortly before daybreak a plan was hatched. Two young male constables from the launch and a young female colleague were asked to change into shorts and a T-shirt and slip quietly into the water. A few moments later the BBC was triumphantly filming three IIs being intercepted and pulled out of the water by the Marine Police. I have the episode on DVD and they do look very tired, and if they weren't real IIs they were very good actors. I doubt if anyone from the BBC will own up to anything now anyway.

In the 1970s there were so many bodies in the Sham Chun River and the surrounding area that the Chinese government recruited labourers to pull the dead bodies from the water. These people were called 'body draggers' by the locals. They were paid a bounty for each body they recovered. It was a nasty job as many of the bodies would be bloated and blackened by decomposition and the stench would be disgusting. There were numerous bodies, some with bullet holes, and dog bites, so that the body draggers prospered. There were four peaks in immigrant numbers, in 1957, 1962, 1972, and 1979. These were usually prompted by turmoil in the Mainland, which created a surge in people seeking to escape. It is estimated that about one million people crossed into Hong Kong between the 1950s to the 1980s. How many people died? Certainly tens of thousands, possibly hundreds of thousands. A Chinese journalist called Chen Bing'an wrote *The Great Exodus* about the illegal immigrants, published in China in 2010. It was the result of twenty-two years of research; a short account was published by the Chinese newspaper *China Daily* in April 2011 and is online. The story deserves a wider audience.

CHAPTER XXXIII

Moving to King's Park

THE YEAR 1989 WAS AN INTERESTING time. The Berlin Wall came down, there was the Tiananmen Square 'incident', the USA invaded Panama, and I married a Malaysian Cathay Pacific flight attendant called Elizabeth. We were officially wed at City Hall in Hong Kong together with a few friends. As neither of us had family in Hong Kong we kept the ceremony rather simple. Later in the summer we had a church blessing together with family and my old friends from England.

The situation in China and Hong Kong in June 1989 was tense. After the Tiananmen tragedy I received a letter from Chief Secretary David Ford: 'We in the Civil Service share with the community as a whole the profound feeling of shock and grief at the recent bloodshed.' I believe all civil servants received the same letter. I still have mine.

It was at this time and with extra housing points as a result of my promotion and marriage, that I decided to move to a bigger apartment in King's Park. I now had a ground-floor flat of over 2,000 square feet in a very convenient area, downtown, not far from Ho Man Tin and Waterloo Road. At first everything went well. It was a nice green space, I had a small garden, with lots of trees, and there were tennis courts nearby. I started playing tennis every week with Dick Lee, my old boss from Sha Tin. After a couple of months though I came to realise there were significant downsides to the location.

For one thing, living on the ground floor meant that any wildlife could easily make its way inside to share my accommodation. These included termites, mice, geckos, and other creepy-crawlies. Termites loved my airing cupboard. They would happily live and lay eggs in its warm, dry confines. When the eggs hatched there would be millions of the little buggers. On opening the airing cupboard door I would be met by a seething black mass of insects covering all our clothes and bedding, it was like a scene from a horror movie. This occurred in two consecutive years and both times I grabbed a large can of insecticide, wrapped a towel around my face, opened the door slightly, held my breath and emptied half a can of Baygon into the small cupboard and closed the door. About thirty minutes later I could go back and use a vacuum cleaner to remove the inch-deep layer of dead insects on the floor.

Then there were feral cats. They might have been pets at one time but had been abandoned and had turned wild. The Agriculture and Fisheries Department put down cage traps and caught many of the unfortunate animals. We had a part-time Filipina helper called Babette to keep the place clean and help me with laundry and so on. Babette was great; my cousin still reckons she made the best roast chicken. One afternoon when I was in the living room I heard a scream. I ran across to the kitchen where I saw Babette's eyes wide open, frozen in terror. I looked across and saw the largest centipede I've ever seen. It was the size of a small snake, thick as my thumb and dark red. It was running along the aluminium draining board and its feet were clattering, tipper-tapper. Somehow I was quick enough to grab a kettle which had been boiling on the stove. I poured boiling water over it which flushed the centipede into the sink where it curled and twisted, thrashing its body in its death throes. It eventually expired. Babette let out a huge sigh of relief as these creatures are venomous and I have known people hospitalised after being bitten by them.

King's Park was also a magnet for human pests. One day, as Elizabeth was walking down the steps to Waterloo Road, she was confronted by a flasher. She shouted out loudly and he ran off. We also had a chap who used to come into our garden and hide behind the bushes. Elizabeth saw him at night once hiding below our bedroom window. I chased him away a couple of times. He was a young chap though and could leap over our nine-foot high fence in seconds. I never found out what his motive was, but I didn't want to leave my young wife alone to find out. So after just eighteen months in King's Park, I decided to take up the government's Home Finance Scheme offer. This meant I could buy my own apartment. With house prices in Hong Kong so high, I had to move to somewhere much smaller. We ended up buying an apartment of just over 700 square feet on Lantau. We had to dispose of many of our possessions, including most of my treasured book collection. I had accumulated over 200 books, but I ended up giving most of them to a charity. Or at least that's where the man with the van said they were going!

CHAPTER XXXIV

Adventure on the Ji Fung

THE HONG KONG GOVERNMENT took training very seriously and I was fortunate to be sent on a number of training and development courses. Shortly after my promotion I was nominated for the Police Intermediate Command Course. I had enjoyed this because it meant some time away from the stress of police work, and an opportunity to see other government departments. One afternoon we were flying in Wessex helicopters from HMS Tamar to the New Territories. When passing over Lion Rock the pilot decided to have some fun. He intentionally put the helicopter into a stall. The chopper lurched up and then seemed to drop like a stone. A female chief inspector called Susie sat opposite me and I saw her hair shoot straight up like something from a horror movie. The look on her face was priceless. Fortunately we were all tightly strapped in and there were no trousers soiled. We all had a good laugh when we arrived in Fanling but it took Susie a while to regain her composure.

About a year after this adventure my cousin Stuart came over from Canada to stay with me in King's Park for a while after he completed his university studies. He was taking a gap year to travel around Asia. However when he saw my liquor cupboard and well-stocked fridge he somehow postponed his travels for a while. I was due to go off on a course designed to develop leadership abilities. It involved sailing a brigantine called the *Ji Fung* from Hong Kong to the Philippines and back. Stuart decided that it would be a good idea to give me a proper send off. So the night before I was due to leave we began to consume dangerous levels of alcohol, mostly consisting of German beer, sake, and schnapps. The next morning, very hung over and having had very little sleep, I climbed into a police Land Rover to take me to the embarkation point in Sai Kung. I wasn't feeling much like sailing as we travelled east. When I arrived I found out we students numbered about twenty, plus the regular crew. I was the only expatriate student. The plan was that we would be taught how to sail en route to the Philippines. Then we would sail the brigantine back to Hong Kong ourselves.

The *Ji Fung* was a sailing ship that had commenced service in 1981 after a generous grant of HK$5.5 million by the Jockey Club. She was used for leadership training by the Outward Bound in Hong Kong. The course members were all introduced to each other and shown the vessel and her cramped living quarters. In no time at all we were required to set sail into the South China Sea. The journey out was uneventful apart from legendary sea-sickness. On the first day almost everyone was throwing up. I was a miserable wretch, retching miserably. When we could stop vomiting for a few minutes we were split into three watches to perform continuous shift duty. When I was not ill there were some beautiful scenes of flying fish, brilliant sunrises and sunsets, and incredible views of the Milky Way at night. After several days sailing we eventually moored at one of the smaller tropical Philippine islands.

I was glad to be able to get onto dry land and have a change of scenery. Even though it was a tiny island with a population of a few hundred people we still had to show our passports to the civil leader who came over to greet us. We took some supplies with us and camped out overnight. The hike through the hills was fun and before heading back on the ship we bought some fruit and fish from the locals at the water's edge.

On the return trip I was voted by my watch as 'captain' for the group. On one night with very little wind we had to use the small diesel engine to make our way. The night was moonless and very dark, and all the regular crew were fast asleep down below in their bunks. I was steering and keeping an eye on the radar and satellite navigation. Fortunately I wasn't required to learn how to use a sextant. Suddenly on the green radar screen I saw a huge black rectangle appear, heading straight for us. I realised it could only be one of the enormous cargo-container ships that ply the South China Sea. As a vessel under sail I knew we had the right of way. I also knew that these giant ships had minimal crew, and at night sailed on autopilot. There were stories of yachts disappearing in the sea at night. If this thing hit us it wouldn't even notice. So I decided to use the engines to dodge around the tanker in a port-starboard-starboard-port rectangular course. The other guys from my watch were understandably worried about the floating city bearing down on us and keen on waking up the regular crew but I felt we could do it ourselves. So as we manoeuvred we suddenly saw the giant ship emerge from the gloom. It was like an enormous blind leviathan as it silently slid past us around 200 yards away on our port side. We stared up at it, thinking of what could have been. All of our watch was super alert for the rest of the night. We returned safely to Hong Kong a couple of days later. I was pleased to have done the trip and glad to get back on dry land, but I have never been tempted to repeat the experience.

After almost twenty years of faithful duty the *Ji Fung* was retired from Outward Bound service in 2002 and sold to John Player Tobacco, but she was wrecked in the Spanish Balearic Islands in May 2003.

CHAPTER XXXV

Race Marshalling

A S IN MOST POLICE FORCES, sporting activities were encouraged and officers could take generous time off to participate. There was an active golf society. Likewise, the police sailing club had an enthusiastic cohort. This was not surprising when it meant they could spend a day on the water instead of doing police work. Later in my career a colleague told me about the motoring society. They were looking for volunteer race marshals for the Macau Grand Prix in November. After training, the marshals would be given time off to travel to Macau on the jetfoil, accommodation, food and even a small cash allowance. It sounded great, so I signed up.

I enjoyed several years marshalling in Macau and I was even sent to Malaysia and China for different motor-racing events. I really enjoyed these trips. The camaraderie and change of atmosphere was refreshing. I marshalled the pit and paddock one year. I loved it, as this was where all the hospitality girls paraded. I also met the drivers including David Coulthard who was then a young Formula 3 driver but later became a successful FI driver. Life was always interesting. Just as the silver cup was being awarded to the winner of a saloon car race I was called over the radio. I was told sternly: 'Pull the winner off from the podium.' I asked why. It transpired there was an allegation, which turned out to be true, that the 'winner' was an impostor. The racer had run into the dressing room immediately after the race, and the impostor had emerged. The impostor was a local triad gangster who had paid off the real racer so he could take the credit. I actually did go up and pull the false racer off the podium. I felt pretty awkward about it all, doing it in front of so many people and the press, but I suffered no retribution.

I also marshalled at the Lisboa Casino corner which was always eventful. The racers would scream down the main straight and the first corner, a narrow ninety-degree right-hander, was the Lisboa. There were always smashes and pile ups at Lisboa corner. The press knew this and would mass there waiting for their scoop. The marshals would have to run out and clear any wreckage whilst trying to avoid being mown down by the next car. One year when I was a marshal at the corner, two motorcyclists were killed over the weekend in separate races. I saw one of the incidents up on the main straight. A rookie racer had clipped the wheel of another bike and been flipped up over the handlebars. It occurred some distance from me so I didn't have to attend the scene. I was relieved it hadn't happened next to my area of the track.

The same year of those accidents, I was out in the evening at a club in downtown Macau having a few beers with some other marshals. We were about 100 metres up the road from the New World Emperor Hotel. In the hotel bar, a well-known Hong Kong triad member called Andely Chan was drinking with friends. Andely was better known as the 'Tiger of Wan Chai'. He was a member of the Sun Yee On, and feared around the Hong Kong nightclub district. Chan had been competing in one of the races. He was with his two mechanics who were also believed to be triad members, and a couple of female friends.

At about 3am they all left the bar and climbed into a red van, with Andely at the wheel. As they all boarded the van, three men wearing crash helmets ran up to the van brandishing Chinese Black Star automatic pistols. They pumped twenty bullets into the van, killing Chan and one of his mechanics instantly, and seriously wounding the other occupants. When I emerged from the club shortly afterwards, the area was swarming with police. I had no idea what had happened. I learnt more about the case the following day. Chan had been wanted by the Hong Kong Police, he was believed to have been involved in several murders, so in one way it cleared up several outstanding case files for my colleagues back in Hong Kong. When I took the jetfoil back on Monday morning I reflected on what had been a very eventful weekend.

CHAPTER XXXVI

Back in Mong Kok

AFTER TWO YEARS HEADING up the Anti-Illegal Immigration Control Centre I was posted back to Mong Kok. At one time it was in the *Guinness Book of Records* as the most densely populated place on earth, having 130,000 people per square kilometre. Mong Kok and Yau Ma Tei are also home to the unfortunate 'cage men' renting bunk beds separated by steel mesh.

A number of markets such as the famous Ladies' Market are in Mong Kok as well as all the various triad societies. Mong Kok was one of the busiest police districts in the colony. The only other place that came close back then was Wan Chai. I was posted to Mong Kok three times in my career and each time I plotted to escape. The first time was when I was a young inspector in uniform, the second time as a senior detective inspector in the district anti-triad squad and the third time as a chief inspector of operations.

The only advantage for me was it had an MTR stop nearby and was easy to commute to, and the officers' mess was quite lively. Everything else I disliked. A young couple, Mr and Mrs Leung, ran the mess and the laundry. They did an excellent job, but they decided to emigrate. The day they left was a very sad one for all of us. I'm sure that whatever they are doing now they are successful. On the wall of the mess was a plaque quoting a senior officer named Quine. On one of his official visits to the station he was informed by a superintendent that the murder rate in the district had increased during the year. 'Oh,' he replied, 'I don't care about the murder rate, they don't affect my statistics at all.' Initially those gathered round thought he was joking. But then he carried on talking without breaking a smile and the realisation dawned that he had in fact been serious. A few of the guys went out and had an official-looking plaque made commemorating the event, including the quote, and placed it on the wall. It was a source of amusement for many years.

The report room in Mong Kok was busy twenty-four hours a day. The duty officer would usually be a station sergeant or a young inspector. There was never a pause in criminal activity, and the report room staff would only be allowed short breaks individually; it was too busy to let more than one person go. I saw people staggering in with knife and machete wounds pouring blood, there were prostitutes, drug addicts, triads, homeless people, and individuals arrested for every kind of offence. Everyone had to be processed individually and all the cases had to be documented. A Friday night resembled a war zone. For the triads, Mong Kok is a sought after (and fought over) area. Every street and every business is carefully controlled and managed by either the 14K, Sun Yee On, the Wo Shing Wo or another triad. Inevitably there were conflicts when someone was accused of straying into another's patch or not giving face.

When a situation boiled over, fights would break out but they were rarely with fists like in the Jackie Chan movies. As firearms were very strictly controlled they would only be used as a last resort. The weapon of choice was either a butcher's meat cleaver or a home-made knife. The knives had blades up to twelve inches long. They were sharpened on a lathe, fixed with a crude wooden handle wrapped in cotton cloth for a better grip that also made it more difficult to lift fingerprints. If an attack was planned on a single person, at least four or five assailants would be arranged. They would wait until the target was away from his triad brothers. The attacks were brutal but rarely fatal, targeting elbows and knees and especially ligaments to disable the victim. The victims would be crippled for months and sometimes years as a result.

There is a lot of nonsense talked about the triads. On the one hand we had our British chief superintendent in Mong Kok telling us they were just unorganised thugs. On the other hand we saw media reports telling us they controlled every aspect of life in Hong Kong. Neither of these is correct. As mentioned, the two biggest triads in Hong Kong are the 14K and the Sun Yee On. The Sun Yee On appears to be the most successful in terms of its business interests. It has retained its roots, but has also acquired a number of lucrative business interests. It is rumoured it even controls several publicly listed companies on the stock market. What is most fascinating is the relationship between the triad leadership in Hong Kong and the leaders of the Communist Party in China. In 1984 Deng Xiaoping was widely quoted as claiming that the 'black societies are very powerful, but not all of them are dark, there are many good guys amongst them'.

In 1993, a minister for public security in China claimed that some members of the triads were 'patriotic citizens' and had a role to play in building up the nation. There were a number of reports of meetings between triad leaders and top members of China's Public Security Bureau. There were claims leading up to 1997 that deals had been done, and that triads had been asked for help in maintaining stability in the territory after the Handover. Who knows how many of these reports are correct? Most of my encounters in the course of my duty were with street-level triads. It's difficult to know how many senior members I met without knowing it. It's highly likely that triads have infiltrated the police, and some of the senior business leaders probably had triad affiliations. Media reports claimed that at least two appointed members of the post-1997 legislature were triad members.

During my time in Mong Kok serving as a chief inspector, a new scam appeared which really annoyed me. When I was off duty and walking down Waterloo Road I saw a Westerner sitting on the pavement begging. He had a cardboard sign which said *Robbed and lost wallet and passport; Please help*. I had stopped and spoken to him. He was British and was staying in Chungking Mansions. I thought it was odd, and questioned why he hadn't gone to the British Consulate and asked for help, but I took it no further. A few days later on my patch in Mong Kok I was out for lunch and saw another one on Nathan Road. It was a different guy but the sign was almost identical. I watched as generous local people feeling sorry for him were placing $10 and $20 notes in his bowl. I called back to the station and requested a police Land Rover be sent to my location. When it arrived I walked over to him and showed him my warrant card. He was an English chap called Rob who was also staying at Chungking Mansions. I told him I was arresting him for mendicancy (begging) and was taking him back to the police station.

At first he protested his innocence saying he really had been robbed, but he had, of course, not reported it to the police or anyone else. When we all got back to the report room I instructed one of my officers that Rob be searched. Over HK$1,000 in cash was in his pockets. Along with his allegedly-stolen passport. I told him that I was detaining him for further investigations and he would be seeing a magistrate in the morning and would likely get a criminal record. Suddenly his cocky demeanour changed and he became very contrite. He was led downstairs and put in the cells and left there for the rest of the day. In the evening I brought him back up to the report room. He was now apparently very sorry for his fraudulent claims and ripping off the local public. In front of all my officers I gave him the biggest and loudest bollocking he'd ever had. I warned him that if he stepped into my district again I would have him sent to prison. He was then given his cash and passport and told to go back and warn his fellow travellers in Chungking Mansions that there would be zero tolerance of such behaviour in future. It seemed to work. I never did see any further British beggars on the streets of Mong Kok after that.

It is common knowledge that Chinese people love to gamble. The two racecourses in Hong Kong turn over more revenue annually than all the racecourses in the whole of the UK. There is also a very popular lottery called the Mark Six, usually held twice a week. In my previous posting in Police HQ a group of us would form an *ad hoc* syndicate for the rollovers or the big jackpots during the holiday festivals. Around ten of us would all put in about HK$50 each, and we would buy HK$500 worth of tickets. The tickets would be 'quick picks' or computer-generated random numbers. Then the tickets were photocopied so everyone had the numbers. If a small amount was won it was often ploughed back into the following week. I had been part of the PHQ Operations Department syndicate for about two years whilst I was in AIICC. My old boss and friend Dick Lee was now an assistant commissioner and was also a part of the group. We never won anything when I was in the syndicate but about three months after I left the department, I received a phone call from an old friend to say that my old pals had just won the previous day's Mark Six Dragon Boat rollover jackpot of 38 million dollars!

Thirty-eight million bloody dollars. At first I thought it was a joke, I couldn't believe it, but then realised it was true. Shit, I thought, so close. I had a sinking nauseous feeling in my stomach for a couple of hours. I closed the door of my office, sat quietly and thought about it. I told myself: I was healthy, I had an interesting career, I had good friends, and I was close to my family. I told myself that I was lucky, and I should consider my life to be fortunate. I composed myself and then rang the group to congratulate them.

There was a postscript to the story. A friend called Bill who was part of the syndicate was tasked with collecting the cheque from the Jockey Club. Once he'd collected it he took it his local HSBC branch to pay it into his account. He said the lady teller had behaved so casually, it was as if he was paying HK$20 into his account instead of $38 million. He then went back to the office and wrote personal cheques to each of his syndicate colleagues. The next day he went back to the bank and was horrified to check his account and discover that he was overdrawn to the tune of HK$35,000,000! HSBC had not credited the Jockey Club cheque paid in, as it was still 'clearing', but had happily deducted all the personal cheques he'd written from his account. He wasn't happy when he discovered he was paying a very high rate of interest on his new overdraft.

On an earlier occasion when I was serving as CID senior inspector in Mong Kok, I was placed in charge of one of the anti-triad squads. There is usually a handover from the previous person in charge. This includes a briefing on the team members, some advice on the district and the major problems, and of course passing on open case files. The case files will tell you a lot about the calibre of the previous officer in charge. So when I took over a team I would spend a lot of time reviewing these files, and then deciding which deserved fresh scrutiny and which were probably close to closure, with no fresh leads likely. Having gone through all of this and having met my new team members I decided to re-arrange my office furniture and move my desk. When I moved the metal filing cabinet a large number of case files were revealed next to the wall where they had been hidden by my predecessor.

I was shocked and upset. There were at least twenty case files and all dated from when the British inspector, I will call him Steve, had been in charge of the squad. He had already proceeded on a long-vacation leave and was now overseas. I closed my office door and locked it. I sat down at my desk and put my head in my hands. I suddenly felt really stressed. I was already in one of the most high-pressure police jobs in the world in one of the busiest postings, and now I had to deal with this as well. I thought about my options. I was really tempted to report him and get the cases off my hands, but I knew if I did it might destroy his career. I would probably be criticised for ratting on a colleague, even though he did deserve the retribution. On the other hand if I did not report it I would have to handle the extra workload myself. I agonised over the situation for fifteen minutes behind my locked door. I eventually decided to take on the cases myself. I pushed the filing cabinet back to the wall. I piled the old files on my desk. At the time I had a very good female station sergeant called Irene Lau working for me. I discussed the situation with her. We agreed to follow up the cases together. I worked even longer hours and asked my team to help me with updating the information and following up with leads and witnesses. It took us weeks to clear the backlog. Steve went on to enjoy a very successful career.

Throughout my time in Hong Kong I was invited to a number of Chinese weddings, although it was the wedding receptions I was invited to. These were lavish affairs held in large restaurants or the ballroom of a hotel. The invitation card was usually in a perfumed envelope with the details written in Chinese and English, often in gold ink on a red card. The legal wedding was often a registry-office affair, but it was the celebration dinner that was the big deal. When I was invited I would often be met by the parents of the bride and groom at the entrance who would usually be wearing Western clothes, and all the male relatives would wear a large flower arrangement in their buttonhole. Apart from the top tables there was not always a seating arrangement so I would scout the room and amongst the hundreds of guests try to find the fellow cops who had been invited.

The custom was to take a cheque to give to the bride and groom as a wedding gift. The special commemorative gift cheques are available from HSBC. I always asked in advance what the expected amount was. The idea was that the total from all the gift cheques paid for the banquet. I feel this is a very practical arrangement. There were often about ten or twelve dishes including some tasty seafood such as prawns, clams, mussels, and steamed fish, and chicken and meat dishes. We always finished with fried rice and noodles. Shark fin soup is an expensive delicacy, and usually the only time I sampled it was at a wedding. We washed the dishes down with beer or Coca-Cola. If it was a very posh affair there might be French wine.

During the banquet the bride and groom would move around the tables with some small cups of rice wine or similar and we would all toast their long life, health and prosperity. For all of us around the table we would also often *yum booi* or toast our good health for each dish. Once when I was at a wedding dinner during my early career I joined the *yum booi* with everyone. The prized steamed garoupa, a very delicious large fish with a delicate white flesh, had arrived. By the time I had put my glass down and picked up my chopsticks the fish was a skeleton. My colleagues had lifted their glasses with their left hands, while keeping their chopsticks poised in their right. The moment the glasses had been raised, the chopsticks went to work in a flash. I didn't make the same mistake twice.

Patrolling in Mong Kok was a trial in itself. When I was walking the streets people would bump into me, even as a uniformed police officer. I used to place my right hand over my gun as I walked as I was so concerned someone could snatch it. The seething mass of the crowds would have made it almost impossible to chase the culprit. The tension of being in such a crazy busy place in the stifling heat and humidity meant that after twenty to thirty minutes I would be exhausted. There were designated cafés for officers to take refreshment breaks. It was necessary to step into one regularly for a soft drink to rehydrate and cool down in air conditioning.

There were many illegal hawkers on the streets and when they saw us they would run off, scattering shoppers. Mostly though we didn't bother the hawkers too much as it was the duty of other departments to deal with them. A lot of the hawkers were recent immigrants trying to make a living, and due to the lack of a sophisticated welfare system this was one of the only semi-legitimate ways to put food on the table. The hawkers were very resourceful; they sold what they felt would be popular during each season. There was a saying that in Mong Kok when it started raining, all the hawkers would be selling umbrellas within ten minutes. Although this was meant as a joke, it was not far from the truth.

Despite some stories in British newspapers and the local crime movies, firearms incidents in Hong Kong are thankfully relatively rare. I only dealt with two directly, both in Mong Kok. The first was when I was out on patrol with one of my constables. We were about to go for lunch when we were alerted over the beat radio that criminals with firearms had been spotted in a tenement building very near us. I drew my revolver as a precaution and after informing the control room we entered the building. It was a labyrinth of passageways, dark, gloomy and smelly, with lots of hidden corners. I kept the volume of my radio turned up so I could hear updates from the control room. There was no way of knowing what was round the corner and what was actually happening. After about fifteen minutes I was told it was a false alarm and we could stand down. I was very grateful to holster my revolver and go for an overdue lunch. The second incident was a couple of months later. I was on duty when I received a report of an armed robbery and open fire incident. I jumped in a Land Rover with a couple of my team and we sped to the scene, sirens blaring. A gang had robbed a goldsmith's shop. A police sergeant nearby had spotted them fleeing and shots had been exchanged. The robbers commandeered a taxi and sped up Shanghai Street. The taxi was later found abandoned with its doors open, several bullet holes, and blood stains on the seats. A few pieces of jewellery had been dropped on the back seat. There was a bullet hole going right through the headrest of one of the seats. The sergeant must have been a good shot. No one had been killed, but one of the robbers had been injured. There was a huge amount of evidence and it wasn't long before arrests were made. The district commander attended the scene and instructed me to compile the open fire report. These cases are taken very seriously and the open fire reports have to be meticulous. The contents are forensic in tone with every incident reported second by second, as every police shot has to be justified. The sergeant in this case had fired five shots.

Mong Kok in the 1980s had a unique individual living in the police station. Bobby was deaf and dumb, and when I was working there the first time, he would have been in his mid-twenties. He was believed to be a local Cantonese man. The story was that he was an orphan who had been unofficially adopted by the local CID guys as a young boy. He had been befriended, fed and allowed to sleep in the barracks upstairs. They would buy him lunch boxes and soft drinks and in return he would run errands for them. I used to see him walking around and he didn't bother me, and I didn't bother him. He was quite strongly built and maybe about five foot eight inches tall. I heard that he had come in useful when the local CID boys had been questioning triad suspects in the early hours, especially when their prisoner was not cooperating. Apparently Bobby would be called in and asked to help. In court when the local triad gangster complained to the magistrate that he had been beaten by a deaf and dumb guy in a T-shirt it's unlikely that the court would have given him much credence.

One afternoon I was in the report room and I saw Bobby walk towards me. He often liked to walk around the station pretending he was a police officer. On this day he was wearing a white Police Tactical Unit T-shirt, with a large Royal Hong Kong Police crest and a pair of blue jeans. He had pinned a home-made police warrant card to his T shirt. His hair was cut by the police barber and he walked in a very confident manner with his hands behind his back. That afternoon there was a young local inspector called Lee on duty. Lee was really tall at about six foot three inches and very slim and gangly. He had been in Mong Kok for about a month and only recently graduated from PTS. He had never met Bobby before, so I watched with interest as Bobby swaggered into the report room and proceeded to check the observation book.

He walked towards the unsuspecting Lee, and as he did so, Bobby naturally not saying anything, opened three fingers on his right hand and tapped his shoulder to indicate the three pips of a chief inspector. At which point Lee, thinking he was facing a senior officer in plain clothes, snapped to attention, saluted, and said: 'Good afternoon sir.' He then started briefing Bobby on all the day's outstanding cases. I ducked out of view with my fist in my mouth trying to stifle my amusement. It was a while before Lee realised something was amiss. As he was wondering who this character really was, one of his constables whispered in his ear and spilled the beans. Lee then came bounding over to where I was sitting, bent over, my sides shaking, and tears of laughter running down my face. He collapsed over my desk and to be fair to him he saw the funny side too and we both degenerated into giggles at the absurdity of the scene. Meanwhile Bobby wandered off to continue his 'inspection'.

There was a very popular American TV cop drama in the 1980s called *Miami Vice;* it all looked very exotic, with the palm trees, Ferraris, and the pastel suits. Yorkshire Television in the UK had looked at this and decided they could produce their own *Miami Vice* in the streets of Hong Kong. It was called *Yellowthread Street,* based on a series of novels by William Marshall. A lot of money was being invested and the producers and the media became very interested in our police force. As I was working in the busiest district I was asked to work with the media and ensure that their perception was positive. Things didn't go quite as planned. The TV series had received high-level police approval, and my chief superintendent was very supportive of the project. When the production company had requested some help with site visits for filming locations I was asked to show them around.

As instructed by my boss I went out with the producers for some scoping visits and answered questions about the crime situation and had my photo taken in street locations. However . . . this was actually the *Sunday People* newspaper from the UK, not film scouts at all. They must have thought we were all mugs, and I guess we were. The following Sunday I started receiving calls from home. This was before the Internet, so communication wasn't so immediate and brutal as it is now. This was fortunate as it turned out the *Sunday People* had printed a full colour, two-page spread on the Royal Hong Kong Police in Mong Kok featuring yours truly. The main story had a colour photo of me about nine inches high in my CID suit carrying my .38 snubnose Detective Special revolver. It called me the 'Triad Buster' in a massive headline and then continued with a completely fictitious story about my heroic actions in shooting dead various baddies and rescuing damsels from burning buildings.

You might imagine the reaction of my family in England. They might have been worried about their son on reading such an account of my perilous adventures. Meanwhile, the ribbing I got from my colleagues was merciless. They naturally assumed that I had told the journalists these tall stories, and I was teased for weeks. I realised the only way I could escape was by pretending it was all true. So I started telling people that, yes, it's correct, I am a real-life hero. They tended to quieten down a bit after that. We were all excitedly looking forward to seeing the TV series, and hoped it would be as slick as *Miami Vice* and match its excitement. Sadly it never did. It lasted one ill-fated series of just thirteen episodes before sinking into ignominy, to be forgotten except for a very few sentimental souls.

CHAPTER XXXVII

Presenting Police Report

WHEN I WAS STILL POSTED to Mong Kok I was reading some official notices one morning when I saw that RTHK, the public broadcasting service, were looking for police officers to present the weekly *Police Call*. This was a programme aired every week on Saturday night on both English-language channels TVB and ATV. It was a programme which requested help in solving various cases, and also gave out crime prevention tips. I thought it sounded interesting and applied. I was requested to go for a screen test in Broadcast Drive in Kowloon Tong. After introductions I was asked to go to a dressing room where a make-up girl was waiting. It was the first time I had ever worn make-up. I was told it was necessary due to the heat under the studio lights. I was introduced to the film crew and to Andy the director and they explained what was going to happen. I was asked to sit in a chair and when they counted down '5-4-3-2-1' I was to look into the camera, smile, relax and read the words on the autocue as naturally as possible.

Well I tried to relax, I really did, but when I saw the director's fingers going from five to one and the lights suddenly being turned on me, and the theme music starting, I think I looked anything but relaxed. I wasn't very happy with my performance when they played it back and I could see it on a monitor. But I must have done well enough, as I was later told I had been successful and would be a presenter. I was very pleased and excited but I didn't tell many people about it. My excitement was later tempered somewhat when I found out that two other people had also been selected, including my colleague Peter Morgan. Peter reminded me of this recently when he found an old newspaper cutting from *Off Beat,* the police newspaper, with the news of the appointments and a picture of the two of us. I found out later that I was to be used mainly as a temporary presenter during holiday periods, but this suited me quite well.

As it turned out this was quite a good arrangement as I had to write and edit the scripts myself and prepare the autocues for every episode. This was a lot of extra work considering this was an unpaid addition to my regular job. What would happen was I would be sent some information on police cases and incidents every Wednesday. I would then write them up in a way suitable for presentation. As filming took place on Friday I only had a couple of days to complete the task. I did eventually present quite a few episodes although I have no idea how many. In some I was dressed in a blue blazer with a tie and in some I'm wearing my police uniform. In some episodes they had people with telephones at the back of the studio answering calls from people with information. In fact they were actors pretending to take calls. It was done to make the public think people were cooperating and encourage them to do the same. I was told the same thing happens during the *Crimewatch* programmes in the UK too.

I have a DVD with some of the episodes. When I watch them now it's funny to see how tense and serious I look in the first episode. In one of my early episodes the regular presenter Paul Gregory interviewed me about a case in Sau Mau Ping. Paul was very experienced and confident, in stark contrast to me. As I filmed more episodes I relaxed more and smiled and I also enjoyed it more. I can't remember many people saying they'd seen me on TV though. I think it's because most people were out on the town enjoying themselves on a Saturday night, or maybe they were actively avoiding it. The other thing I notice now is how young I look!

CHAPTER XXXVIII

Police Training School Instructor

I WAS ON MY THIRD POSTING to Mong Kok and looking for other possible postings. So when I received a call one day in 1994 offering me a posting to Police Training School as a course instructor I jumped at the opportunity. I then spent two of the happiest years of my career back at the place where I started out. I was back in uniform but I didn't care. Before I was allowed to be let loose with my own probationary inspectors I had to participate in an instructors' training course. This lasted four weeks and enabled me to hone my teaching skills to an acceptable standard to be able to lead my new students.

It was nearing the end of an era. When I arrived at PTS the last British inspectors were already under training. A decision had been made to end recruitment three years before the Handover so that their first tour would be completed within British rule. The decision would then be made by the new administration as to whether to extend the contracts of the expat inspectors. In the event, contracts for all those who wished to continue service were extended exactly as they had been before.

From the beginning of my time on PTS staff, I loved the role. I enjoyed training the new young inspectors and found that I had a talent for training and teaching, which carried over to my later career. We had a strict curriculum but we could manage our own lesson plans and presentations and impose our own style on the lessons. For me, taking twelve young fresh-faced inspectors and watching them develop and grow over nine months was a very rewarding experience. I could also use all the training facilities during the non-teaching hours and I was able to regain some of my earlier fitness.

This was important when I was leading the squad on leadership exercises where we were taken by helicopter from PTS and dropped off on some remote hillside up in the New Territories. We had moved on from the old Wessex helicopters by now to Sikorskys and then to Blackhawks. When we were up on the top of the hillside I would appoint one of the squad as leader and give them a task. Everyone would be in jungle gear – green fatigues, rubber and canvas boots and floppy hat. The staff would often still wear their blue berets. These exercises formed a very important part of the training for the local officers. Generally they were all quite studious and could pass the academic exams. Most of them would manage to get themselves through the fitness or at least do enough to pass. The weakness often was in leadership ability. Encouraging them to be decisive and assertive enough to lead was critical. Once on top of the remote hillside the squad would be told to take out their Ordnance Survey maps and compasses, to take bearings and try to figure out where they were. The leader had to get the entire squad to a specific grid reference before an allotted time. In the early stages we would often select as leaders the students who we considered might be weaker in this area.

The task was designed to put the leader under pressure. Although students were not required to run to the muster point, the group would have to move at a brisk pace. Once the leader was appointed it was always enlightening to observe the reactions of their peers in the group. Were they happy? Or did they look disappointed? Did they offer to help? Or did they shy away and leave him to it? From watching the group it was possible to ascertain how popular the leader was and how well respected. I had to observe the events closely and I would make notes as the exercise progressed. Once the task had been set it was common for everyone to crowd round and for lots of views to be expressed.

For the weaker members this could be intimidating and some-times a squad mate would start to become the de-facto leader. It was always fascinating to see these incidents unfold. If there was a lot of dithering at the beginning it would eat into their allotted time and I would shout out 'thirty minutes to go' or whatever time to put pressure on the leader. If they could not find, or did not reach the target point in time it would be recorded as a failure. Once the time got down to the last fifteen minutes or so the leader would often try to get everyone to break into a jog which on hilly terrain when they were carrying packs was not easy. This would also stress the squad and the less fit would get upset at the lack of direction. At the end of the exercise I would debrief the team and point out the strengths and weaknesses of the leadership. The other squad members were also invited to air their views too which was often enlightening.

We would have rudimentary accommodation arranged in the form of some military-style Nissen huts with dorms and bunk beds; we usually stayed for one night and would be taken back to PTS by police trucks or buses the next afternoon. When we were staying overnight, the PTS commandant would sometimes fly in by helicopter to check out how we were managing. My fellow squad instructor Cheung, who later became an assistant commissioner, and I would escort him to the accommodation block to review the squad's performance. One day, I was standing watching the helicopter descend slowly onto the 'H' that marked the landing area. The draught from the rotor blades became so strong it blew my police beret off my head and it flew off like a Frisbee into a bush on a nearby hillside. Of course my fellow instructor Cheung thought this was hilarious. As the commandant marched stiffly towards us, Cheung saluted smartly with beret firmly attached. Whereas I was red-faced, and feebly explaining 'Sir, sorry I cannot salute you, my beret has flown off.' It was now half way up a hillside resting nicely on a thorn bush. Fortunately the commandant saw the funny side of this as I scrambled up the hillside to recover it.

In the first squad I led, we had a young man named Mak who was struggling in a few areas. If a probationary inspector failed any aspect of training, be it written exams, fitness, drill, musketry, or leadership they would be given an initial written warning. Then a second warning and then if it happened a third time they would be removed from training. Sometimes it was something more serious and they would have to be removed from training with immediate effect. One morning when all the squad were on roll call and on the parade square in gym kit, there was no sign of Mak and no one had seen him at breakfast. After the squad leader had led the squad off the parade I went in search of Mak. I took one of the drill instructors with me and went into the male accommodation block.

There we found Mak in an unfortunate state. He was in his PE kit, curled up on his bed in a foetal position sucking his thumb and mumbling to himself. The poor chap had suffered a nervous breakdown. We called for medical attention and he was quietly withdrawn from training. It was a very sad situation. A couple of years later when I was not on staff any more I was asked to go back to PTS to assist with recruit assessments during an extended interview process. To my surprise I saw Mak; he was going through the recruitment process again from the beginning. I had a quiet word with the person in charge of selection about his possible mental frailty.

During my time in Hong Kong I was able to meet a number of well-known people, some by invitation, and some by simply recognising people on the street. One day I was reading the *South China Morning Post* in the mess and saw a small advert saying that Michael Palin from *Monty Python* fame would be signing books in the bookshop next to the Star Ferry in Central District. I was quite excited on reading this and that afternoon on leaving PTS I went over to the bookshop expecting to join a long queue and get my book signed. To my surprise there was hardly anyone around. I walked in and saw Michael sitting down next to a table staring into space and smiling amiably to himself. There were maybe two or three people in the bookshop and none of them seemed to know who he was. This was before he appeared in *A Fish Called Wanda* and his many BBC travel documentaries.

So I went over and we had a very pleasant conversation. I then bought a book about the British film industry in which he wrote quite a long acknowledgement with thanks for supporting the industry 'which needs all the money it can get'. Michael became a regular visitor to Hong Kong after that, during his various travel programmes, but sadly I never met him again. The other person I got to know quite well was Sir David Tang, of Shanghai Tang fame. I met him when he was married to his first wife and simply called 'David'. We were staying at the same resort in the Philippines. He was a keen photographer and when we had all got back to Hong Kong, he rang me and we had *yum cha* together in Central District. He handed me some of the photos he'd taken. He was very keen on photography and had a good eye for a picture. After that he invited me to his house in Sai Kung where I enjoyed lunch sitting next to the late Alan Whicker of *Whicker's World* on ITV. David was an entertaining raconteur who claimed to have signed an exclusive deal with Fidel Castro to have the sole agency for importing Cuban cigars, and then opened his own cigar shop in the Mandarin Hotel. He was rarely seen without an expensive Cuban cigar himself. David seemed to know everyone, and was probably the most amazing networker I ever met.

When off duty from my instructor role at PTS I would still try to socialise with friends outside the force. One of my good friends was Damian who was the food and beverage manager at the Park Lane Hotel in Causeway Bay. Sometimes on my way home I would call in at the Park Lane for refreshments during happy hour. I was taking the MTR early one evening when I saw an elderly Chinese lady. She was quite small and slightly stooped, with grey hair in a bun and was wearing a black jacket and wide traditional dark trousers with cotton slippers. What caught my attention was that she was carrying a white stick and was tapping the floor amongst the huge throng of commuters. She seemed quite lost and no one was stopping to help. I was looking at her and thinking, this is maybe where I need to do my 'Good Samaritan' bit so I went over to her and spoke to her in Cantonese.

She replied quickly, but I really couldn't catch what she said. It was very noisy amongst the massive crowds. The Causeway Bay MTR station is an interchange and there are several levels of platforms. Even for a normal-sighted, able-bodied person it's a challenge. So whilst I continued to talk to her in Cantonese telling her: 'It's okay, I will help you,' I gently led her by the arm onto the escalator. Up we went climbing the huge escalators, and all the time I was trying to comfort her while we moved. Fortunately she could not see the suspicious looks I was getting from the commuters on the opposite escalator. At the top of the escalator we had to move around another level, and because she moved so slowly it was a long process.

Gradually we made our way around, and up onto yet another escalator. These escalators were quite long but eventually we made it to the top and through the barriers and out into the street. Phew, I was relieved. I said to the old lady: 'It's okay. Now we are safely out of the MTR, near Hennessy Road.' She suddenly began shouting and beating me over the head with her white stick. I was shocked, what had happened? I cowered and tried to avoid the blows and at that moment a young Hong Kong man came over who evidently understood the old lady's dialect. He turned to me and said in excellent English: 'She says she was only trying to get onto the opposite platform.' My embarrassment was complete. I had taken her all the way up two escalators for nothing. I turned, and headed off quickly to the Park Lane Hotel for a stiff drink. I felt like Inspector Clouseau from the *Pink Panther* movies.

When the first mobile phones were introduced in Hong Kong they were the size and weight of a house brick and cost over HK$20,000 each. They were a status symbol and paraded like a Rolex watch. By the time I got one, the prices had come down significantly and Nokia was the popular make. One night mine slipped off my belt when I was travelling in a taxi. I only found out when I was back in Discovery Bay on Lantau. So I walked into a 7-Eleven convenience store near the bus station, and rang my number from a pay phone to see if anyone had picked it up. A foreign female voice answered. She sounded pleased when she heard my English accent. She sounded quite sexy and told me her name was Anya and it was okay, my phone was safe and she would return it to me. We agreed to meet the next day in a restaurant in the Sheraton Hotel called 'Someplace Else'. The next day I made my way to Tsim Sha Tsui and looked out for the mysterious Anya. After about fifteen minutes in she walked. She was about twenty-four years old, five feet five inches tall, slim, with long red hair and was wearing a smart charcoal grey trouser suit. She was immaculately turned out and looked like a successful businesswoman.

She sat down and I ordered drinks. She immediately took my phone out and handed it to me without saying anything. Naturally I was very grateful and I suggested I buy her lunch as a 'thank you'. She ordered a salad and a fruit juice; I had a burger and a beer. Anya was quite curious about me as I was about her. The ensuing conversation was very strange. When I told her I was a police officer, she seemed intrigued and looked at me with a faint smile. Anya told me she was Russian. She asked if I was married, I told her I was, and again she looked pleased. I was interested to hear that she was Russian, as at the time there were very few Russian people living in Hong Kong. Naturally I asked what she was doing in the colony and she calmly replied that she was an escort and was living in Whampoa Gardens near Hung Hom.

She looked at me the whole time possibly to gauge my reaction, so I tried to keep my face as blank as possible. She added that she had a number of regular clients, and by her appearance I would guess they paid well. I couldn't understand how she had entered Hong Kong as I knew it was very difficult for Russians to get visas. So I asked her how she had obtained a work visa. 'Simple,' she replied, 'I have come in using a forged Swedish passport.' She explained that the Hong Kong immigration officers did not speak Swedish and did not see many Swedish passports so it was quite easy. I realised that here I faced a conundrum. I was sitting and talking to a charming young woman who had just kindly handed me my mobile phone, but then confessed to an offence. After lunch, she asked me if I would accompany her to the California fitness club. We walked there and outside the club we said our goodbyes. I walked back to the Star Ferry and then caught a ferry back to Discovery Bay. I never saw her again and I never resolved the moral dilemma.

Since the Hong Kong Police had achieved 'Royal' status, Princess Alexandra had been our commandant general. The princess was a great supporter of the force and a regular visitor. In the months leading up to the Handover one final visit was arranged for her so she could say her farewell; it was a very emotional affair. As part of this last tour of the colony a visit to PTS was included on her itinerary. I was into my second training squad and was the intake director. I was also on the officers' mess committee and in particular I was responsible for the wine and other mess beverages. This meant I had to arrange the ordering of beers, wines and spirits and ensure we had sufficient stock, and that everything was priced correctly. The princess and her entourage including her husband Sir Angus Ogilvy arrived by helicopter and landed on the cricket pitch.

I was stationed in the mess as part of the welcoming committee. We had arranged a formal lunch and I had personally ordered a very nice Chablis for the fish course. As part of the arrangements, private lavatories were prepared for the princess and they were closed off and guarded to avoid any smelly accidents before her arrival. Immediately on entering the mess Sir Angus was looking around to see where the loo was. I happened to be standing in the right place and was able to talk to the princess. Princess Alexandra was radiant and very gracious; she asked me about 1997 and my intentions after the Handover. Meanwhile an official photographer was on hand to record the moment of our conversation. In the back of the photo you can see Sir Angus desperately looking around for the gents.

The lunch went well and thankfully all the speeches were short and reasonably sweet. I was sitting next to the princess's lady in waiting, Lady Mary. Lady Mary was very attractive and had similar features to Princess Diana. As the lunch progressed I noticed that Lady Mary was not drinking the expensive Chablis I had ordered. I pretended to be upset and told her that I would 'lose face' if she did not have a glass. Lady Mary had a good sense of humour and sportingly drank her wine followed by another glass. As things loosened up she asked: 'Simon, where in Hong Kong is a good place to go shopping?' I replied that I liked Pacific Place near Admiralty as they had many high-end designer brands there such as Chanel, and Louis Vuitton, etc. Lady Mary looked at me and said, 'Do you mean the original genuine brands?' I replied: 'Oh yes Lady Mary, they are all certainly genuine, the real thing.' Lady Mary then said: 'Oh no, I don't want that; I want the other stuff.' I tried to stifle my surprise and then rather sheepishly said that Ladies' Market in Kowloon was possibly a good place. I later heard from their bodyguard, that the next day they all headed out for Stanley Market.

Before the Handover the last British expats passed out from PTS. I was there to witness the event. It was all rather low key. Everyone knew this was the last ever batch of British inspectors. But although it was mentioned in the speeches there was no fanfare. For those like me it was more poignant. The Brits understood the significance and it reminded us yet again that the day of the Handover was looming. We tried to forget this, hoping that as long as the Union flag still flew from government buildings, and the Queen's portrait looked down on us from the walls of the mess, everything was alright with the world.

CHAPTER XXXIX

The Marine Police

L ATE IN MY CAREER I was posted to Marine, the place where I had initially wanted to go as a junior inspector. This meant during my career, I had served in Kowloon in uniform and CID, and New Territories in uniform. I had also served Marine in uniform, and enjoyed plainclothes staff and CID postings in Police HQ on Hong Kong Island. My posting to Marine was largely desk bound but I was still able to go out on the Marine launches and was able to enjoy the excellent hospitality in the renowned officers' mess. Unfortunately this was in the new premises on Hong Kong Island at Sai Wan Ho, and not the beautiful old colonial building in Tsim Sha Tsui which later became part of a shopping centre. I also became a commissioner for oaths which was a great honour, although I had no idea what it meant. I don't recall uttering any oaths at this time but I did swear a lot. But it was nice to know that if someone fancied making a deposition that I could hear the oath if I wanted to.

The culture in Marine was different from the rest of the force. It was slightly more laid-back. It was not regarded as a great place to be if you yearned for rapid promotion, but this changed somewhat as the force developed. The Marine Region had a massive fleet of launches of various descriptions which before 1997 was backed up by the Royal Navy. Altogether around 3,000 officers of all ranks served in the Marine Police. They policed over 260 islands, from more than 140 vessels. My first regional commander was Assistant Commissioner Spencer Foo, who was later replaced by Cheung Chi-sum. Both of these senior officers had their own leadership styles, but I got on well with both of them and appreciated their guidance and mentoring. I also remembered Spencer Foo appeared as a young inspector in the BBC *Hong Kong Beat* programme in 1977.

The two biggest challenges facing the Marine Police were illegal immigration from China and Vietnam, and smuggling of goods between Hong Kong and China. I have mentioned the issue with the bodies washed up in remote coves. The bodies were a nasty problem for the Marine launch commanders. To haul a black, bloated, decomposed body onto a launch was not easy. Even if the body was caught it might disintegrate and fall apart. Some of the bodies were caught in nets and towed behind the launch. If a body was found it would be necessary to get back to port as early as possible. There were stories of launch patrols turning a blind eye to dead bodies in the water because they were so common, and it took so much time out from a patrol's schedule.

Smugglers realised that by fitting a 40hp engine to the back of a small, flat *sampan* they could zip along the water at high speed. They would have a very low profile so were undetectable by radar. Painted black and with no lights, they were almost invisible, even to night-vision goggles. Sometimes the *sampan*s were used to carry illegals, in particular those of higher value who could pay a premium, such as girls working in the sex industry.

Things became more serious in the late eighties and early nineties when smugglers started building powerboats in southern China. The snakeheads and smuggling bosses copied the designs of racing offshore powerboat hulls. Speedboats were made from moulds using dark-grey fibreglass. These were about twenty feet long and designed to be as light and simple as possible. There was a small open cockpit near the bow big enough for two or three crew. This would have only a steering wheel and throttle, there would be no lights or safety equipment. At the stern there was a large empty space. These vessels had only one purpose, the smuggling of luxury cars from Hong Kong to China. These were the *dai fei*s, literally 'big-fast'. These illegal high-speed powerboats would be the scourge of the Marine Police for years.

The scenes that faced the police in those early years were like something from a Hollywood movie. It was *Gone in 60 Seconds* in real life but on water. The organisation and coordination of the criminal gangs was spectacular. Rich businessmen in China wanted the latest luxury cars, but due to import restrictions, obtaining one was almost impossible. To meet that demand, the criminals stepped in. Cars were stolen to order. The most requested models were the Mercedes S-Class and the Lexus 400 series. The *dai fei*s had been designed exactly to fit the luxury car size specifications.

So when an S-Class Mercedes was placed in the back of a *dai fei* there would be only a few centimetres gap to the side and the front and back. Once an order had been placed for a specific model and colour a crack car thief would be tasked to go out and steal the exact model requested. This was a skilled job because the thief had not only to break into the car, but to defeat the built-in alarms and security devices. After that, once he was in the car the objective was to drive as quickly as possible to a designated location. From the beginning, the gangs used mobile phones to communicate, even when the old brick-sized phones cost HK$20,000 each from Hutchison. The gang would select a small quiet cove which would have a suitable slipway. The car would be driven, whilst keeping in constant contact with the pilot of the *dai fei* to coordinate their respective arrival times. Neither group wanted to hang around.

The *dai fei*s were usually powered by four in-line 200hp engines giving a total power output about the same as a Formula 1 car. They could scream across Mirs Bay from China in thirty minutes or less at speeds of fifty knots or more. It must have been exciting but was very dangerous as there were many hidden dangers and a lot of floating debris in the water. Once they had reached the designated cove they would reverse into the slipway. The stern of the boat was fitted with a hinged ramp. When lowered, it was a simple matter to drive the stolen vehicle straight up and onto the back of the *dai fei*. It was strapped in, the ramp raised, the engines engaged and they were off again screaming across the bay. In slightly longer than one hour the whole venture could be completed and the new car could be driven up the streets of Guangzhou to its proud new owner.

The sale price for each car was about HK$120,000, much less than it would cost in China considering the punitive import duty, certainly a very tasty profit for one hour's work for the smugglers. The work was extremely risky but the adrenalin rush for the young guys in the gangs must have been like a narcotic. In the early days of this criminal scheme there was not much the Hong Kong Police could do. We had rather slow, heavy-duty launches that if pushed might struggle up to twenty knots, and semi inflatable 'rigid raiders' which were usually launched off the backs of the larger vessels. The rigid raiders had powerful outboards and were manoeuvrable but they could only reach speeds of about forty knots. The guys in the *dai fei*s knew they could easily outrun them.

Before 1997 we had the backup of the Royal Navy. They deployed helicopters which could keep up with the powerboats, and had an incredibly powerful searchlight called 'night-sun' that illuminated the smugglers and might distract them into making mistakes. Some of the Royal Navy chaps were very brave. They would swing down on rope ladders from the choppers and drop smoke bombs or other devices to try to stop the criminals. In some cases the Navy guys actually rappelled down into the fleeing boats travelling in excess of fifty knots and then tried to overpower the smugglers. After one navy guy smashed his leg, they were ordered not to try to board the *dai fei*s when they were in motion.

Those of us in the police knew about some of the tactics used by our Royal Navy counterparts, but they never got out into the press. They had our admiration for their bravery in trying to tackle these gangs. Gradually the coordination between the police on land, the Marine Police, and the Royal Navy improved, and various ambushes were laid. This resulted in a couple of the criminals' *dai fei*s getting seized. We later had permission to appropriate these for ourselves. This seemed to be the most practical solution although they were not particularly safe. But after a re-fit and the installation of basic safety equipment and navigational lights they were given the okay to be used by our colleagues. So we put five in-line Mercury engines on the back and turned the boats back against the smugglers. There was no shortage of volunteers among our guys to being paid a salary to drive fast powerboats around Hong Kong waters. But because of the nature of the work, it was mainly the younger and fitter guys that were deployed on these boats.

The odds were still in the smugglers' favour and even after using *dai fei*s ourselves the chances of apprehension were small. However, cars in Hong Kong are right-hand drive as we drive on the left, and cars in Mainland China are left-hand drive. So even after re-registering the cars in China, it was obvious that they had not been imported legally. Some of the new owners did convert the cars to left-hand drive but many didn't bother. Liaison between Hong Kong and China started to grow as 1997 loomed closer. The issue of theft of luxury cars was raised with the Chinese government. Some prominent Hong Kong businessmen with good connections who had had their cars stolen complained to their Mainland friends. Gradually the Chinese government started to acknowledge the problem.

In 1993, over 1,000 Mercedes cars were reported stolen. If the gangs were getting HK$120,000 per car sold in China, then the annual income of HK$120 million was a decent return, and that was only Mercedes. The Hong Kong Police were also embarrassed by the inability to prevent such thefts and realised that after 1997 the Royal Navy support would be lost too. Approval was given for some new vessels to be purchased to counter the threat. After significant research the boat that was purchased was the Cougar Tek Sea Stalker 1500 Interceptor. This was a beast of a powerboat. It was similar in dimensions to the *dai fei*s and was built from aluminium and specifically ordered to counter or exceed the criminals' capabilities. They were powered by three 500hp engines. The boat was light and streamlined, and had no seats. The pilot and crew all stood up or leaned against a small padded backrest. They wore small light buoyancy vests and held on tight. Holding on tight was necessary as these ultra-high-speed vessels could reach seventy knots. At last we had something that could outrun the *dai fei*s.

I went out a few times on the Cougar Teks. It was always a thrill ride. I was told to keep my knees and arms bent and clench my teeth. This was to stop me biting my tongue. I heard that when they were first tested in Hong Kong waters one chap did not bend his legs, the boat hit a wave at high speed and his shin bone shattered. The first time I went out a typhoon was nearing Hong Kong. The No. 1 signal went up, and then as we were out on the water near the Lei Yue Mun channel the No. 3 signal was raised. The sky went black; the dark-grey waves seemed to grow. I stood with my teeth clenched, and looked straight ahead, whilst holding the padded handrail in front of me tightly. We were hitting the tops of the giant waves, then falling down between the troughs. We had a skilled pilot but whatever he did was not going to help much. Every time we went over the top of a wave there was a strange quiet for maybe one second. As we flew over the top of a wave I looked down into the hole and tried to estimate the time before we bottomed out. When we hit the bottom of the next incoming wave it seemed I had jumped two or three floors down into a lift shaft. Thump, we hit the next wave, thump, again. I wondered if my knees would survive. This was not as much fun as I'd expected. Then the rain started coming down. We were still travelling at high speed in spite of the conditions and the rain was hitting me straight in the face, it felt like glass splinters stinging my eyes. I was relieved when we turned around and returned to our base at Sai Wan Ho.

Our new boats started having an effect. As our tactics and equipment improved so the numbers of *dai fei* sightings started to reduce. Two other changes helped reduce this type of smuggling. Firstly the Chinese government made it illegal to drive right-hand drive cars on the Mainland, and secondly a number of foreign manufacturers started to produce cars in China. On my final trip out on a Cougar Tek a group of us decided to dine out our leader Spencer Foo. We heard he was transferring to a land region. We decided to go to a small island south of Stanley and Hong Kong Island. Po Toi is a very pretty little island and very famous for its seafood. There is a ferry on Sundays from Stanley, but most people go there by private boat.

It can get quite busy at weekends but is almost deserted during the week. We took two Cougar Teks on a marine patrol which culminated in a seafood farewell lunch for our regional commander. We had the restaurant to ourselves and the food was fantastic. Plates of steamed fish and prawns and fried squid arrived which we all scoffed greedily. One amusing incident occurred when we found an old well in the village and decided to look down to see if it had water. Dom, one of our British police colleagues, forgot he had his personal mobile phone in the open pocket of his tunic. As he bent over, his phone dropped out and fell straight into the well. We all waited for the 'plop' when it hit the water. It was quite a few seconds, and the phone was never recovered. He was not amused, it was an expensive phone.

One chap took a small Sony Handycam video camera with him and filmed the return trip on the Cougar Teks. I have a copy of the video and it's still amazing to see the power and speed of these boats.

In the Marine Police we also had to patrol a large number of outlying islands like Po Toi. This was usually quite pleasant as the air was fresher, the countryside prettier, and there was not much crime. Often the policing was more related to community relations. Many people don't realise that there are over 260 islands in Hong Kong, although the vast majority of these are tiny, uninhabited outcrops. Apart from Hong Kong Island itself, the main inhabited islands are Lantau, Peng Chau, Lamma, and Cheung Chau. For the police patrolling these islands on foot it seemed like an idyllic environment. But there was one place with a darker side. Cheung Chau to the west of Hong Kong is famous for its Bun Festival. This is a very colourful event with paper effigies, bamboo towers, young girls dressed in traditional costumes and of course the baking of thousands of white buns. Cheung Chau is listed by the official tourist agency as 'packing a powerful punch when it comes to the good times'. But for many people over the last fifteen years it has also provided the last time to be alive.

There are many holiday villas on the island. These can be rented out by the day and became very popular with young lovers. Many young couples still head over on the ferry on weekends to get away from their families. They can relax, play music, have a barbecue on the beach and spend the night together in a private room. But the island's villas have become infamous. Some people say it started in the Bela Vista villas in 1989. A mother dressed herself in traditional red robes, she stabbed her young son to death, and then hanged herself. After this it seemed that suicides on Cheung Chau became more common. Most of them use the same method: 'death by charcoal'. People intending to kill themselves will take masking tape, and seal all the windows and doors to make the room as airtight as possible. Then they will take a large wok and put it in the middle of the room. Charcoal is then burnt in the wok. This is the same charcoal used in the barbecues so it is easy to buy. As the concentration of carbon monoxide rises everyone in the room falls unconscious and then dies.

For the Marine Police this would be horrible work. To discover a young person or couple lying on a bed, or in a bath, dead, but seemingly asleep was harrowing. Once this suicide method was reported in the press it quickly became the most common method of suicide in Hong Kong, and Cheung Chau became one of the preferred locations. By 2001, 25 per cent of all suicides were from burning charcoal. It was believed this method was fairly painless, which could not be said about the other popular method which involved jumping from the top of a high building. Cheung Chau's Bela Vista Villa has become notorious as it believed that up to twenty people may have committed suicide there over the last fifteen years. Some young people now go there as a dare, as it's widely believed to be haunted. As recently as 2012 a young couple who were having an affair committed suicide in the Bela Vista by this method and were found dead the next day lying together in the bathtub. Cheung Chau is now often known as 'Suicide Island' or 'Death Island'.

As for the Marine Police they continue onwards and upwards, and are now very well equipped. The chaps carry Heckler & Koch MP5 machine guns, and Glock 17 automatic pistols. The Finance Department approved the replacement of the Cougar Teks with five brand-new improved ones at a cost of HK$150 million so we can expect to see them around Hong Kong waters for a few more years. I really enjoyed the camaraderie in the Marine Region. I was properly dined out when I left and very kindly awarded a very nice engraved plaque which is now on my office wall.

CHAPTER XL

Countdown to the Handover

As 1997 APPROACHED THE MAIN topic of conversation amongst the expat police was: 'Should I stay or should I go?' It reminded me of the song by the same name, sung by the Clash in 1982. Although I'm not sure that trouble would be doubled if we stayed. Every phone call, every chance meeting in a corridor, every chat over a beer in the mess seemed to be about 1997. I became a bit bored with it. I was still really enjoying my job. I had bought a small flat using the housing scheme. I was happily married, and I had a young daughter called Isabella. I was still fairly young, but I hadn't really considered the next step. I was still content in Hong Kong.

I had made some commitments to the place. I had gone onto the 'permanent and pensionable' establishment and I was quite settled and enjoying life. Some of my colleagues decided to leave and start a life overseas. Quite a number of people left for Canada, especially Vancouver. Many Hong Kong Chinese had also emigrated there because of fears of what would happen after 1997. They were also attracted by the Canadian government's tax advantages for qualified talent from the colony. I knew people who left with no jobs to go to. I knew of others who decided to leave because their friends were leaving. I thought this was very silly.

There was a lot of stupid jingoism as well. I heard some older expats saying they weren't staying because they made an oath to serve the Queen, and weren't going to work for the communists. I felt this was a load of rubbish. The ones saying this were mostly the older chaps who had pensions, loads of money in the bank, and no kids. It was easy for them to go; they didn't have to work for the rest of their lives. Some people did very well out of the Handover financially. I know of one British chap called Mike who I was quite friendly with. He had shared the Dragon Boat Mark Six jackpot at PHQ, he had invested in properties, and he had gone onto pension terms. He was able to take all the tax-free government compensation. He was not yet forty years old yet walked away in 1997 with around HK$12 million in his pocket.

But there were others not so fortunate. Many expats had stayed on gratuity contract terms. This was very tempting because every two or three years they received a lump-sum cash payment. They also stayed in large government quarters because they were comfortable, cheap and convenient. The problem was though, what were you left with when you reached fifty-five, the statutory retirement age? You would have needed to invest the gratuities very well indeed to provide a decent pension and you had to find somewhere to live after leaving your luxury government flat. In his book *Hong Kong Noir,* Feng Chi-shun relates the tale of 'Clive' a British officer in the ICAC who did not take up pensionable terms. When he retired he had less than HK$2 million in his bank account. That might sound a lot to some people but it's not if you need to buy a house and live off the remainder. However, he frittered this money away in a failed business venture in Australia and then returned to Hong Kong to look for a job. He failed to find anything and descended into alcoholism and an early death in Chungking Mansions. In the UK I was told by a person from the Royal Hong Kong Police Association that there were a number of similar cases in Britain where former expatriate police officers were in serious financial difficulties.

The Hong Kong government had been busy identifying local officers to be fast-tracked for promotion. The police personnel department did an excellent job of forward planning to ensure that the force would be in good shape when there was the inevitable exodus of expat officers. There is no doubt that for a local police inspector or superintendent the lead up to 1997 were good years for promotion. The position of the force was understandable. No one wanted the force to be left with a vacuum in the senior ranks. Naturally some expats resented this and moaned when younger local officers gained promotion. I took a more sanguine position, I thought it was necessary. For many years we had already had a local police commissioner. In fact the last British police commissioner was Raymond Anning who had retired in 1989. He was succeeded by Li Kwan-ha.

I had worked with Li Kwan-ha when I had been a young inspector and he was an assistant commissioner in PHQ. I liked him, and I was happy when he was promoted as the first local commissioner. Li had a hobby: he liked to collect antique jade. He would often be seen walking around the office rubbing a piece between his finger and thumb. I had asked him once about a piece of white jade he was holding. He told me it was from a broken sword scabbard dating to the Ming dynasty. When I was a young inspector I had been caught in the office in PHQ when a powerful typhoon hit. We were told to stay behind because the No. 8 signal had been raised. But I was bored and keen to go home; there was nothing to do. I cheekily asked him if my colleague and I could leave. He initially said: 'No,' and walked off. After an hour he was walking around the office and I asked again. The second time, with a glint in his eye, he said: 'Okay PUFO.' I was a bit bemused, so I asked what he meant by 'PUFO'. He said with a small smile: 'Pack up and fuck off.' I grabbed my coat and hurried out the door. Li served as commissioner for five years, until 1994.

I don't think people really thought about 1997 much until Margaret Thatcher visited China in 1982 to meet Deng Xiaoping. Certainly I had not considered the 1997 issue at all when I joined the police force. But Mrs Thatcher's visit put the issue in the international media spotlight. By all accounts the meeting did not go well. Mrs Thatcher thought that perhaps the colonial administration could be extended and somehow there might be some kind of power-sharing arrangement. Those present claim that Deng did not take this idea well, and became quite angry. How much of what he actually said was translated to English during the meeting is subject to conjecture. Reports later said the translator had omitted the swear words. Deng's views were that the treaties were unequal and unjust, but at least they had stuck by them. Deng told her China would take over on the 1st of July 1997, and that was that. Mrs Thatcher famously tripped on the steps of the Great Hall of the People in Beijing when leaving a meeting. This was viewed as an ominous omen. For a short while people discussed this and thought of the future, but not for too long. Even though a poll had shown 85 per cent of the population wanted to stay as a British colony, nothing would alter the course of history and everyone simply went back to work.

To be fair to the Chinese government they stuck to the treaty. Historically they have a good record in abiding by treaties. There were many occasions that they could have easily taken Hong Kong by force. The Japanese invasion during the Second World War had shown that Hong Kong was almost indefensible. By the 1990s China was also becoming a formidable military power. As the Hong Kong population grew the demand for water grew too. Although a number of reservoirs had been constructed they could not meet the entire demand. Hong Kong began to rely more and more on importing water through giant pipelines from China. Even during the serious troubles in 1967 the water supply was never turned off although this could have brought Hong Kong to its knees quite rapidly.

So negotiations began and the proposals for the new administration were created. The concepts of 'one country-two systems', a Special Administrative Region (SAR) and 'no change for fifty years' were coined. Meanwhile the best description of the British administration I heard was that it was a 'benevolent autocracy'. Both sides knew the huge economic importance of Hong Kong now that it had become such a financial powerhouse. Chris Patten compared the Handover to 'gifting Cleopatra's dowry'. In the police, the expats were all concerned about compensation and protection of their pension benefits. I had gone onto pensionable terms in the 1980s and had enrolled as a member of Her Majesty's Overseas Civil Service. I had received my confirmation in a letter from the Government Secretariat in October 1985. Attached to the letter was a copy of the Special Regulations by the Secretary of State for the Colonies. It claimed that appointments to membership of 'Her

Majesty's Overseas Civil Service' shall be held during Her Majesty's pleasure. I was pleased to know that I had given Her Majesty some pleasure.

Once I was accepted into the HMOCS, I also joined SPOS. There were so many acronyms to remember. This stood for 'Supplementary Pension for Overseas Service'. It was a kind of pension guarantee from the UK government. Joining HMOCS and SPOS was voluntary but it was also free. It was beyond me why anyone would not join. From about 1992 onwards the various staff associations lobbied the British government for compensation for loss of sovereignty protection and for protection of pension benefits. I have kept some of the letters and correspondence concerning these negotiations, some dating back over twenty years. It's quite interesting reading them now.

Before the Handover, Steve Wordsworth was a chief inspector and the chairman of the Expatriate Inspectors' Association. Steve worked very hard for the association and its members and lobbied hard for full benefits for us all. He and the association encouraged us to write letters to the government to protest and complain and most of us did. I think the Overseas Development Administration must have become rather fed up with us. Some of the earlier offers by the British government for deferred payments and with various complex calculations were rejected. As there had been precedents set with other colonial administrations, the British government knew that it should not provide any less compensation in this case. In the end, due to the excellent efforts of Steve and the other associations, the British expats on pension did receive a one-off tax-free lump sum. My letter shows mine was paid just one week before the Handover in June 1997.

Chris Patten had been appointed as the last governor of Hong Kong; it was quite an honour for him. I'm not sure the Hong Kong people knew what to think about Mr Patten. As an ex-politician he liked to be seen as a man of the people. He enjoyed being casually dressed and walking around markets eating egg tarts. It sometimes seemed though that the local press were more interested in Patten's three pretty young daughters. The sisters, Laura, Kate and Alice were all in their early teens when they arrived in Hong Kong, and to some extent they matured into young ladies whilst living in the rather luxurious confines of Government House. The three young women were always in the spotlight, and the media were particularly taken with the youngest daughter Alice, who was also considered the prettiest.

I had an Asian colleague called Raj who worked part-time as a tennis coach. He was hired to teach tennis to the three sisters. I don't think he could believe his luck. He was playing tennis with the Patten girls at Government House and getting paid. He seemed to have a permanent grin on his face. Chris Patten did not endear himself to the Mainland Chinese government however. In 1994 he decided to change the voting rights to the functional constituencies to allow a wider public democracy. Whilst the pro-democracy lobbyists in Hong Kong loved him, he was violently rebuked by the Mainland. They called him names like 'serpent', 'whore of the East' and 'a wrongdoer who would be condemned for a thousand generations'. And those were some of the kinder attacks. Although I admired what he was doing, I also felt some sympathy for the Chinese position. The colonial administration had not provided any democracy of note in the last 150 years. But here we were three years before the Handover saying, what you need is democracy. I felt it was shifting like the goalposts after the match had already started.

Sir Percy Cradock, a career diplomat, who had sat through ten years of negotiations with China regarding the tricky 1997 question, was very upset by Patten's proposals. He had the support of many senior civil servants in London who questioned the benefit of such changes so late in the process. It was widely felt that Patten was being a populist and not considering the long-term implications. China was an emerging superpower that was opening its doors and would become an important trading partner. What was the benefit for the UK from upsetting China now? As someone who had lived in Hong Kong for over sixteen years my views were closer to Sir Percy's. I felt Patten was just trying to bolster his standing with the Hong Kong people. But he was no longer standing for election. He was never going to get another term.

One thing Patten tried to do was modernise the Civil Service and introduce concepts like service quality, transparency and accountability. In particular he wanted departments to adopt service quality, and measure customer satisfaction. He told all departments that they must introduce ways to collect data from the public on their satisfaction with the service they received. A few months later I had to see a government dentist on Hong Kong Island. I was having a new crown fitted and was very grateful for the benefits I received for being in a government department myself. The dentist was excellent and the crown he fitted is still working today. As I left the dentist's surgery and went back into the waiting area the young female receptionist handed me a form. I looked at it; it was one of the new customer satisfaction forms. The options for my opinion of the dental service were; a) very satisfied b) satisfied c) fairly satisfied. So the worst possible feedback anyone could provide was that they were 'fairly satisfied'. In spite of my painful mouth I couldn't help smiling. I don't think it was what Chris Patten had in mind.

In the months before the Handover I received a phone call from the UK Conservative Party in Hong Kong. They were holding a cocktail party in the prestigious Hong Kong Club in Central and wanted me to invite Sir David Tang to attend as a special guest. The VIP guest of honour was Sir Edward Heath. Sir Edward had been the prime minister from 1965 to 1970, and by 1997 he was already eighty-one years old. I called David and asked if he could attend. To my surprise, David said he couldn't because he was meeting a 'VVIP' that evening, he was terribly sorry. I was quite surprised to hear this; I wondered who could be more important than Sir Edward Heath in Hong Kong? My wife and I still attended the cocktail party and enjoyed a wonderful evening. Ted Heath was still the consummate politician and mixed with, and spoke to absolutely everyone.

As he walked around I noticed a very smart white-gloved waiter following him. This waiter carried a silver tray with a bottle of Macallan twelve-year-old single malt, a silver ice bucket and a cut-glass whisky tumbler. His only job that night was to keep Mr Heath's glass filled. I had watched as the new bottle had been opened, and I watched as the contents were consumed. By the end of the evening the bottle was almost empty yet Sir Edward was still very lucid and made a short off-the-cuff speech about his views on the future of Hong Kong. The next day I was still wondering about who the top-secret person David had met was. He confided later that it was Princess Diana. He had gone to Kai Tak Airport to the VIP arrivals to pick her up and take her to Government House where they enjoyed dinner with Chris Patten and his wife. No cocktail party could have matched that.

The big news for me was that two weeks before the Handover I received a letter saying I had been promoted to a gazetted officer and could now wear a crown on my epaulette. I could now also now dine in the gazetted officers' mess; I was now a superintendent. I had never expected to amount to much, and certainly had never expected to become a police superintendent. Perhaps getting married and having children had made me more responsible. It made me think that I had done the right thing by deciding to stay on in the force. I was a gazetted officer for about twelve days before the colonial term was dropped and the term 'senior officer' replaced it. I believe I was one of the last British officers to be promoted before the Handover. Fortunately I was allowed to keep my crown, and other Royal Hong Kong Police badges including my cap badge. I still have them today.

The eve of the Handover arrived. During the day I tried to keep busy with a lot of menial little jobs to keep my mind off things. The weather was terrible; it started raining and just didn't stop. The Handover was officially at midnight on 30th June 1997, so that by one minute into the 1st of July sovereignty would have transferred to China. In the evening I went out with Elizabeth and some friends on Hong Kong Island. We all tried to pretend it was a normal night out but we couldn't. The rain continued and my mood was low. The world's media was focussed on Hong Kong. Every news station was in place with their satellites beaming live images around the world. On June 30th all the police stations had quietly removed all the portraits of the Queen that had been mounted on the walls of government buildings and our own officers' mess. The crockery that had the Royal badges was also placed in boxes. Many of the cups and plates were later sold to expat officers and I bought a set.

The British Union and Hong Kong Blue Ensign flags were taken down and removed and replaced with the red five-star flag of the PRC and the new Hong Kong bauhinia flag. Shortly after midnight, as I wasn't in the mood for partying, I took a taxi back to the ferry pier in Central. I boarded the Discovery Bay ferry from the old pier in Central district. I climbed the steps to the upper deck and went outside on the open deck at the stern. The rain was still lashing down. The sky was black, the clouds were low, and there were fire boats spraying water out of their hoses into the sky, as if we needed even more water. Many helicopters were hovering overhead, and there in front of me was the Royal Yacht *Britannia*. I could see Prince Charles, Chris Patten, and his family waving to the crowds from the deck to the crowds onshore. Slowly the *Britannia* pulled out from the dock and headed east towards the Lei Yue Mun channel. As it did so, the Discovery Bay ferry I was on also slowly pulled away heading in the opposite direction. It was as if the two vessels were synchronised. As I watched this, the enormity of the situation suddenly hit me. It was truly the end of an era: 150 years of British colonial rule was finished and was sailing away in front of me. I was overwhelmed by the finality of it all and I started to well up with tears. I stood alone on the outside upper deck leaning against the rail and cried.

CHAPTER XLI

Life after 1997

A FEW MINUTES AFTER the British Union flag was lowered, the People's Liberation Army rolled into Hong Kong in a convoy of armoured vehicles. Some later accounts claimed they had crossed before midnight. Well, no one was going to stop them. It was remarkably well choreographed. The move had not been publicised to avoid media attention. It might have come as a shock for those living in the New Territories who were still awake and out and about. I wonder if they did feel liberated. The PLA were an impressive sight. Hong Kong was a plum posting for them; these guys looked like the elite. They sat to attention, upright in their trucks holding their machine guns tightly to their chests as if to say: 'Don't even think about messing with us.' They moved quietly into the military bases that had been vacated by the British Army. There were not going to be any more fist fights between the army squaddies and the military police in Wan Chai. No more stupendous street battles with the US Navy. The PLA drove their trucks into the camps, closed the gates behind them and virtually disappeared. They were under strict orders, there would be no fraternising, and they were only in the SAR for national defence.

A week or so after the Handover I was on the twentieth floor of PHQ in Arsenal St. I was in an office overlooking Admiralty. I looked down and there was one of the smaller military bases the PLA had occupied. I saw the troops in the yard. A squad of them, stripped to the waist, practising *kung fu.* They were behind the locked gates and a high fence, hidden from street view. I watched them go through their moves which involved smashing pieces of wood with their fists and kicks. It was impressive.

After my promotion I was transferred back into CID. My new posting was superintendent crime in PHQ, working for Mike Dowie.

I was up on the twenty-fourth floor of the new Police HQ, I enjoyed it, and life was good. One morning my team came in for our regular morning briefing, usually referred to as 'morning prayers'. I told them we had a 'DF meeting'. They looked a bit surprised; I think they thought I was talking about departmental finance. I told them to follow me and led them down in the lift, out of the yard, and across the road into Délifrance café for coffee. It became a regular occurrence after that. If anyone asked where we were, we were 'in a DF meeting'. I wasn't in PHQ long before Mike came into my office one day and asked: 'How would you like to head up the Crime Prevention Bureau?' I hadn't even known there was a vacancy but it seemed the previous incumbent had left under a bit of a cloud. The CPB was located in an office building in Tsim Sha Tsui East. It was responsible for security company licensing, physical security advice, architectural design security, IT security, and promotional activities and public relations in schools and so on. It took me about three seconds to say: 'Yes please, sir.' The following Monday I was on my way to my new role and my new command. I had a large corner office overlooking the harbour and my own secretary and driver. I felt as if I'd arrived. It was probably the best posting in my career.

Because of some incidents that had occurred before my arrival I decided my new office needed to be given a *fung shui* inspection. *Fung shui* literally means 'wind and water', and is a mystical method of checking if places are auspicious or prone to bad luck. My local colleagues happily agreed to the suggestion. A qualified geomancer was located and I duly paid out a couple of thousand Hong Kong dollars from my own pocket. The result was I had to move my desk around, place a large green plant in a corner, and a world map on the wall behind me. Fortunately I avoided having to buy an expensive fish tank. Order was resumed and now hopefully my luck would remain.

In order to prepare me for my new responsibility, my boss Trevor Oakes kindly nominated me for a specialist crime prevention course. Police HQ agreed and so together with my colleague Adrian we headed over to Louisville University, Kentucky for a three-week course in crime prevention and physical security. We were the only two overseas students. Everyone else was from US law enforcement. We both enjoyed our time there except unfortunately it was in February and the weather was freezing. Our American colleagues were friendly and we enjoyed some great nights out in the Bluegrass Brewing Company, which was a micro-brewery with a bar. I found these beers much more palatable than the tasteless mass-produced stuff. What we found interesting was that the cops carried firearms even off duty. One day in the classroom one of the female cops was rummaging through her handbag looking for her lipstick when her 9mm automatic fell out onto the desk with a loud 'thud'. We both completed the course okay and have certificates to prove it. On the way back we even stopped by at the FBI in San Francisco, before catching a Cathay Pacific flight back to Hong Kong.

After Chris Patten, there were no more governors. The new position was 'chief executive'. The first CE of the Hong Kong Special Administrative Region was Tung Chee-hwa, a businessman selected by Beijing. He was seen as a safe pair of hands. In reality, he would not be able to make many decisions anyway. One thing he did decide was that he was not going to live in Government House. Apart from the colonial legacy, the house was seen as having bad *fung shui,* as the sharp pointed lines from the new Bank of China building were pointing directly at it, creating negative energy. We were used to having our leader living in Government House and all the security arrangements were designed around this provision. Tung had decided he was going to continue to live in his own apartment in Mid-Levels. To make the area more suitable for formal receptions he purchased the adjacent apartment and knocked down the dividing wall creating a sizeable living space.

I'd found out that some of the guys from the Security Branch were over in the newly renovated apartment to sort out the security details. There were all sorts of headaches with the CE sharing an apartment block with ordinary citizens. I heard that some of the other residents were unhappy with all the noise, and comings and goings which created quite a lot of disturbance for them. I decided to go over to take a look, so I took Inspector Tsang, one of my experienced inspectors, with me. We pulled up and parked in the visitors' car park. Tung's flat was on one of the lower floors, and as the lift doors opened the place was still busy with builders and Security Branch officials. I don't think they were very pleased to see me, they felt that the arrangements should be theirs alone. It didn't bother me; I walked in with Inspector Tsang and looked around.

Most of the physical security arrangements, such as alarms, cameras, and so on had already been decided. One of the Security Branch guys led me through the details. After he had finished his short briefing I realised that they had concentrated on the main doors and front windows. As I looked around I noticed that, like most luxury apartments in Hong Kong, Tung's had servants' quarters at the back. When I looked out of the maid's bedroom window I saw that there was a grassy slope leading up the back of the building. Next to the bedroom there was a drain pipe leading up past the window frame. As the apartment was only on the second floor it was an easy climb up the hill and the drain pipe and in through the window. There were no alarms, no cameras, no window bars. The rear of the apartment was completely unprotected.

I thought it was ironic that these guys had felt that the back of the apartment didn't matter because there would only be a Filipina sleeping there. I went back into the living room and told them that if I was a burglar or someone who wanted to kill Tung I could easily get in through the maid's room. They looked a bit shocked but I heard later that they took my advice and got it sorted. Inspector Tsang and I joked about it on our way back to the office.

All of the cap badges, badges of rank, and uniforms changed after 1997. The force did a good job of making the changes as subtle as possible. The new cap badge replaced the crown and the (alleged) opium clippers with a bauhinia and skyscrapers that from a distance looked very similar. The green uniforms and the Sam Browne belts were also quietly retired in favour of something more modern. The only criticism I heard was that the new baseball caps were a bit too casual-looking for a police force. I had my old Royal Hong Kong Police badges and after the Handover I was allowed to keep them. They are in a box in my garage. I keep saying one day I will take them out and display them. Apart from this the only other obvious change was the red bauhinia flag flying on government buildings. Wan Chai continued to provide nocturnal delights; Lan Kwai Fong still rocked the night away. There was still horse racing in Happy Valley on Wednesday nights. Taking the MTR, and looking at the people, they all looked the same too. I'm sure everyone woke up on 1st of July 1997 wondering if everything would be the same. People were waiting to see if China would keep its promise. China knew though that the world's media were still closely watching too.

In my new role I had a number of interesting duties, one of which was ensuring the security of the Buddha's tooth. I don't know how the Buddha had lost his tooth but it was believed to have been carried from India to China in the fifth century. It was kept safe in a pagoda in Beijing. The Hong Kong Buddhist Association had been wanting to display the tooth in Hong Kong for many years. After the Handover their prayers were answered. It is considered so valuable that it cannot be insured. When it was transported from China a private plane was chartered just to carry the tooth, and a special security detail was arranged to guard it. The Buddhist Association approached the police about security in Hong Kong.

My bureau was tasked with providing advice and support for the physical security measures whilst it was under escort and on display. From the airport it was brought with armed guards to the Coliseum in Hung Hom. There it was placed in a special display, with giant screens and all the fanfare that you can imagine. The whole event went off without a hitch and tens of thousands of people filed past to admire the relic and show their respects. Eventually it was time for the tooth to go home and another chartered plane took it back to Beijing. The Buddhist Association seemed very pleased with all the arrangements and presented me with a certificate of appreciation.

As part of the growing ties between China and Hong Kong there were more frequent visits from officials from the Mainland. These were to learn about us and our administration, although I felt we gave away a lot too cheaply. We had spent years developing best practices and software programmes but when the Chinese officials came down and asked for it we were told to give it to them. It was not my place to question the new administration. But as we had proven ourselves to be incredibly successful and prosperous we should not have been handing out our intellectual property and competitive advantage for others to copy. There were visits in the other direction too. During my time living in Hong Kong I had made over ten visits to China, the first being back in 1980. Not long after the Handover I had the opportunity to attend a security conference in Beijing, during which I visited the Public Security Bureau and some of the major government buildings and institutes.

I thought my hosts were very gracious and I was impressed by their hospitality. It was one of those events where I was led into an enormous hall with only six chairs, and I was asked to please take a seat. This was a protocol minefield – one of the chairs was the 'top' chair, but which one? So I moved very slowly and looked around at my colleague and hoped he might guide me with his eyes. It was so easy for a *gwailo* to commit a faux pas in such places. I was introduced to Mr Zhu En Tao, the vice minister for public security, and a very senior person indeed. We drank tea and made small talk. He didn't ask me many searching questions. I suspected he, correctly, viewed me as a small potato who knew nothing. Twenty years earlier I had looked nervously across the border at Sha Tau Kok at the serious Chinese soldier who had eyed me suspiciously. Now here I was drinking tea with senior officials in Beijing. It was wonderful to see how far China had progressed.

Back in Hong Kong, Trevor moved on and my next boss was John Bicknell. I liked John, he was a very affable chap who gave me a lot of support. The biggest talking point in CPB for some time was the curious story of a senior member of the Hong Kong Security Association who decided to change sex. We had become accustomed to dealing with Charles, a married man with three children who ran a sizeable and profitable security company. He was not the easiest person to deal with. He always seemed to question everything, and complain about every decision made. He became very grumpy if he didn't get his way. I don't believe any of us were prepared for what was about to happen next though.

Charles was tall, slim and sandy haired. He was in his early forties and a member of the Mormon Church. We met often as my bureau had direct liaison with the security companies and associations. I noticed during one of the meetings that his appearance and demeanour had changed and I mentioned it to my colleagues, but they had not noticed anything. Then I heard he was due to return to London in February and would be away for several weeks. When he came back he announced that he was now a woman and should be called Cecilia.

It's fair to say that a lot of people were in shock. Amongst these were his wife and children, and the Mormon Church. He still came into my office regularly, sometimes unannounced. Only this time 'he' was a 'she' and was wearing a frock and high heels. It took some getting used to, especially as she was about six feet tall even without the high heels. Many people, including me would still call her 'Charles' out of habit. Then it became 'Char-Cecilia' for quite a long time. She later decided to sell her security company and I believe did well financially from the sale. I understand she is still in Hong Kong, running a new business, and living with a Thai woman. I wish them well.

A major infrastructure project had begun in 1991, six years before the Handover. It was one that China initially was not happy about because of the cost. It had been hoped it would be completed before the Handover but was so enormous and complex it was not completed until a year after: Chek Lap Kok Airport. This was a fantastic project built on a small island and reclaimed land next to Lantau Island. It is based on a Norman Foster design, and had Mott Connell and Arup as partners. It took six years to build and cost about HK$160 billion. It's a fantastic achievement and the associated infrastructure, including giant bridges, and a new MTR rail line, were all designed, built and coordinated with precision. So in 1998 Kai Tak Airport would be no more: no more last-minute chequer-board approaches, or last-minute turns onto the tiny single runway.

But with the airport operating twenty-four hours a day and seven days a week how could the transition be arranged? Eventually what happened was that in the early hours of the morning in 1998 an enormous fleet of heavy goods vehicles left Kai Tak in a massive convoy. They were carrying all the essential equipment to ensure the smooth transfer of the airport operation.

There are videos showing how fantastic the whole operation was. I was in Iran at Tehran airport and visiting Customs officials at the airport a few years ago. One of the officials took out a DVD of the Chek Lap Kok construction and played it on a TV in his office, he was so amazed by the whole thing, and I was happy to sit and watch it with him even though I'd seen it before. The project was also a testament to superb British engineering expertise and a great showcase for the skills the country still possessed. Ironically it also relied on British labour too. A lot of the grass-roots construction was carried out by imported British labourers who lived in a large communal camp near the new airport. Quite ironic when I considered that over a hundred years earlier Chinese labourers had been imported to the USA to build the American railroad. How the world had changed.

In Hong Kong in 1999 we were not immune to what I still consider was a massive scam. Computer consultants around the world were able to convince companies and even governments that at midnight as we entered the year 2000 all our IT systems would crash due to the Y2K or millennium bug. Suddenly everyone was in a panic. I read that aircraft would suddenly believe it was the year 1900, and fall out of the sky. Whilst it was correct that internal computer clocks had often not been set up to register the year 2000 correctly, the predictions of Armageddon were wildly exaggerated. As head of the Crime Prevention Bureau, I had responsibility for the technical security equipment and therefore had to complete a detailed audit of all our systems. It did not take long for IT specialists to emerge promising to fix the millennium bug for a large fee.

The 1st of January dawned on the year 2000, and precisely nothing happened. Once our hangovers had receded, and we switched on our televisions, the news was only concerned with which country had the best celebrations and firework displays. As for the millennium bug, a bus-ticketing machine malfunctioned in Australia and some court summons with the date 1900 were issued in a few countries. It was hardly worth the massive cost and effort.

Eventually things slowly changed in the SAR of Hong Kong. I noticed that as expats left and more people took up the home finance scheme, more of the old government quarters were falling empty. These blocks usually stood on prime real estate and the land alone was worth a fortune in the booming property market. This was very canny foresight by the government. To those of us in the civil service and disciplined services jobs it seemed very generous to offer us money to buy our own place. The allowances though were only for ten years. I'm sure the sums were calculated very carefully. Selling land is one of the major sources of revenue for the Hong Kong government. Some plots could raise billions of Hong Kong dollars. But it was still a shock to me to see virtually all the places I'd lived in being demolished. First the Beacon Hill Road flats were knocked down, and then the King's Park flats where we had seen the giant centipede, then the Ede Road quarters, where I had enjoyed the warm bean-curd desserts.

In 2013 even the lovely, privately owned New World Apartments were demolished. The developer could build a giant skyscraper in its place now that there are virtually no more height restrictions in Kowloon. I have heard of some retired soldiers and police who served in the 1960s and 1970s returning to Hong Kong with their wives to make one last post-retirement visit. They walk around the streets looking for the same old bar, or restaurant or hotel, or shop they used to frequent and find absolutely nothing they recognise. I think this is terribly sad, and perhaps they leave wishing they had never come back. I have been returning to Hong Kong regularly in the last ten years, but on each visit I feel more and more like a foreigner as old landmarks disappear.

In the police things were going well for me, and at home we completed our nuclear family when my son Henry was born. This meant we had a daughter and a son, and decided we needed a bigger apartment, so using the home finance scheme we moved to a larger split-level flat in Discovery Bay. But just as we thought everything was great, Hong Kong was hit by SARS. The cases in Hong Kong were believed to have been spread via a Chinese doctor from Guangzhou. He had stayed in the Metropole Hotel in Kowloon when he was visiting relatives. He later died, and then over 200 people living in Amoy Gardens, a housing complex in Kowloon also contracted the disease. Things were getting serious. Hong Kong is such a crowded city and most people rely on cramped public transport. The shops, flats, hotels and offices all use air-conditioning to keep residents and guests cool in the hot and humid climate and few ever open their windows.

The World Health Organisation became involved in trying to stop the spread of the disease. People started wearing surgical masks in public and were avoiding public places. The streets looked like a post-apocalyptic movie set. Expat families started to take their children out of school and relocated them back to the USA, the UK, and Australia. So suddenly we were in a situation where we had two little children and around us people were dying from a mystery respiratory illness. It was extremely worrying. So we went to Japan, and enjoyed one of the best unplanned holidays ever. We cycled through paddy fields, admired the cherry blossom, and watched the spectacular drum festival. But it was short-lived. When we returned to Hong Kong we found that many schools were still closed, so we kept our children at home most of the time. Altogether 299 people in Hong Kong died from SARS, forty-two of them in Amoy Gardens. We started thinking that it might be time to consider alternative places to bring up our children.

This coincided with me reflecting on my life and career. I enjoyed my career but it was not something I ever planned on doing for the rest of my life. I decided I would start to look at alternatives outside of the force. I had been awarded a medal from Police Commissioner Eddie Hui Ki-on for 'long and meritorious service'. When I made up my mind to resign I went to my regional commander, Cheung Chi-sum and told him I had decided to move on to a new career in the private sector. Mr Cheung was very understanding and gracious about my decision. He wrote me a flattering valedictory letter recognising my twenty-two years' service in the force which I am still proud of. I will always remember that in my final interview he said: 'I wish you well in the future,' and then added: 'I'm envious of you moving to another career.' I thought it was an unusual comment from an assistant commissioner.

I was given a proper farewell in the messes, including the senior officers' mess in PHQ. As a gazetted or senior officer I had the option of being presented with a ceremonial sword on resigning. I decided to take the cash equivalent instead. On reflection, I wish I'd taken the sword. I then left my government job, sometimes referred to as an 'iron rice bowl' because it was secure, and made my way into the scary world of the private sector. I was told by a friend at the time that many of my colleagues thought I was stupid to leave such a safe, well-paid job.

I have been able to survive the cut-throat corporate world though, and have no regrets. I was back in the UK two years later, and was saddened when I heard that my last boss, Assistant Commissioner Cheung had committed suicide by jumping from the top of his apartment building in the early hours of the morning. He was fifty-four years old.

CHAPTER XLII

The British Legacy

I ALWAYS THOUGHT that the Brits and the Hong Kong Chinese make a good team. Like any great team, all the players have different attributes that together are better than the sum of their parts. I was happy making decisions, and I didn't mind if I made mistakes. I did not like to refer to Police General Orders every time I decided to do something. I strongly believe that the Hong Kong people liked to see British police on the street. I think it reminded them that Hong Kong was special. It was a little bit of the United Kingdom perched out on some rocks on the edge of China. In all my years in the force I never experienced any animosity on the basis of my being British.

I made many friends amongst local people and my Hong Kong colleagues in the force. I had, and still have, a tremendous respect for the local guys in the police. They do a fantastic job. But I do also think that together we had the best combination, and the best times. The crime rate compared to the size of population was always low. I'm pleased to see that continues today.

There was also a lot of charity work and sponsored activities that supported the underprivileged in the community. Many of us participated in swims and runs to raise money. Each year local and expat police officers raised funds for many different charities. One of the most successful long term charitable organisations is 'Operation Breakthrough'. Expat police like Dave Grant, BJ Smith, Danny Lawley and others worked incredibly hard to make it the success it is today. Operation Breakthrough is a testament to the collaboration in the community which helps young people succeed through sport. They work with disadvantaged youth and try to turn their lives around for the better. All of the founders and directors should be proud of their achievements.

In 1990, the Royal Hong Kong Police had around 900 expat officers. This was the peak figure in the force's history. By 2014 this number had dwindled to about 100. I never wanted to be the last expat to switch off the lights, I'm glad I left when I did. I knew that however long I was out in Hong Kong my own contribution would make little difference. My presence over twenty-two years in the force changed nothing. Everything carried on as normal the minute after I left. It's difficult to guess what the legacy of the expat police in Hong Kong will be. In other ex-colonies any vestiges of the British police seemed to have been mostly obliterated. In fifty years from now I wonder what memories will remain. Will the services of our expatriate police in Hong Kong only be remembered in a few fading photographs, and by a handful of members of the Royal Hong Kong Police Association? I would be happy though if charities such as Operation Breakthrough were still around, and people remembered the British police who helped create it. Perhaps this might be the longest and proudest legacy.

I enjoyed new challenges in the private sector, and embarked on further studies to continuously improve and to learn new skills. I became an immature student and a lifelong loser, I mean learner. I realised I was never too old to learn something new. Although I was quietly pleased when I sometimes embarked on a course and found out I wasn't the oldest student in the class.

A few years after leaving the police, when I had some spare time, I decided to search out my family tree. I realised that I knew almost nothing about my ancestors, especially on my father's side. My father was ninety years old by this time, but he started to open up more, and talk to me about family history which helped me look back a bit further. I also received assistance from genealogists and the Internet. After believing for decades that I was the first in my family to have been in the police, and visit Asia, I found I wasn't. Thirty five years after taking the fateful long flight out from London, I discovered that I had a great-grandfather called Joseph who had left Ireland aged fourteen to join the British Army. At the age of seventeen, in 1879 he had left England on a troop ship and served in Afghanistan. He had later become a policeman in Liverpool. My father gave me copies of Joseph's original army records from the year 1876. They were fascinating. What I then learnt spooked me even more. He was the same height as me, he had my build, and he had the same chest measurement, and shoe size as well. Sadly, having survived travelling to South Africa, India, and Afghanistan with the army, he succumbed to tuberculosis in Liverpool aged only thirty-two.

I always considered myself to be quite a lucky person, despite missing out on the Mark Six lottery win. I enjoyed a fantastic life in Hong Kong and really loved being part of the Hong Kong Police. I might have had some 'ah wells' but not many 'what ifs'. I made the most of the opportunities I had. I set out with little ambition other than to have an adventure, and was pleased to reach the rank of superintendent. I made many friends; I married a lovely lady, and had two wonderful children. I know my own contribution amounted to no more than a grain of sand in a desert, but I wouldn't change a thing. I'm happy to say that I will always be proud to have served, and to have patrolled the *Hong Kong Beat*.

POSTSCRIPT

IN 2015 I WAS LIVING IN the UK, and I was a member of the Royal Hong Kong Police Association (RHKPA). I was still working in a security role for a large logistics company in the private sector. My new career had taken me all over the world and I had lived in Dubai and Bahrain for a few years. One day I was reading my e-mails when I noticed a message from the RHKPA saying that the Hong Kong government office in Grafton St, London was moving. It had been there for decades and I can still clearly remember my interview there in the 1970s. The message went on to say that there would be a final farewell cocktail party held for invited guests from the Hong Kong government from different departments who had served over the years. Our RHKPA chairman Keith Lomas was asking in the mail whether anyone would like to attend. My friend and ex-colleague Carl got in touch and he suggested it would be worth going together so we both arranged to get invites via Keith.

On the day of the function I arrived a few minutes late. So after entering the grand building and walking up the broad curved staircase I tried to slip into the back of the room unnoticed. There were probably about fifty people in the room and someone was making introductory welcoming remarks. I grabbed a glass of wine and tried to stay out of sight. At the head of the room there was a chap called Lee making announcements and calling people forward to say a few words in turn. I realised that he was calling names of people representing different government departments. Clinton Leeks, a former secretary for security, was called out to make a short speech. I looked around the room; there were a number of very senior ex-RHKP people including Keith Lomas and Eric Blackburn. So after Clinton had finished I was shocked to hear Lee say: 'So next, I would like to invite Simon Roberts to say a few words on behalf of the police.' I had nothing prepared, and had been enjoying the wine and thought no one had noticed me. I had no idea why I had been called out. As I looked round, I could see Carl grinning, enjoying my embarrassment. The first thing I did as I moved to the front and took the microphone was to apologise to all my senior colleagues present. I then spoke off the cuff for about ten minutes reminiscing about my first long flight over to Hong Kong, Kai Tak Airport, and the smell of the nullah and a few words about the tough training in PTS. I finished by wishing everyone well and good luck with the move to the new premises.

As I finished I received some polite applause, and could see people smiling, so I thought I had not gone on for too long. Later Keith very kindly came over and put his hand on my shoulder and said: 'Well done, I'm really glad they called you out as I hate doing those speeches.' Carl also said it seemed to have gone down well, so I felt a bit more relaxed and had another glass of wine. I was curious though, why had my name been called out? Then I found out. It transpired that Lee had played in the same football team in Hong Kong as I had thirty years earlier; the team was called 'Dynamos'. He either recognised me or saw my name on the guest list. I think it was his way of playing a little joke on me, as he would have known there was no way I would be expecting it. Later, as I made my way home on the train, I smiled to myself. What a curious evening. My life seemed to have gone full circle.

Bibliography

Chen Bing-An. *The Great Exodus,* 2010, Guangdong Provincial Publishing Group; 2011, Open Page Publishing, Hong Kong. Excerpted in *China Daily,* http://www.chinadaily.com.cn/hkedition/2011-04/20/content_12358785.htm.

Austin Coates. *Myself a Mandarin,* 1969, John Day, Hong Kong.

Feng Chi-shun. *Hong Kong Noir: Fifteen true tales from the dark side of the city,* 2013, Blacksmith Books, Hong Kong.

Hong Kong Government. *Hong Kong Yearbook 1979 – A Review of 1978,* 1979, Government Printer, Hong Kong.

William Marshall. *Yellowthread Street,* 1975, Hamish Hamilton, London. First of 16 novels published between 1975 and 1998.

Jan Morris. *Hong Kong: Xianggang,* 1988, Viking, London.

Royal Hong Kong Police Association. *Stories from the Royal Hong Kong Police: Fifty accounts from officers of Hong Kong's colonial-era police force,* 2020, Blacksmith Books, Hong Kong.

Francis Wellman. *The Art of Cross-Examination,* 1903, Macmillan, New York.